SHIPWRECKS of the IRISH COAST

VOLUME 3

1582-2000

EDWARD J BOURKE

AN CHOMHAIRLE OIDHREACHTA

THE HERITAGE COUNCIL

This publication was supported under the Publications Grant Scheme 2000.

Front cover illustration, Marechal de Noailles wrecked near Mine Head on 14-1-1914

Rear cover illustration, figurehead representing a Spanish soldier, carbon dated to 1550. Found on the Connemara coast. Believed to have come from an Armada ship. Photo: Lucius Emerson.

Published in Ireland by the author 33 Rushbrook, Dublin 15.

Typeset and design by Bernard Kaye

Printed by Powerprint, Rush, Co Dublin 8437130.

ISBN 0 9523027 2 1

CONTENTS

Introduction

In the introduction to volume one I estimated that some 12,000 ships were wrecked on or near the Irish Coast. Initially I believed that the available records had been exhausted in the preparation of volume one. Further research resulted in volume two and now volume three. This exhausts the material in the readily accessible records. Local lists have again demonstrated that the Lloyds material covers only about a quarter of the incidents. I have had no reason to revise the approximation of 12,000 shipwrecks on the Irish Coast but have only located accounts of some 7,000. It is possible that a trawl week by week through all the newspapers would reveal more, but that task would be truly impossible. Some papers have been covered for a specific area and data for that area and period is near complete. This completeness depends on rare comprehensive coverage by a local paper. The main development in the last two years is the computerisation of wreck data both in Britain and Canada. The prospect of a world wide ship register with unique ship numbering will make the assembly of comprehensive data possible at some time in the future. I have no doubt that a detailed study will at some time approach a complete list of the wrecks mentioned in written sources. A useful index to the Freeman's Journal was located but it only covered the years 1763-1780. The weakness of newspaper indices is that the reader is at the mercy of the indexer. Shipwreck topics may be covered in detail or not at all depending on a whim. The index served to illustrate the level of loss in Dublin Bay for those years and provided the usual large number not covered in Lloyds List. Unfortunately coverage of shipwreck news in various papers is uneven. This means that absence of a report on a certain date does not guarantee that an event did not happen. At certain periods especially the 1700s some newspapers devoted their pages entirely to political news. Similarly in the 1920s and 1930s local Irish newspapers often fail to mention shipwrecks as their reportage did not seem to extend beyond the County Council chambers.

Some additional chapters are added on loss of life in emigrant ships and troopships, Lusitania legends, salvage and the location of maritime artefacts in Irish museums and collections.

Organisation of Data

The wrecks are listed in county order clockwise around the coast from Antrim to Derry. The reason for this is that most users are searching information by locality especially if they are trying to identify remains of a vessel found underwater. Wrecks are not in chronological order but are grouped in locations. Ships with similar names within a locality are also kept together for easier reference. In cases where a large amount of data was discovered in other publications a special chronological list has been assembled bringing together data from all available publications in a summarised format. An alphabetical index by ship name is at the end of the book.

INTRODUCTION

Customs Data

A chance discussion with Maighread Ni Mhurchadha lead to the material in the Minute Books of the Commissioners of Customs and Excise for Ireland. The Commissioners met on each working day and their minutes have survived in the Public Records Office at Kew. Details of personnel and petitions by merchants form the bulk of the data recorded. The minute books would have been lost in the Dublin Custom House fire in 1921, except that unlike most government departments, the Custom & Excise were controlled from London. Even the Irish Commissioners Minute Books were held there. The excise men were responsible for prevention of smuggling, collection of duties and safeguarding salvaged goods. In this latter role there are several mentions of shipwrecks in the minute books. Unfortunately only books from 1766 are held on microfilm at the National Archives in Dublin.

Photographs

One discovery during the course of preparation of this volume was several unpublished collections of shipwreck photographs. These are very rare in Ireland and I was most surprised to find so many more in the course of preparation of a separate book "Irish Shipwrecks" for the Images of Ireland series. It is tantalising to be aware of other inaccessible sources like The Nautical Photo Agency. This service was mentioned in Sailing Book IV, published by Chatto & Windus in 1935. They must have assembled a huge archive now believed to be lost. One tantalising search tracked down a copy of a photograph described as men tending to bodies of Tayleur victims on Lambay in 1854. Luckily it looked somewhat familiar and turned out to be an inquest on shipwreck victims in Cornwall in 1883 published by Richard Larn in his Shipwrecks around Mounts Bay.

Acknowledgements

The preparation of a volume such as Shipwrecks of the Irish Coast has involved the assistance of a widely dispersed group of enthusiastic historians who generously contributed information, photographs and advice on sources. I am pleased to acknowledge the help of Michael Kirwin of Limerick, John Kelly of Drimoleague, Neil Dardis the Dublin Port archivist, Roy Stokes, Des Quigley, Cormac Lowth, Tom Kelly and Jim O'Dea of Dublin, Lucius Emerson of Ballyshannon, George Morisson, Frank Pelly of Irish Lights, Nicholas Tweedy of Hotel Naomh Seosamh, Paddy O'Sullivan of Bandon, Val McCarthy of Dunmanway, Frank Madden of Limerick, Bernie Colclough of Waterford, Tony Caulfield of Tramore, Elizabeth Balcombe of Skerries, Iris Freeland daughter of TH Ensor, Gerald Lewis of Cork and England, Richard Palmer, Ian Wilson of Bangor, Jim Blaney, Vic Foster and Stanley McKeown from Northern Ireland. The Librarians and staff of the National Library, Dublin, Public Record Office at Kew, Dublin Port Archives, The National Archives. The help of the Heritage Council towards the printing of the book is acknowledged.

References

The items on each shipwreck come from Lloyds List (166) of the date indicated unless another reference is indicated. Some items of information come from personal communications and these are also referenced where possible. Each reference is indicated by a number in brackets and a full listing is given at the end of the book.

Ireland's Heritage and Long Term Future

The importance of shipwrecks as heritage material was identified by UNESCO who described all wrecks over 100 years old as heritage objects. This concept was introduced into Irish legislation in 1987 when the National Monuments Act required permits to dive on 100 year old ships which were wrecked. Further protection of modern vessels was given by the Merchant Shipping Salvage and Wreck act which allowed the boarding of a wreck only by permission of the captain or owner. Shipwrecks have a unique contribution to make to our historical landscape as they lie intact on the bottom of the sea as a time capsule freezing their contents as they were on the day that the vessel sank. This will allow archaeologists study their contents at leisure in the future. This is why it is so important that divers do not disturb the contents of shipwrecks as they lie in their archaeological context. In less informed times historic buildings such as the Colliseum or the Parthenon were used as quarries for their marble. This would not happen today because people are convinced of the value of the ruins as they stand. The climate regarding shipwrecks has also moved on with the times and now all wrecks over 100 years old are treated with the same respect and care. Divers are therefore encouraged to visit wrecks with a permit from Dúchas and enjoy their visit without any form of disturbance or barbaric pillage. Shipwreck heritage can only be preserved and enhanced by divers who are in a unique position to appreciate the underwater material. Data can only be gathered by divers who fulfil their obligation to make reports to the Gardaí when something is found. This is the same as for land based material. The development of a sense of pride in the national heritage is essential for its preservation because no amount of legislation can instil a cultural appreciation for what is our children's inheritance.

Archaeological research

Both Duchas and the Northern Ireland Department of Environment hold databases of shipwrecks; the Duchas database is part of the Register of Recorded Monuments.

Disclaimer

This book is not intended as an invitation or prospectus to members of the public or other interested parties to dive on any of the sites that are mentioned in the text and anyone intending to do so should take appropriate advice with regard to the safety and viability of their proposed actions. In Irish waters boarding a wreck requires the permission of the owner. Diving on a 100 year old wreck requires a Dúchas permit.

ANTRIM

Friends
The Friends was lost at Glenarm on 21-9-1844. She carried coal for Belfast. The captain was McCulloch. (177)

Orion
The *Orion* was wrecked at Larne on 21-2-1831. She was from Alicante and Derry bound for Larne. 126 bales of cargo were saved one day and 113 the next. The Captain was Campbell. (177)

St Tammany
On 5-11-1799 the *St Tammany* was wrecked at Cushendun. She was bound for Virginia. (177)

Susannah Kelly
The collier *Susannah Kelly* owned by Kelly's of Belfast sank in Belfast Lough on 17-6-1897. There was a gale blowing and she was seen to heel over by the crew of the *Grouse* which had just over taken her. The *Grouse* turned back to investigate but there was no trace of the crew. The vessel carried coal from Ayr for Belfast. Captain Brigs and all hands were lost. The ship sank about 14 miles from Black Head. (28)

Regitze Thorstrup
In January 1974 the *Regitze Thorstrup* went ashore at Larne with its cargo of butane. The crew were lifted by RN Helicopter and the ship was eventually refloated.

Neptune
The 400 ton, *Neptune*, was lost at Ballycastle Bay in 1786. The vessel was returning from Liverpool where she had discharged the products of three whales caught by the Greenland Fishery Company based in Londonderry. The event is mentioned in Irish whales and whaling (4)

Alert
The *Alert* of Donaghadee was lost off Portrush on 9-9-1844. The Captain was McFadden. (177)

Ella Hewett
The trawler *Ella Hewett* struck the wreck of the *HMS Drake* and sank on 22-1-1980. The wreck leaked oil and was blown up in 1978 to release the fuel which was polluting Church Bay.

Henry
The *Henry* sank at Rathlin on 12-1-1840. She was from Derry bound for Glasgow. The captain was Mr Black. (177)

Rival
The *Rival* was wrecked on the South side of Rathlin on 18-1-1840. She was from St John, New Brunswick for Liverpool. The cargo was saved. (177)

Margaret Browne
The *Margaret Browne* went to pieces on the East side of Rathlin 15-3-1841. She was from Irvine bound for Ballina captained by Shaw. (177)

Andrew Forbes
The *Andrew Forbes* struck Magee Island and filled on 25-1-1831. She was bound for Liverpool from Ballyshannon Captained by Sutton. (177)

The Fleetwood trawler *Shakleton.*
Photo: George Morrisson Collection.

Shakleton

The Fleetwood trawler *Shakleton* was wrecked at Grennan Bo on the North side of Rathlin on 1-3-1930. The crew were rescued from the bottom of 200 foot cliffs by the Rathlin rescue team. The *Shakleton* was built in 1913 at Selby. She was returning from fishing grounds at St Kilda.

Lerwick

The *Lerwick* was wrecked at Ballyferris on 26-1-1842. She was en route from Dublin to Lerwick.
Two schooners were wrecked at Dunluce Bay at the same time. (177)

Hope

The *Hope* was wrecked on rocks at Belfast on 20-1-1838. She was from Chepstow bound for Greenock. The Captain was McLoughlin. (177)

Phoebe

The *Phoebe* was wrecked on the East side of Rathlin on 15-3-1841 She was from Liverpool for Derry captained by Thompson. (177)

Scotia

The *Scotia* was wrecked on rocks at Cushendall on 11-2-1842. She was bound from Glasgow to Gibraltar and Malta. Her Captain was Malcom. (177)

Matthew Bell

The *Matthew Bell* was ashore in Church Bay, Rathlin on 15-3-1841. The cargo was being discharged. (177)

William

In 1739 two Scottish Lairds hired a ship to take their tenants to America. This would have been during the Highland Clearances when it was common for the landlords to evacuate their tenants to make way for sheep farming. The ship stopped at Donaghadee for rerigging and several of those aboard escaped. When they were rearrested it became clear that they had been falsely imprisoned. The ship set sail again but was wrecked on the North Coast of Ireland. Details of the story are unclear and the story forms part of Scottish emigration folklore.

Princess Victoria

The roll on ferry *Princess Victoria* sailed from Stranraer for Larne on 31-1-1953. Soon after leaving Lough Ryan during a NE gale a heavy sea burst the stern vehicle doors and caused damage so they could not be resecured. The first message after sailing at 07.45 was a message that the *Princess Victoria* had hove to at the mouth of loch Ryan at 09.46. An attempt to return to Stranraer exposed her damaged stern doors to the waves which burst at 10.32. The ship turned towards the Irish coast and the call for the help of a tug was answered by the dispatch of the *Salveda* and the destroyer *HMS Contest* from Greenock. The life boat was launched 11.00 when the *Princess Victoria* gave a position 4 miles NW of Corsewall Point but nothing was found. An incorrect position was deduced from the direction finding applied to the radio messages. In addition the mountainous seas and yawing of the destroyer at high speed rendered radar useless. The *Contest* searched until at 13.15, a radio message reported that all were abandoning ship which was on her beam ends 5 miles East of the Copeland Islands. Bangor lifeboat launched at 13.40. The trawler *Eastcoates* recovered bodies, mailbags and a survivor 4 miles NE of Mew Island. The *Princess Victoria* carried 127 passengers and 49 crew. Only a total of 42 survivors were picked up by the *Contest* and the other vessels. The 2694 ton ferry was built by Denny on the Clyde in 1947. (98)

Smuggling vessel

On 7-11-1781 the London Chronicle reported that a 250 ton smuggling cutter, carrying 16 guns, from Kintyre was wrecked on the Maidens. She was supposed to have come from Gottenberg with 1400 chests of tea, silk and 60 ankers of spirits. Thirty one of the 47 aboard were saved. The cutter had fought Captain Crawford's naval vessel in the Bay of Benluce during September. (177)

Tea wreck

On 19-12-1766 a buoy was reported to have been attached to Farrens large decked wherry which sank in Dundrum Bay. The buoy was put there by smugglers who hoped to recover the cargo of tea. The Commissioners of Customs and Excise were most interested in this attempt at salvage. (115)

Clyde

The Clyde was lost on the Maidens on 21-11-1832. She was from Belfast for Demerera. The master was Robertson. The crew were saved. (177)

Hope
The *Hope* went on the rocks at Ballycastle during an ENE gale on 11-11-1832. She was bound for Limerick from Glasgow. The master Mr Prentice and crew were saved. (177)

Royal Tar
The *Royal Tar* went ashore at Church Bay on Rathlin on 6-9-1830. The vessel was refloated and tied up at the pier. She broke loose and beached again. She was from Belfast for Portrush Captained by Hunter. (177)

Agnes
The *Agnes* was wrecked on a reef at South Rock, Belfast on 6-1-1844. She was from Ichiboe bound for the Clyde. The captain was Bryer. (177)

Julia
The *Julia* sank at the Copeland Islands on 13-10-1830. She was bound for Belfast. (177)

Flying Fish
The *Flying Fish* was wrecked in Larne Bay on 9-11-1830. Some of the cargo of wheat from Liverpool was saved. (177)

Agnes
The *Agnes* struck Mew Island on 9-11-1830 and broke up. She had come from Demerera bound for Belfast. The master was Haswell. (177)

Albertina
The *Albertina* was wrecked at Belfast Lough on 9-5-1839. The Captain was Petersen. (177)

Fortune
The Killough sloop, *Fortune*, went ashore at Kilroot on 14-2-1764. James Perry was master. (90)

City of Derry
The *City of Derry* was stranded at Larne on 3-3-1764. Captain McClaverty of the Hind stationed at Larne salvaged part of the wreck and cargo. (90)

Mary, Jane
The *Mary* and the *Jane* were stranded at Portrush on 2-1-1744. They were en route from Dublin to Londonderry. (115)

Lady Mary
The *Lady Mary* collided with the Glowworm of Ardrossan and sank in Belfast Lough on 8-1-1844. On 26-2-1845 she was raised and brought in to the Harbour. The Lady Mary was from Moville for London captained by Jones. (177)

Friends
The *Friends* went aground at Church Bay, Rathlin on 2-11-1830. A report on the 22-11-1830 indicated that she would not be refloated. She had come from Mulroy captained by Gallagher. (177)

Shannon
The *Shannon* was lost at Church Bay at Rathlin on 26-1-1844. She was from Sligo bound for London. Three men were drowned. (177)

Unknown
Two unnamed ships were wrecked at Larne on 25 & 26-1-1844. One carried lime, the other coal. The same storm saw a schooner wrecked between Ballintoy and the Giant's Causeway. Another vessel was lost between Ballycastle and Portrush. A sloop with iron for Belfast was lost at Garron Point. (177)

Data supplied by Peter Steele, North Irish Lodge dive centre

Name	Location	GPS	Notes
Empire Tana	Strangford Lough	54 23 36 N 05 34 35 W	The Lees Wreck
Alasdair	Strangford Lough	54 27 06 N 05 37 71 W	motor yacht at 20m
Zarina	Strangford Lough	54 23 35 N 05 33 50W	the Pins wreck
Hunsdon	Strangford Lough	54 19 13 N 05 27 30 W	2899t at 37 m
Bangor	Strangford Lough	54 19 74 N 05 26 60 W	stone blocks at 38m
Arantzazu Mendi	Strangford Lough	54 22 46 N 05 26 49 W	6,600t on Yellow Pladdy
Chirripo		54 45 938N 05 40 651W	
Tiberia		54 46 476N 05 38 653W	
Lagan		54 43 049N 05 35 243W	
Normanby Hall		800m S of Kilroot	
Housatonic	Maidens	54 57 255N 0544 805 W	
Albia	Maidens		
Smuggler	Maidens		7-11-1781
American Trader	Maidens	N Side of Allan Rock	
Dalnada	Maidens	E Side	
Sumatra	Maidens	E Side of Highland Rock	
Maria	Maidens		
Norseman	Maidens	54 55 780N 05 43 533W	
Overton	Maidens	54 55 558N 05 43 515W	
Industry			
Pembury			
Raylight			
Zetland			
State of Louisiana		54 52 911N 05 45 118W	
Alcedo		54 48 695N 05 41 402W	
Black Diamond		54 47 252N 05 41 315W	
Peridot		54 51 608N 05 45 691W	
Ailsa		54 51 204N 05 44 302W	
Roberts	Browns Bay		1811
Hudson	Skernaghan Point		1827
Alpha	Skernaghan Point		1827
Tuskar	Skernaghan Point		27-11-1891
Harrington		54 51 124N 05 47 355W	
George		54 51 052N 05 47 355W	20-12-1876
Ferric		54 52 502N 05 49 185W	16-1-1905
Rose II		54 44 307N 05 38 756W	WW1
Karanan		54 42 805N 05 31 768W	20-1-1942
Teanua		54 49 691 N 05 45 754 W	1976
Berbice		54 51 221 N 05 46 187W	1-1-1827
Cannons		54 50 424N 05 46 903W	1559-1580
Woods		54 50 773N 05 42 786W	March 1827
Ulrica		54 41 750N 05 31 660W	7-1-1897
Troutpool	off Bangor		20-7-1940
Annagher			
Tobago	Skernaghan Point		
Pembury	Maidens		
Susanna & Anna	Maidens		Schooner 13-8-1873
MTB no 75	North of Maidens		66 t 8-8-1892

The destroyer *HMS Mystic* and the *Oriania* aground at Torr Head.
Photo: courtesy of Sea Breezes

Mystic

The destroyer *HMS Mystic* and the *Oriania* went aground at Torr Head during the First World War along with several more ships. An outbound convoy from Liverpool lost its bearings in fog. The intention was to pass between Rathlin and the British coast. Four steamers and a destroyer went ashore and were lying parallel under Torr Head when the fog lifted. Two further merchantmen went ashore on Rathlin. A rescue tug *HMS Sonia* and a destroyer pulled all the ships off without serious damage. (99)

Elizabethan cannon

Cannon were found at Larne Harbour about 1975 in position 54 50 424N 05 46 903W. They date from 1559 to 1580 and have a large Tudor rose emblem. The cannon were made by the famous London gunfounders, Owens brothers. These are extremely rare and represented the height of technology in Elizabethan times. They are now in the Tower of London collection. Just like the similar cannon found at Tramore they must have come from a Royal ship but no definite information exists of such a loss. An extensive survey of the area by John Peacock and a team from St Andrews found no associated shipwreck material.

Jewellry find

Finds at wreck sites continue and the importance of retaining the context is illustrated by this example. In 1998 a single gemstone was found at a Northern Ireland shipwreck site. Careful archaeological work guided by the original diver who located the gem, led to the recovery of 11 more, completing an exquisite piece of jewellery owned by a nobleman in 1588.

DOWN

Belisle
The *Belisle* was wrecked at Kearney Point on 15-1-1845.She was from Maryport for Dublin captained by Huddart. (177)

Molly
The *Molly* of Glasgow was wrecked at Donaghadee on 5-3-1750. She carried tobacco from Maryland. The bales of tobacco were scattered and the excise-men were ordered to gather it into hogsheads. A condition of the sale of the tobacco was that it had to be exported. At the salvage auction nobody would bid for it under these terms. The Lord of the manor James Echlin claimed rights to the tobacco washed ashore at Ballyhalbert. (115)

Hamlet
The *Hamlet* went ashore in 1819 at Ballywalter. Looters attacked the ship and the master committed suicide before the revenue men arrived to take charge. (177)

Adonai
The *Adonai* was wrecked at Portavogie on 28-2-1842. She was from Ardrossan bound for Plymouth. The Captain was Roche. (177)

Phoenix
The *Phoenix* of Irvine was wrecked at the entrance to Donaghadee on 6-12-1763. All but a passenger, John Calwell were lost. She was Captained by Robert Fulton. (90)

Unknown
On 12-3-1765 there was a severe gale which cost three vessels on the Down coast. A sloop from Milford for Belfast was stranded at Donaghadee. She was bound for Belfast with wheat and flour. A sloop from Whitehaven with coal was wrecked at Ballywalter. A vessel from Dublin for Whiteabbey was wrecked at Ardglass with the loss of all aboard. (90)

Three Vessels
Three ships were lost on the East coast of Ards on 23-1-1768. (90)

Ann
The *Ann* went to pieces in Dundrum Bay on 16-11-1830. She was bound for Aberdeen from Newport. The master was Littlejohn. (177)

New Diligence
The *New Diligence* from Newport went ashore in Dundrum Bay on 7-1-1832. The master Mr Wale and crew were saved. After unloading cargo the ship was refloated. (177)

John
The John was wrecked on a reef off South Rock on 12-1-1832. She had sailed from Liverpool for St Thomas and St Domingo. The master was Mr Scotland. (177)

Unknown
An unknown brig was seen to sink by the crew of the *Lively Fell* 10 miles WNW of the Copeland Islands on 26-11-1841. (177)

The *Ulrica* wrecked on the Copeland islands.
Photo: courtesy of Stanley McKeown

Ulrica

The bell from the *Ulrica*, wrecked on 7-1-1897 on Old Lighthouse Island at Belfast Lough, was sold in 1990 from a shop in Francis St, Dublin. Apparantly it had been used in a Mission Hall which was demolished. She was built at Barclay Curles on the Clyde in 1884.

Surprise

The *Surprise* went ashore in 1794 at Annalong. Looters gathered from miles around. An eyewitness said they numbered nearly 1000. Troops were at the scene and fired on the "country rabble". The Surprise was engaged in the notorious triangular trade. This consisted of a trip from Liverpool to Guinea for a cargo of slaves who were taken to the Caribbean. A cargo of sugar and rum was loaded to complete the round trip to Liverpool. The condition of the slaves was dreadful and their life in the plantations no better. The suppression of slavery became a priority and was eventually wiped out by the Wilberforce act. The shipping wealth of Liverpool was founded on this disreputable business and the Liverpool trade connections with the West coast of Africa and Caribbean continued until the decline of the Liverpool Port. (177)

Durham

The snow, *Durham* was wrecked at Donaghadee on 5-3-1750. The cargo was flax seed. (177)

Brutus

The *Brutus* was bilged when she went ashore at Ballywalter on 26-1-1842.

She was from the Clyde bound for St Thomas. Two schooners were ashore at the same time. (177)

Isabella

The brigantine *Isabella* of Drogheda was wrecked at Dundrum Bay on 26-2-1785. She was from Cowes, Isle of Wight bound for Belfast with a cargo of wheat. The crew were saved but the vessel was completely lost. (155)

Great Britain

On 22-9-1846 the *Great Britain* left Liverpool for New York with 180 passengers. The newly established light at St John's Point apparently caused confusion as Captain Hoskin's chart had not been updated since 1 May when the light was lit. The ship just missed rocks at either side of the Bay which would have destroyed the ship. The crew and passengers spent an anxious night aboard. In the morning the passengers were lowered over the side and brought ashore on carts. The tug *Dreadnought* took the mails and baggage to Liverpool and was instructed to return with the biggest ropes and anchors available. The wind increased to a gale and the anchor cable which was holding the ship off the shore parted. The tug had to take shelter. The *Great Britain* was driven further ashore and broadside to the waves. Refloating was impossible in the short term, and every effort was made to prevent further damage. Captain Claxton took over the salvage operation. Water was able to enter the ship through the damaged bottom and this helped prevent strain. A breakwater was built around the ship using saplings and wattles anchored by chains and rocks. The saplings were particularly effective as they flexed with the strain. The ship was thus protected from winter gales and suffered no further damage.

Work recommenced at the end of the winter. Boilermakers strengthened the cargo deck by shoring it from the deck above and coal was off loaded. At high tide the ship lifted four feet and stones were packed under the hull. At the same time the stern was pulled to one side. Then levers were used to raise the ship as stones were tumbled through chutes to fill the gap under the hull. Twenty, 25 ton boxes of sand were used to balance the ship. By 13 July a spring tide was used to make a first attempt to refloat the *Great Britain*. The ship rose rapidly but was reflooded by valves as a precaution against strain damage. Further piles and supports were placed and, on 29 July she was raised to the required height. She was released from the rocks which had penetrated the hull by levering the whole ship up 20 feet onto a platform of piles to allow navvies chip away the boulders and boilermakers patch the holes.

A tide of thirteen and a half feet was needed to refloat the ship and on 27-8-1847 she was towed off. The accident bankrupt the Great Western Steamship Company. The salvage alone had cost £22,000 on top of a cost overrun on the building of about £50,000. In addition despite a huge publicity campaign she failed to attract sufficient passengers. After a period tied up, the ship was sold and refitted for the Australian emigrant trade which she served for some 20 years until her A1 passenger certificate was withdrawn by Lloyds. Then she spent a time in the coal trade before being abandoned at Port Stanley as a hulk. The *Great Britain* was recovered from the Falkland Islands in 1970 and carried to Bristol on a barge. She is undergoing preservation in the very dock at Bristol where she was built. Some £7M in UK lottery funds were made available for her restoration in August 2000.

Unknown

A large ship was wrecked at Tyrella on 29-11-1838. Cotton came ashore at Kelly's Cove, East of Pier Head. The crew were all lost. (177)

Lady Downshire

The *Lady Downshire* went down off the Copeland Islands on 14-2-1839. The crew were saved. (177)

Mary Gordon

The *Mary Gordon* was abandoned at Black Head, Donaghadee on 22-3-1840. She was from Derry bound for Whitehaven. The Captain was Canning. (177)

Aurora

The *Aurora* sank two miles off Strangford on 3-1-1841. She had come from Wexford captained by Welch. (177)

Newry Customs List

A list of vessels driven on shore in the Newry customs district in the years 1832-1852 between St John's Point and Cooley Point was submitted to the Harbours of Refuge Commission (80). The list was prepared by Captain Leonard Watson the Lloyds agent. The following were described as total losses.

Name Date Type value location crew lost *Minapia* 16-12-1836 Schooner £1000 Off St Johns Point all hands *Stranger* 23-10-1838 Brig £1000 Dundrum Bay - *Bloom* 23-10-1838 Schooner £600 - all saved *John Stamp* 17-2-1839 ship £20,000 Lestone Mourne seven *Trevor* 18-1-1840 schooner £3000 Tyrella all saved *Clytie* 2-5-1841 Schooner £600 Ballagan Point *Louisa* 7-11-1852 Brig £3,600 Cranfield Point saved

Warrenpoint

The *Warrenpoint* was lost at Killough on 5-3-1832. She was from Portrush for Liverpool. The master Mr Westmoreland and crew were lost. (177)

Hannah

The *Hannah* was wrecked at Cloughey near Strangford on 10-3-1767.She was from Port Glasgow bound for Holland. The cargo was 405 hogsheads of tobacco. The customs took great precautions to prevent smuggling of the tobacco. (115)

Wachlaren

The *Wachlaren* of Stockholm was wrecked at Strangford on 31-7-1783

Peggy
The *Peggy* of Glasgow was lost at Cloughey on 22-9-1783. She had come from New York and the customs were interested in the wine in her cargo. (115)

St John Baptista
The *St John Baptista* was wrecked at Strangford on 2-3-1782. She carried wine and fruit from Oporto to Dublin. The cargo was saved. (115)

William
The *William* of Liverpool bound for Liverpool was wrecked at Portaferry on 27-4-1784. The cargo was salt. Her master was Mr Bell. (115)

Unknown
A ship was wrecked at Newry on 7-2-1784. The customs were interested in the 43 rolls of pigtail tobacco that were salvaged. (115)

Emanuel
The *Emanuel* was wrecked in Dundrum Bay in June 1767. The merchants Currie, Beck of Kircudbright petitioned the Commissioners of Customs and Excise to allow them ship deals from the wreck. (115)

Sally
The *Sally* was wrecked at Dundrum Bay on 9-3-1830. The master was Rodham. She was from Maryport for Dublin. (177)

Friendship
The *Friendship* filled and sank after striking Ballyberries Rock on 4-4-1830. She was bound for Dublin from Cushendall. (177)

Meridian
On 10-11-1901 during a blizzard and a fierce NE gale, fishermen at Donaghadee were surprised to see a full rigged barque coming from the South. She missed the rocks at Coal Pit Bay and the reef at Robby Dyke. Then she struck the Foreland spit having just grazed the South Pier. She managed to anchor in the clear hole at the Warren. The lifesaving rockets were brought to the scene but could not reach the wreck. Then the Groomsport lifeboat was brought by road to the scene. By this time another disaster had occurred when another ship foundered in Bangor Bay with the loss of all aboard. This loss prompted local fishermen to launch the 21 foot yawl, Lucy. This boat was drawn by horse to the *Warren* and launched over the sand hills. The fishermen rescued the German crew of the Meridian after a titanic struggle. A tug saved the ship towing her clear of the ill fated Whiteabbey. (39)

Eclipse
The *Eclipse* foundered off Donaghadee on 6-11-1886. This 180 ton schooner was owned by Captain Frances of Bangor. The Liverpool boat picked up all but one crewman who was lost. (39)

Minnie Ha Ha
This regular trader to the port of Donaghadee was lost on Briggs Reef. The Captain Alan Bell and all hands were lost. She was owned by Mr James Kinstry of Mount Charles. (39)

Eldorado, William Bell
The 400 ton barquentine *El Dorado* foundered at the back of Lemon's Wharf, Donaghadee. She was owned by John Neil of Bangor. The 200 ton William Bell Owned by R. Dunn of Newtownards foundered at the same place. Her Captain was John Gunning. (39)

Zephyr
The 210 ton brigantine *Zephyr* foundered at Dormans Bush at the back of Donaghadee pier. Local fishermen saved the crew. She was owned by Rippet and Dunn. (39)

Irishman
On 14-9-1877 the 23 year old iron steamship, *Irishman*, was wrecked at Burial Island, Ballyhalbert Co. Down. She was en route from Dublin to Glasgow. Owned by Lairds, the Captain was T. Morisson. (177)

Helen Burnell
The schooner *Helen Burnell* was wrecked at The Quoile river used to allow ships reach Downpatrick but is now silted. Some remains survive near a picnic area on the shore. (177)

Richard Pope
The barque *Richard Pope* was ashore and in distress at Newcastle in Dundrum Bay 6-3-1826. The vessel was among the breakers. Fishermen launched a boat from Newcastle but they drifted back to the shore and beached after a struggle as approaching the pier was impossible. A sturdy yawl was put on a cart and launched from a proper spot manned by six from coastguard station and Captain John Row Morris RN (author of a letter to the paper describing the events) She got alongside but none of the ship-wrecked men could board the yawl. A boat from the Richard Pope was launched but overturned and four of five aboard were lost. During the night one more seaman died of cold. Then Lieutenant Usher of the coastguard launched his boat and brought the Captain and four crew ashore. The next day the shore boat brought the remaining crew ashore. In all five were lost and 11saved. (35)

Catherine Corrigan
The schooner *Catherine Corrigan* was wrecked at Dundrum Bay on 21-1-1854. David Davison was master. She carried coke from Cardiff to Cork and was driven North by the Easterly gale which wrecked the Tayleur. The wreck was described as near Tyrella watch house. (17)

Lively
The *Lively* of Preston was wrecked at Dundrum Bay also on 21-1-1854. Her Captain was Whittle and she carried coal. (17)

Fanny
The *Fanny* struck Ballyferris Point near Ballywalter on 16-11-1831. The vessel quickly broke up. She was en route from Wick to Dublin. The master was Sangster. (177)

New John
The *New John* was wrecked at Bushford Strand, Killough on 14-3-1831. The crew were drowned. She carried a cargo of coal. (177)

The wreck of the *Mary Anne* at Strangford about 1900 with McCausland salvors at work.
Photo: courtesy of James Mackey

Zarina

Just inshore of the *Empire Tina* at Strangford lie the remains of a wooden vessel known as the pins wreck by divers. Some sources think that she is the *Zarina*. This was the name of the barque which sank about 1700 in Ballyhenry Bay at North end of narrows. Others believe that the remains are the Nimble, a large two masted schooner which caught fire in the Bay on 9-2-1850. The *Nimble* carried general cargo from Glasgow for Dublin. The colloquial name derives from the copper pins which fixed the ships timbers together. Copper sheeting has also been found at the bottom of the slope at Ballyhenry. Copper bottoming was introduced to warships about 1790 as an anti fouling measure. A photo exists of McCausland divers working on a sailing ship wreck c 1900 just out from the shore, this is thought to be the *Mary Anne*.

Alasdair

The *Alasdair*, a large motor yacht, lies at 17-23 metres in Ringahaddy Sound. She sank after a fire but is largely intact. A feature of the wreck is the quantity of fire damaged tiles which indicate the intensity of the blaze.

Cooley Boats

On 2-11-1825 the Cooley boats were in Carlingford fishing for herrings. A storm arose and most of the boats threw their catch overboard in order to survive. Two boats were lost and ten bodies washed ashore. Another boat took shelter at Derryvogue two miles to the East of Cranfield Point. They had so much fish aboard that there was not room. They cast lots

The *Davaar* went aground at Briggs Reef on 7-7-1895. The steamer was refloated, but while working to free the wreck, the tug *Ranger* of the Liverpool and Glasgow Salvage Association struck the wreck of the *Emily* and sank.

Photo: courtesy of Jim Blaney

and two men landed and went home. The boat was dashed against rocks and the remaining two aboard were lost. (17)

Minerva

The *Minerva* was wrecked at Cranfield Point on 2-12-1825. The Whitehaven brig was Captained by Morisson who survived along with his crew. They escaped by casting the cargo overboard. The Captain reported that he had seen the distress signals of two more vessels went down with all hands off the Bar. Timbers were washed ashore. A Carlingford vessel with a cargo of coal from Liverpool was lost at Carlingford Bar. A father, his two sons, and one other were lost. (69)

Margaret

The *Margaret* was wrecked at Newry on 20-1-1838. The Captain was O'Neill. (177)

John Stamp

The *John Stamp* was wrecked at Kilkeel during a SE gale on 17-2-1838. Seven of the crew were drowned. The voyage was Bombay to Liverpool. (177)

Antrim

The *Antrim* was wrecked at Cloughey Bay on 17-2-1839. The cargo of 2000 bales of cotton was saved. The Captain was McCracken. (177)

Hope, Thomas

The Hope and the Thomas were both wrecked at Ardglass on 21-2-1838. The Hope had come from Cambletown with barley. (177)

Kennedy
The schooner *Kennedy* of Balbriggan was wrecked at Ardglass on 17-2-1838. (177)
Good Intent
The *Good Intent* sank off Donaghadee on 21-11-1841. She had been abandoned by Captain Gutherie and the crew and foundered after striking a rock. She was bound for Troon from Dublin. (177)
Farnham
The *Farnham* was wrecked at Cranfield Point on 7-11-1838. The Captain was Wylie. The materials were saved. (177)
Bonnie Lass, Rushden Castle
The *Bonnie Lass* from Dundrum and the *Rushden Castle* from Isle of Man sank at Ardglass Harbour on 7-1-1839. (177)
Eagle
The *Eagle* was wrecked at Ballywalter on 20-2-1838. She was en route from Dublin to Fort William. Captain Trellis and crew were saved. (177)
Ellen, Waterloo
The *Ellen* and the *Waterloo* were wrecked at Portaferry on 8-1-1839. The *Ellen* was from Belfast and the *Waterloo* from Carlingford. (177)
William & Mary, Margaret
The *William and Mary* from Maryport Captained by Race and the *Margaret* from Irvine Captained by Patton were wrecked at Strangford on 7-1-1839. (177)
Northumbrian Maid
The *Northumbrian Maid* was lost at Strangford on 21-2-1844. (177)
Caledonian
The *Caledonian* grounded at Strangford on 6-3-1846. (177)
William
The *William* of Donaghadee went ashore at Ballyhenry on 6-3-1846. (177)
Shannon
The *Shannon* was wrecked at Ballywalter on 14-2-1839. She was from Maryport bound for London Captained by Little. (177)
Fruitful Vine
The brig, *Fruitful Vine* of Northam drove on Bembridge Ledge in Carlingford Lough. She carried beef, pork and candles from Cork for Havre Le Grace. While the cargo was saved the vessel was a total loss. The report was from Newry on 18-11-1783. (121)
Trevor
The *Trevor* went to pieces in Dundrum Bay on 25-1-1840. She was from Marseilles for Belfast. The crew were saved. (177)
Clarence
The *Clarence* was wrecked on Blockhouse rocks at Newry on 14-2-1840. She had come from Runcorn Captained by Hughes. (177)
Susannah
The *Susannah* was bilged when she went on Garter Rock at Strangford on 11-11-1840. She carried coal from Maryport for Strangford. The crew were saved and the ship got off but was badly damaged. The captain was Rule. (177)

The schooner *JMK* was wrecked at Bangor in November 1905.

Photo: North Down Heritage Centre, Bangor courtesy Ian Wilson

Susannah
Another Susannah was badly damaged at Bangor on 19-11-1840. Her Captain was McKenzie.

Neatsfield
A mention is made in the log of the armed trawler *Aracari* where she and another patrol vessels went to an area off the Antrim coast, 7 miles ESE of Skullmartin lighthouse, on 9-10-1918 to investigate the loss of the "*Neathhead*". A ship called the *Neath* was requisitioned by the Admiralty. The entry is in Lloyds register 1918-19 but does not continue in 1919-20. The ship was built in 1906 by Rickmers at Bremerhaven. She was a steel auxiliary screw measuring 410 feet in length and 5548 tons. The 4000 ton collier *Neatsfield* was torpedoed off Ballywalter on 13-9-1918. Divers say the *Neatsfield* has a particularly large gun on the stern. This vessel is suspected to be a Q ship or anti submarine mystery ship. Data is therefore sparse as these disguised, heavily armed anti submarine vessels do not appear in lists as merchantmen or warships It is unclear why a search was instituted for the sunken vessel.

Industry
The Fleet Auxiliary, *Industry,* left Kingstown on 18-10-1918 escorted by the armed trawler *Persian Empire*. The *Hunsdon* preceded her out of the Harbour. That night about 21.30 the *Hunsdon* was torpedoed and sunk three-quarters of a mile SE of Strangford Light Buoy. Nothing was seen or heard by the *Persian Empire* or the *Industry* sailing a mile and a half ahead. The *Persian Empire* reported that The RFA *Industry* had been torpedoed and sunk and that she was taking four survivors along with the 30 survivors of the *Hundson* to Belfast. No record indicates that the *Industry* was either attacked or sunk nor was her name removed from the fleet list until 1919. It was not until a year later that the deaths of six crewmen from Mersea were published as in memoriam notices in the local paper. No explanation for the secrecy has been found. The *Industry* was formerly the *HMS Glasgow* and was renamed after a major conversion to storeship at Beardmore of Glasgow in 1901. The *Hunsdon* which is known to divers as the hay boat was launched in 1911 as the *Arnfried* for the Hamburg Amerika Line. She was captured at Duala in German West Africa and managed by Elder Dempster Line. The *Industry* is believed to lie at position 54 23 40 N, 05 19 36W. (157, 158) The Admiralty records indicate the position as 54 22 00, 05 20 00 and that she was torpedoed by UB 94 captained by Lt Cdr. Haumann. The wreck of the *Hunsden* lies in 35-40 metres a mile outside Strangford. The 2899 ton vessel was torpedoed on 18-10-1918 by a German submarine. One of the crew was lost. The wreck of the *Bangor* is nearby.

Iron Hulled Sailing Vessel
An iron hulled sailing vessel lies at 54 15 44 N 05 27 26 W at a depth of 52 metre. The bow sprit has been dragged off. No name is known for this wreck. (159)

The motor vessel *Samanco*

Photo: David Masters

Samanco

The motor vessel *Samanco* was driven ashore on 19-1-1945 in a snowstorm at the entrance to Belfast Lough. She was bound for India with 6,000 tons of cargo. The ship was severely damaged and the bow was in danger of breaking away from the stern. Rocket lines were sent to the ship and a rope bridge made to the wreck. By February 18 she was refloated with compressed air and beached at a safer place. A rubber patch was attached and the vessel salvaged. (89)

Cannons

Some cannon were found at Sheepland Harbour on the South side of Strangford toward Ardglass. There is no recorded wreck at this spot.

Collier

A collier from Scotland was wrecked on rocks below Bangor on 13-12-1784. There were no survivors. (155)

Solway Harvester

The trawler *Solway Harvester* was lost with all hands on 13-1-00. The wreck was discovered by sidescan sonar in 38 metres about ten miles off Ramsay in the Isle of Man when an oil slick was spotted by helicopters searching for survivors. A salvage vessel prepared to raise the wreck and observed bodies when inspected with remote cameras on 31-1-00. The *Solway Harvester* was raised and taken to Ramsay, Isle of Man on 27-6-00. The reason for the loss was not understood at the time. When the wreck was surveyed damage was observed indicating that it had collided with a large object. Theories suggested that she might have struck another boat or submarine. The British Ministry of Defence denied the latter, although it is known that the nuclear submarine *HMS Vigilant* arrived at Faslane base some days later for repairs.

LOUTH

St Patrick
The *St Patrick* sank at the mouth of the river Dee on 19-9-1840. She went to pieces on 30-12. She was bound for Dundalk for Flint. The Captain was Murray. (177)

Unknown
An unnnamed vessel from Irwin was wrecked near Drogheda on 22-2-1766. Captain Boyd and crew were safe but a woman was lost. Two further vessels were lost between Drogheda and Dundalk. (90)

Leviathan
The *Leviathan* sprang a leak at sea and went down off Dundalk on 29-12-1764. Her Captain was Grisdal. (90)

Nightingale
The *Nightingale* was lost at the North Rock, Dundalk on 9-6-1767. She was from Dundalk for Belfast with oatmeal. Her master was John Rice. (90)

Wrestler
The Liverpool tug, *Wrestler* went aground at Dundalk on 24-12-1895. It is not clear if she became a total loss or was refloated. (177)

Boyne
The *Boyne* went ashore at the South Bull, Drogheda on 9-5-1839. Captain Hudson and crew along with some materials were saved. She had come to Drogheda from Ardrossan. (177)

Minerva
The *Minerva* went ashore at Drogheda on 1-4-1839 Two crew were drowned. She was from Bangor for Dundalk. (177)

James
The *James* went onto the Nutt and Louth Rock and sank en route to Drogheda on 29-11-1837. She was commanded by Pattison. (177)

Jane
The *Jane* leaked and foundered off Drogheda on 9-5-1839. Captain Clarke and crew were safe. (177)

Jane
The brig *Jane* was wrecked at Nanny Water, at Drogheda reported 16-2-1841 (1).

JessieThe Jessie was totally wrecked at the entrance to Drogheda Harbour on 2-6-1840. She was bound for Troon from Dublin. (1)

Castor
The *Castor* went ashore at Dundalk on 26-1-1832. It was feared that she would not be got off. (177)

Eagle
On 8-11-1877 the smack *Eagle* was wrecked half a mile North of Laytown coastguard station. The vessel had been fishing from Arklow. (177)

Eagle
The *Eagle* of Drogheda sank off the quay at Dundalk on 10-7-1837. She had come from Ayr. (177)

Prince George
The remains of the *Prince George* were auctioned at Soldier's Point Dundalk on 9-4-1847. They consisted of the barque's hull and materials. (177)

Swallow
The *Swallow* of Bristol was wrecked near Rath, Drogheda on 1-12-1825. All aboard were lost. She carried tobacco, turpentine and palm oil. Lieutenant Beatty of the coastguard at Clogher recovered three bodies and cargo. Rathbournes of Liverpool claimed the palm oil and turpentine washed ashore. The topmast of a 400 ton American ship came ashore at Clogher Head. (123)

Nancy
The *Nancy* of Whitehaven was wrecked at Annagassen on 1-12-1825. The crew climbed the masts and remained aloft all night until boats from the shore rescued them next morning. The cargo of coal was unloaded into carts. (177)

Mary Ann
The *Mary Ann* was wrecked at Dunaney in May 1783. The cargo was tobacco, turpentine and timber. Expenses were claimed by a party of army sent to guard the cargo from pillage. (115)

Adeline
The *Adeline* was lost at Drogheda on 7-12-1830. She became dismasted and was wrecked. The crew and passengers were saved. She was bound for Liverpool from New Orleans. The master was Bunker. At the same time the *Union* and the *Fancy* were ashore but expected to be refloated. (177)

Eliza Knightly
On 20-11-1830 the *Eliza Knightly* went on shore at Drogheda during a SSE gale. She was en route from Liverpool to Drogheda Captained by Roggan. (177)

Raven
The *Raven* sank near Drogheda on 20-11-1830. She was from Bangor bound for Dundalk. The master Mr Dale and crew were saved. (177)

Juno
Wreckage was washed ashore at Greenore on 28-11-1838. A sealed bottle with a message was found on the Strand at Carlingford. It described the plight of the *Juno* offshore with her masts gone, floating on her beam ends with a jury rig. There were no survivors. (124)

Jane
The *Jane* was wrecked at Drogheda on 4-2-1841. She had come from Troon bound for Dublin captained by Clarke. (177)

Clytie
On 3-5-1841 the *Clytie* and another unnnamed vessel was lost at Cooley Mountain, Dundalk. Both came from Workington bound for Drogheda. Captain Jackson and crew were saved from the unknown ship. Captain Lemon commanded the Clytie. (177)

Samarina
The *Samarina* of Kilkeel sank on 22-6-2000 off Clogherhead. She had collided with another Kilkeel trawler the Golden Bell. The crew of three were taken off by Clogherhead lifeboat. The wreck lies at 30 metres depth in position 53 50.48, 6 06.90.

Sir Milne

The steam tug Sir Milne was beached at Clougherhead about 1988. The tug which was originally powered by steam had a diesel engine fitted for the voyage from Malahide. She had been abandoned at Malahide for some 20 years. Originally she was inside the harbour at Clogher Head but broke loose and was beached. The intention was to prevent damage to trawlers in the harbour and eventually to dismantle the tug on the beach. It is believed that she was built in 1897 and operated in Belfast harbour for many years. She would have assisted at the launch of many vessels at Harland & Wolfe including the Titanic.

DUBLIN

St Antonio & Almas
The surveyor of Skerries was permitted to return pipes of wine which had been salvaged from the *St Antonio & Almas* to the merchants. The charge for salvage was 6 shillings per pipe. The ship had been wrecked on 11-5-1782. (177)

Vanguard
The *Vanguard* was wrecked at the North Bull at Dublin on 18-10-1844. (177)

Six Brothers
The *Six Brothers* was wrecked on Bennets Bank, Dublin Bay on 7-8-1831. The master Mr Hughes and crew escaped and the topmasts remained above water after she sank. (177)

John Dugdale
The *John Dugdale* was wrecked off Lambay. A board and figure head were washed ashore on 5-2-1838. (177)

Dublin Port derelicts
Various documents in Dublin Port Archives describe vessels abandoned around the port area. The first 1895 list is a list of wrecks or derelict vessels which may be broken up. It contains a list of wrecks that may, unless already in an unsuitable position for firing like the Elizabeth, could be placed close together on the Eastern breakwater for destruction, either by fire or explosives or by both.

No	Date	Name	Type	Location
1		*Elizabeth*	Schooner	Alexander Basin
2		*Orion*	Trawler	Alexander Basin
3	6-7-1895	*Racer*	Trawler	Alexander Basin
4		*Eliza*	Stone hacker	Alexander Basin
5		*Margaret & Anne*	Stone hacker	Alexander Basin
6	5-7-1895	*Mary*	Trawler	Alexander Basin
7		*Wave*	Stone Hacker	West of Gouldings
8		*Earne*	Trawler	West of Gouldings
9		*Margaret*	Schooner	West of Gouldings
10		*Cornet*	Schooner	West of Gouldings
11	24-6-1895	*Little Harry*	Trawler	Below Ringsend Bridge in Dodder
12	27-6-1895	*J T Y*	Trawler	Ditto
13	14-6-1895	*Whitehorse*	Herring boat	Ditto
14	12-6-1895	*Cloud*	Herring boat	Ditto
15	20-6-1895	*Club boat*		Ditto
16	13-6-1895	*Salmon boat*		Ditto

List of Derelict Vessels or wrecks in Harbour at date August 1894

Name	Description	Location	Details	Owner
Argo	Trawler	Alexandra basin	Sunk in river 10-12-1893 lifted by Mr Boyd	Port & Docks board
Elizabeth	schooner	Alexandra basin	1-7-1886 beached by owner	Batey & Co
Jane Doull	3 masted schooner	Alexandra basin	beached and scuttled 30-8-1890	Jas Kirwan
Orion	Trawler	Alexandra basin	placed by owner on slob	Mr Burnham
Racer	Trawler	Alexandra basin	placed by owner on slob	Mr Power
Eliza	Stone hacker	Alexandra basin	placed by owner on slob	
Margaret Anne	Stone hacker	Alexandra basin	placed by owner on slob	
Mary	trawler	Alexandra basin	placed by owner on slob	Mr Good
Wave	stone hacker	West of Gouldings	placed by owner on slob	
Erne	trawler	West of Gouldings	placed by owner on slob	Mr Good
Lea formerly Dove	herring boat	West of Gouldings		
Margaret	Schooner	West of Gouldings	nearly broken up	Bewley Webb & Co
Comet	Trawler	West of Gouldings	placed by owner on slob	Mr Shea
Little Harry	Trawler	In Dodder	placed by owner on slob	
JTY	Trawler	In Dodder	placed by owner on slob	
Whitehorse	Herring boat	In Dodder	placed by owner on slob	
Cloud	Herring boat	In Dodder	placed by owner on slob	
Club Boat		In Dodder	placed by owner on slob	
Salmon boat		In Dodder	placed by owner on slob	
Unknown Boat		In Dodder		
Relief	3 masted schooner	In Dodder		
Maid of the Mist	3 masted schooner	In Dodder		
Fishing boat		In Dodder		

Wrecks or Derelict vessels which have been brought to Alexandra Basin since August 1894

Name	Type	Details
Ondine	Trawler	Memory owner
Citizen	Trawler	unknown owner
Gannet	Trawler	M Curran owner
Admiral	Trawler	M Curran owner
Crusader	Trawler	John Murphy
Lillie	Trawler	Pullen owner
Commodore	Trawler	Fulham owner
Emerald	Trawler	Probably Coastguard
Swift	on yard ships	Dec 1894
Brunette	Schooner	7-7-1899
Water Lily	Trawler	7-7-1899
Sea Searcher		not in report book
Merry Lass		not in report book

Derelicts in Alexandra basin October 23 1899

Name	Type	Location
Jane Coull	schooner	West of concrete wall
Elizabeth	schooner	West of concrete wall
Orion	Trawler	West of concrete wall
Comet	Trawler	West of concrete wall
Cloud	Smack	Broken up Boyd report
Whitehorse	smack	Broken up Boyd report
Salmon Boat	smack	Broken up Boyd report
Club Boat	smack	Broken up Boyd report
Little Harry	trawler	Broken up Boyd report
JTY	trawler	Broken up Boyd report
May	trawler	Broken up Boyd report
Racer	trawler	Broken up Boyd report
Margaret & Anne	Stone hacker	Block Wharf
Undine	trawler	Block Wharf
Citizen	trawler	Block Wharf
Admiral	trawler	Block Wharf
Gannet	trawler	Block Wharf
Relief		Block Wharf
Maid of the Mist		Block Wharf
No 4		Block Wharf
Commodore	trawler	Block Wharf
Lilly	trawler	Block Wharf
Crusader	trawler	Block Wharf
Emerald	trawler	Block Wharf
Brunette		Block Wharf
Waterlily	trawler	Block Wharf
Sea Searcher	trawler	Block Wharf
Swift	trawler	On yard slip
Merry Lass	trawler	West of concrete wall

John & Susan

The *John & Susan* hit Dollymount Bull, capsized and filled on 31-3-1844. She was from Whitehaven and Newry bound for Dublin. Her captain was Merriman. (177)

June

The *June* of Yarmouth was wrecked off Shennick Island at Skerries on 21-1-1831. The captain, Tolver Silvers and five crew were drowned. Their headstone is in Holmpatrick burial ground.

Tudor Wrecks

In December 1582, seven vessels were lost off the coast of Ireland, including two carrying provisions from Chester and Bristol. (134)

Brig

A coal brig from Workington was wrecked near Skerries on 3-3-1786. She attempted to enter the Harbour at low water but was driven ashore and all aboard perished. Three bodies had been found but women's clothing was found as well indicating that more had died. (121)

Janietta

The *Janietta* was wrecked a mile from Skerries on 2-12-1825. She carried cotton, calico and muslin for Java. The cargo worth £70,000 was owned by Evans of Liverpool. Captain Kirk and the crew survived and were reported to have gone to the American consul at Balbriggan.

Lovely Silvia

The *Lovely Silvia* of Yarmouth was wrecked at Balbriggan on 22-1-1831. Barley, oats and herrings were washed ashore. The crew was lost. A further account suggested the vessel was the yawl Lovely June captained by Silvers.

Moelfre Rose

On 2-10-1946 the *Moelfre Rose* foundered in Dublin port. She carried coal bound for Donnelley's coal merchants. The port assisted with salvage by hiring a dredger to the coal firm. The sum of £442 was billed by the port for their services. Coal was dredged from the sunken vessel and loaded onto lighters for discharge. (71)

Sandycove Lifeboat

There were lifeboats stationed from 1800 around Dublin port by the Ballast Committee, at Clontarf in 1801, Sandycove in 1803, Sutton 1805, Pigeon house (Poolbeg) in 1815 and Howth 1816. Several changes of location occurred and three at Kingstown, Howth and Poolbeg were retained to attend the numerous shipwrecks in the Bay. One of these the Sandycove boat was upset 28-12-1821 with the loss of four of the crew of 14. The boats were manned by pilots of the port. They had launched to save the crew of the brig *Ellen* of Liverpool. (95)

Echo

On 10-11-1806 Ann Shurben of Pool petitioned Trinity House for a pension. Her husband was formerly Captain of the brig *Echo* lately lost with all aboard off Lambay. The petition (74) describes him as "bred to the sea and served there as a commander in the merchant service many years in the

Newfoundland, Portugal and Spanish trade". His 61 year old widow describes herself as not now able to support herself without the charity of the Corporation of Trinity House. Prior to the merchant shipping act of 1854, the corporation of Trinity House had at its disposal certain charitable funds to be used for the benefit of seafarers and their dependants. In order to benefit from these a seafarer (mostly mercantile mariners) or his dependants had to make application to Trinity House. This application took the form of a petition which gave details of his circumstances. The *Echo* disappeared from Lloyds register between 1806 and 1807. The 66 ton, *Echo* was built in Newfoundland by Neuve & Co in 1800.

Nicholson

The *Nicholson* was wrecked at Blackrock on 1-12-1825. She carried coal for Drogheda or Dublin. During the gale she lost her rudder and became waterlogged before her stern was beaten in. Captain Carr and his crew were saved. (177)

Sloop

A Wexford sloop was wrecked on Dalkey Island on 11-9-1786. Shortly after she went ashore the vessel went to pieces. The crew and most of the cargo were saved. (121)

Success

On 29-4-1838 the *Success* of Whitehaven was run down in the Liffey by the Victoria. (177)

Muglins Island

Wreckage lies on the Northern side and Southern tip of the Muglins Island off Dalkey but no record survives of a wreck in that location. On 1-4- 1838 the Darerera struck the Muglins and lost her rudder. However Captain Miller succeeded in getting her off. The Arab ran on the Muglins on 21-11-1837. She also got off. Wreckage was also found in 2000 just off the steps at the Muglins.

Nancy

The *Nancy* struck the South side of the lighthouse wall at Dublin and sank. Captain Bloer and crew were saved. She was from Whitehaven for Dublin. (177)

Unknown

The travel tales of John Gamble relate a journey from Liverpool to Newry in July 1812 which ended in shipwreck near Skerries. A strong gale arose during the voyage and the captain suggested that the port of Drogheda was the nearest place of safety though he did not know the port except that the entrance was dangerous. He is referred to as Captain K, a Welshman. The vessel struck about two in the morning and luckily held together. About six fishermen from Skerries took off the crew and passengers numbering 38 in a boat and conveyed them the village. The survivors expected not to eat but to be eaten and were pleasantly surprised. The final comment was that Ireland was not the worst country in the world to be shipwrecked in. (119)

Wexford brig

A brig from Wexford was wrecked at Portrane on 15-10-1784. She carried a cargo of salt and coal. There was only one survivor from the crew of six and one passenger. The bodies were found and buried by the inhabitants of Portrane. The captain named Hayes was washed ashore at Rush and buried at Kenure. (155)

Collon

The *Collon* sank at the East pier at Kingstown on 30-1-1837. She was from Troon for Dublin. (177)

El Gallo

On 20-4-1947 the *El Gallo* was in distress off the Kish Bank. She was taken in tow by the Dublin Port tugs off Kish and brought to safety.

Steamer

On 30-11-1838 an unnamed steamer was wrecked at Balbriggan. The vessel was from Belfast for Dublin. There was a great gale and many vessels were wrecked on the East coast. Reports of this wreck were somewhat vague. (177)

Elizabeth

The *Elizabeth* of Glasgow captained by John Morisson went ashore on the Kishes at Dublin on 3-8-1751. The cargo was pottery and tobacco. The customs and excise permitted the cargo to be discharged into gabbards but under strict supervision to prevent smuggling. (115)

Gainsboro

The *Gainsboro* left Liverpool on 25-11-1838 with cargo valued at £11,000. She was driven North of Ireland's Eye and went ashore at Carrick Hill, Baldoyle on the morning of 27-11-1838. The crew tied themselves to the rigging for 16 hours. Several died of exposure. Captain Jeffries and his young brother survived. During the same gale a Skerries fishing boat was upset off the Harbour and six men were lost. Their bodies were washed ashore at Laytown and the remains of the boat at Termonfeckan. She had left Liverpool on 25th and tacked off the Arklow Banks, she attempted to reach Kingstown but swept past Ireland's Eye and was driven ashore. The Master of a collier at Malahide, Mr Begg assisted by the coastguard rescued some of the crew from the surf.

The Freeman's Journal 6-1-1839 reports that the Ipswich brig, *Gainsboro*, was wrecked at Carrick Hill Baldoyle.

The Police report on 28-11-1838 is in National Archives Chief Secretary's Office Papers 14268. "I have to state that on the 26th instant about the hour of 4 o'clock report A schooner laden with coal was driven ashore on the Strand at a place called Corbalis in the Donabate sub district and that the vessel being in a bad state and likely to become a total wreck. Acting constable James Drumm at Donabate was called upon by Charles Cobb of Newbridge esq. JP to render assistance in taking charge of the property and upon the acting Constable proceeding to said place, he found, three of the coastguards in charge of said vessel and who told the acting Constable that they would give up the charge of said vessel as the cargo did not, pay duty, and upon the circumstances being reported to me I gave directions to the Acting Constable and his party to have a most sharp lookout about said vessel and to keep up a constant patrol at and about said vessel both night and day. Let the coast guard give up the charge of the vessel or not and to use all means in his power in protecting the property thereof until I would receive instructions and orders from the sub inspector to whom I reported the circumstances on yesterday morning the 26th instant and received his answer thereto on this day. The acting constable and his party in acting in this case under the orders of the above named magistrate. Benjamin King 27-11-1838".

A further Police report was made on 28-11-1838 (Chief Secretary's Office Papers 14272) "I have to report that on yesterday 27th instant about the hour of 10 o'clock a vessel was wrecked at a place called the Velvet Strand, Malahide laden with a general cargo. Some of the crew were clinging in the rigging until last night when three of them were lost. Four of them ventured to swim ashore at low water and there is one man hanging in the rigging yet dead. There is a great quantity of the goods washing on shore and Andrew Ball of Malahide Castle JP is constantly on the spot in attendance and has required the assistance of all the police I could send him to protect the property as the country people are there in great numbers. I have fourteen men in attendance on the spot from my Headquarters and out stations acting under the direction and orders of said magistrates in protecting the property. The coastguards are also in attendance. I have undertaken to send all the men there that I possibly could until I could receive instructions from the sub inspector to whom I have reported the circumstances on this day. Benjamin King Head Constable in charge of Swords district."

The police again reported on 29-11-38 (Chief Secretary's Office Papers 14274) "I have to state in continuation of my report which I have on this day forwarded to the Inspector General concerning the vessel that has been wrecked near Malahide on yesterday the 27th inst. That Andrew T Ball Esq JP has told me on this day that the number of constabulary (fourteen) which I have accommodated him with at said place and acting under his orders are quite sufficient to protect the property, belonging to said vessel and that he does consider a few men will now be sufficient for that duty, on this night and tomorrow, as the agent from Lloyds has come down on this day to load and convey the goods (as washed on shore) to Dublin. He (Mr Ball) has sent one of the constabulary and two of the coast guards, to protect and escort, ten carts laden with some of the goods, to Dublin, consisting of wine, rum, wool and dyed cottons. He gives great applause, to the constabulary so employed for their exertions in protecting the goods when washed on shore from said vessel. One of the crew who died (and mentioned in my former report on this day) is still hanging in the rigging. No boat can venture out the sea is running so high. Benjamin King Head Constable Swords. "

Lord Camden

The *Lord Camden* drifted onto the South Bull on 14-2-1784. She carried a cargo of flax seed and flour from Philadelphia to Newry. Captain Griffith, the crew and passengers were saved but the vessel was plundered and went to pieces. The Commissioners of Customs & Excise ordered their men at Ringsend, Clontarf, Baldoyle and Dunlaoghaire to save the cargo. A few days later a sloop with bark was driven on the piles in the Harbour. She missed her course in a heavy fall of snow and sank with all hands. (155,115)

Portmarnock wrecks

Portmarnock beach is the site of many wrecks. Six were visible at a low tide on 19-3-99. Five were wooden, the sixth was metal. The wreck high on the beach has brass pins indicating some antiquity. The sand level on the beach is sufficiently variable to conceal the brass pins wreck to a depth of three feet in sand or expose it on other occasions.

This is one of six wrecks were visible at a low tide on 19-3-99. Five were wooden the sixth was metal. This wreck high on the beach has copper pins indicating some antiquity and quality of building.

Photo: Author

The wreckage of the *Dusty Miller* appears from time to time on Portmarnock beach. A revenue cutter with a cannon also appears from the sands. The *Jamaica Packet* (1887) seems to be another of the wrecks (81)

A beachcomber walking on Portmarnock beach describes beach movement revealing black sand where over the years he had found several gold rings and a 16th century spoon. (18).

Submarine Yarns

The story is told that a submarine was scuttled by the crew after putting in to the gut of Rockabill for repairs. She sailed and may have sunk a ship before scuttling. Another account relates the story that the crew of a scuttled sub came ashore and surrendered at Donabate. One story relates that about 1970, two Englishmen came to Rush and went out diving from a small boat, they were dropped on a wreck which turned out to be a submarine. The same boatman brought out others. U35 was underlined and marked at a position SE of Lambay.

The Evening Herald carried a story in 1963 described as sourced from Mr W Blood Smith whose father John was a local historian. He related that a German submarine surfaced at Rockabill during World War One. The crew entered the lighthouse and held up the keepers. Then the submarine beached between the two rocks at high tide, carried out repairs when the water fell and floated off the next tide. The details are further embellished by the suggestion that the submarine was UB 123 which sailed off to sink the Leinster. The damage was supposed to have occurred when the submarine was attacked by a vessel towing an explosive sweep. The story though oft repeated cannot be confirmed either by reference to a date or the records of Irish Lights. A further story from Castletownbere describes an interview with the captain of a German submarine which beached on a rock nearby. There is a further story from the Second World War that a submarine struck Dhulic Rock and was seen to sink backwards by watchers from Galley Head. The story is attributed to a man called Hoskins. The official censor deleted a story about to be published in the Freeman's Journal from a resident of Tory who asserted that a German submarine base was found there in 1916. Colourful though these stories are they cannot be confirmed. The common factor is the absence of any date to place the incident firmly. Given a date there would be the possibility of research to discover unexplained submarine losses around that time.

U 1172

A submarine is supposed to lie half a mile outside the Leinster, East of the Kish Bank. So Said by a fishermen from Howth who used take out divers to the Leinster for Shane Gray. John Small also believes it to be true. The German submarine *U 1172* was sunk on 26-1-1945 20 miles off Kish in position 53.39, 05.23

Crew of the American brig *Edward* landing from the sea on the North Bull, in Dublin Bay, 1-12-1825, Drawn and lithographed by J.S. Templeton working in London 1820-1845 Printed by Engleman.

Print: Cormac Lowth Collection

Edward

On 1-12-1825 the *Edward* was lost on the North Bull at Dublin. The American vessel was outward bound from Liverpool to New York. The crew were saved, but the next day a man was drowned while salvaging the timbers. (17) A fine lithograph depicting the rescue was made at the time.

Betsey

On 13-8-1829 the *Betsey* was lost in Dublin Bay. Initially she tried to reach Bulloch Harbour but put about when a Bank obstructed her course. Then she tried to reach the Liffey but a high sea drove her towards Kingstown. As she neared the East Pier her mast was blown off and her rudder was lost and the seas dashed her against the pier. Master and three crew were saved including a boy Keenan aged 10. Six crew and four passengers were washed overboard. (177)

Eva

The crew of the *Eva* were saved by the fishing smack *Emerald Isle* in December 1853. The *Eva* sank near Dublin while en route from the Clyde to Australia. A fund was established to reward the fishermen involved in the rescue. (17)

Belgioso

On 21 June 1787 the Freeman's Journal reported: It is said that Mssrs Braithwaite will make an attempt to recover some of the chests of dollars in the wreck of the *Belgioso* sunk on the Kish Bank on 5-3-1784. There have been many attempts including the one during which Mr Spalding and his nephew perished on 3-6-1784 due to the drunkeness and negligence of those who tended the bell. A negro who worked on the Belgioso borrowed a convenient barge and sold it on the Welsh coast. He has not been heard of since.

The Freeman's Journal of 21-7-1787 reported " Monday afternoon Mr Spalding (note brother of Spalding drowned in 1784) made an experiment from Champion, frigate in Leith Roads during which he used an air pump, each stroke of which supplied air sufficient for one minute. Mr Spalding remained down for 15 minutes and his friend Mr Small submerged for 10 minutes". Another adventurer who descended at Essex bridge has since drowned. The Freeman's Journal of 7-8-1787 reported that the Grace and Peggy of Cardigan (Capt. Phillips) came to Dunleary with the same bell as Spalding being worked by Charles Spalding.

There is an account of Mssrs Braithwaite in the London Times of 22-9-1786. "Mssrs Braithwaite, the divers are not Scotchmen, as mentioned in the Dublin papers: the father is an Englishman, by profession a fire engine maker, and has a factory near Soho square, London: His eldest son is an ingenious mechanic: he obtained the gold medal from the Society of arts for the best model of a crane of his invention for raising weights: the younger son got the medal of the Royal Academy for the best model of the human figure in clay. The father conceived that a chamber supplied with atmospheric air by means of a hose, or leather tube, he got an account of the loss of a Spanish register ship at Peniche in Portugal, and instantly determined to proceed to that place; but in his eagerness he ventured to cross the Bar of Sallee at an improper section. His vessel struck, lost her keel, was with difficulty got off, and it was near three months before he could proceed for Portugal, where when he arrived the treasure had been already fished up, and he thus lost the opportunity of making upwards of thirty thousand pounds sterling, for such would have been his premium.

His bell would answer the purpose of exploring wrecks better than Dr Halley's diving bell and having by a very ingenious contrivance devised a method of working on the wreck, which he keeps a secret, he caused a small ship to be fitted up with proper apparatus for his purpose, and accompanied by his sons proceeded in her to Portsmouth, where he raised the great anchor, weight 20 tons and some smaller ones, of the Royal George: but conceiving he would find superior advantages by raising the ordnance of the Spanish gun boats sunk before Gibraltar, he went thither and raised on them a stipulated share of the value of the brass: the iron guns were entirely given to him, with which, finding no sale there he proceeded to Sallee and made a present of them to the Prince who rewarded him as already mentioned in this paper.

He was now determined on his way to England to explore the *Belgioso,* East Indiaman, wrecked on the Kish, near Dublin, but was prevented by the threats of the person who had entered into some engagement with the insurers, for the purpose of working on the wreck, about two years ago, after the ingenious but unfortunate Mr Spalding and his nephew were suffocated in their diving bell.

Mr Braithwaite having good testimonials of his abilities, and a strong recommendation to a merchant in Dublin, through him, applied to the agent of the underwriters for liberty to explore the wreck, offering gratuitously to take on board his vessel such persons as the agent should appoint, to whom he would deliver, free of expense any article he should bring up, and that he would make a report of the state of the wreck : the agent received him with great civility, but could not grant him the permission o account of the previous contract; therefore, after a few days, Mr Braithwaite and sons sailed for England.

The nature of this artist's apparatus is peculiar to himself: his general practice is to remain at work under water for six hours consecutive. He declares he could without inconvenience remain in his chamber underwater for six weeks or any length of time, as the air he there breathes is of the same temperature of the external atmosphere, by the constant supply through the tubes.

This extraordinary genius is very expert at raising water from great depths. He contrived and water from great depths. He contrived and executed the pump or fountain at St Albans, 20 miles from London, about four years ago, since which it has received no repairs and was never once out of water. The well is near 100 feet from the surface, yet a girl of ten years old pumps the water easily with one hand. He is now about to execute a new improvement in engines for extinguishing fire, which he thinks will render them less liable to be out of order, and worked with greater facility, the machinery will be much simplified".

In the early stages of Belgioso salvage there is no record of silver coins being salvaged. Spalding was lost in June 1783 and an attempt at diving was made later that summer. The Customs and Excise men did not record this activity though it was mentioned in the newspapers. There is no mention of coin salvaged at the auction.

On 16-9-1783 the Commissioners of Customs and Excise for Ireland were petitioned. "Blacks & Murray of this city merchants, their memorial setting forth that there is in the care of the store keeper 9 casks of damaged ginsing and 6 casks free of damage, one puncheon of rum, two whole and one ullage cask of porter and two casks of tar which were saved out of the ship Count Belgioso wrecked on the Kish Bank. That they have received a letter from the underwriters in London to have the ginsing etc. sold by auction which they intend to do on the 10th of next month and praying that the board will grant an order to the storekeeper to sell it on that day by auction and the money arising from the sale to be lodged in the Collector's Funds until the salvage and duties be settled and paid out of the produce and Mr Gardiner Surveyor of the stores having reported that he does not imagine that there is any objection to the petition being granted." The decision of the Commissioners was :Write to the storekeeper that on the memorial signing consent in the name of the underwriters He may comply with the memorials request and he is to pay the amount of the sale to the collector of this port of which acquaint Mr Jones" It would appear that all these items would have floated free from the wreck and were not recovered by diving.

Unknown

On 15-1-1767 a ship with a valuable cargo stranded at Merrion. The customs men were instructed to apply to the army for assistance in saving the cargo. (115)

Duke

On 14-8-1829 the 92 ton wooden coal brig, *Duke* was wrecked at Sandycove Point. The lifeboat based at Bulloch Harbour launched under William Hutchinson and saved the crew from the seaward side. Mr Hutchinson figured prominently in several rescues. (35)

Smuggling

As recently as 16-3-1854, 105 bales of tobacco were seized by the customs cutter at Rockabill. The goods were brought to the Dublin customs house by Mr Wade the leading surveyor. They were found in a deep chasm. The Freeman's Journal pointedly posed the question: How did the coastguard not find the hoard as their station is so near? (72)

Mayro

The pleasure sloop *Mayro* was wrecked at Skerries on 13-9-1976. She broke from her moorings in a gale and was driven on the rocks. The craft was part owned by John Boland then a senator and later a government minister.

Queen Of Ulster's vessel

In the Bank covered with grass close to Malahide Castle a mound is reputed by legend to be the resting place of the Queen of Ulster. The legend relates that in the 6th century the Queen was sailing down the Irish Sea and encountered a storm. The ship with the Queen and her entourage was driven ashore on rocks close to the castle and all aboard lost. The bodies were buried in the mound measuring 15 x 3 x 2 feet. This could be a Viking style longship burial. There is also such a burial reported at the highest Point on Lambay. (81)

Anne

The 36 foot yawl, *Anne* of Malahide capsized in Malahide Harbour on 14-11-1828. Four local fishermen, Michael Gaffney, Tim Gaffney, Pat Dunne and Michael Finn were drowned. Michael Gaffney's widow, Rose walked the shore until she found his body personally. He was buried within the nave of Malahide Abbey. The yawl was raised and reused until the skipper died in 1864. Though built in 1809 she was registered in 1845 probably to apply for compensation for loss of fishing rights when the railway was built across the Malahide estuary. (81)

William & Sarah

The *William and Sarah* was buried West of the Green at Malahide until about 1918. She had been owned by the Malahide shippers Gaffney's and was used to trade coal from Whitehaven. The skeleton had lain abandoned for some 40 years from 1878. (81)

Fishing Boats

Two fishing boats with seven men on board were lost on 1-8-1785 off Howth Head and only one man was saved. They were fishing for soles when a gale came on and raised a great surf on the shore. (155)

Unknown Shipwreck

The remains of a shipwreck in Dublin Bay are described in proposals for the improvement of Dublin Port published in 1801(or 40th year of George III). The location is mentioned as having her masts above water in five and three quarter fathoms. Bearings were given Bailey N68E, 3 7/8 mile, Lighthouse N15W 2 1/4 mile, Dunlaoghaire pier S69W,1 7/8 mile, Dalkey Island S5W 3 1/4 mile. (31)

Isabella

The *Isabella* of Liverpool sank near Rockabill before Christmas 1912. The vessel was raised with difficulty by McCauslands and brought to safety on 28-7-1913. (32)

Docena

The Guinness lighter barge *Docena* sank near the Custom House on 18-8-1927. The skipper B. Holcroft describes meeting a sudden squall as he passed under Butt bridge. He discovered he was in danger due to the amount of water shipped. He made for the pier but the mooring ropes had only been fixed when the barge sank. The men aboard scrambled ashore without injury. The cargo was 200 hogsheads of Guinness of which 167 were salved. The barge was raised by the Dublin Port and Docks Board two days later and found to be undamaged.

Vartry

Even shipwrecks have lighter moments. This ballad refers to the *Vartry*, one of the fleet of large steam barges or lighters which were used to transport Guinness stout from the Brewery wharf at Victoria Quay on the Liffey, down river to ships at Custom House Quay whence it was transported to Britain. The barges operated until 1963. The *Vartry* was built in the Liffey dockyard in 1902 and apparently sank in 1907 but was raised shortly afterward. The ballad was collected by Colm O 'Lochlainn and published in More Irish Street ballads.

It was the good ship Vartry
That sailed the sweet Liffee,
And the skipper had taken the casks aboard,
A goodly companee.

Blue were the labels, and azure blue,
Proclaiming double x,
But nather the skipper or the crew
Had dreamt of storms or wrecks.

Now as she steamed by the Ha'penny Bridge,
The engine raised a row,
While a cloud no bigger than a midge
Loomed up on the starboard bow.

And as they steered by Aston's quay,
The lookout man grew pale,
"I feared we'd not escape" says he,
"McBirney's summer sale".

And ere they reached the Customs House,
Down in a wild vortex,
The Vartry plunged, the cause was plain,
She'd too much Double X.

All you who drink of James Gate,
(No matter what your sex),
Take warning by the Vartry's fate,
Thro' too much Double X.

Wales Queen

On 21-8-1891the *Wales Queen* was lost four miles North East of Codling.

Sloop

On 20-3-1786 a sloop was wrecked at Balbriggan. In order to lighten her some 4000 slates were thrown overboard. The customs supervised the salvage of the cargo. (115)

Unknown

Late in 1933 a contractor working on a road bridge in North County Dublin discovered a body. It was buried in what was thought to be armour near Daws bridge at Turvey three miles North of Swords. On close examination the armour proved to be an elaborate framework of body fetters. These are known as chain and were used to hang criminals especially in cases of piracy well into the 19th century. Local folklore was able to supply an explanation. About 1760 an English ship bound for Dublin was driven ashore in the neighbourhood. The survivors were killed by the locals but a ship's boy was spared and taken in by a local family involved in the affair. The youngster, Joseph Daw having grown up, murdered the entire family consisting of Barnaby Sherwin, his wife and son and badly injured a grandson. The minutes of the trial are not available and no reason was given in the contemporary newspapers like the Leinster Journal 8-9-1770 for the horrible murder. Daw was apprehended, sentenced, and the report that he was hanged and gibbeted was published on 15-5-1771. A passing clergyman had him buried on 11 May. The account is related in the Dublin Historical Record which cautions that two folklore tales, one of wreck and adoption could have been combined with another of murder. Nonetheless there is enough evidence to substantiate significant elements of the tale. (30)

London

The smack *London* of Strangford went ashore at the North Wall at Dublin on 7-11-1825. She carried furniture from Kilkeel. The vessel sank and was expected to go to pieces. The master, John Cavan, and crew were saved. (17)

Scotland

The wreck of the 565 ton, *Scotland*, of Liverpool was sold at Dollymount on 31-1-1854. Her cargo had been transferred onto the steamer *Mona*. The vessel had been driven ashore by the Easterly gale which wrecked the Tayleur. (124)

Mary & Elizabeth

The *Mary and Elizabeth* from China for Liverpool was lost off Skerries (maybe the Skerries near Holyhead) a few days before 23-2-1841. The crew were saved. (1)

Duke of Bedford

On 14-12-1759 the customs men saved the cargo of the Chester ship, *Duke of Bedford*. The vessel had run foul of an anchor. The Skerries Surveyor, George Watson and his men prevented pillage of the cargo by locals. (117)

Petrus

The *Petrus*, formerly the Grove, was wrecked at North Strand, Dublin on 16-1-1972. She was used as a pleasure boat based at Malahide. The vessel was built by Skinner of Baltimore in 1937 as a 27 footer with a 30 HP former naval engine. She was lost when she broke from her anchors and filled.

Prince

On 3-8-1846 the *Prince* struck rocks and was badly holed about a mile North of the Bailey. No lives were lost. (8)

Betsey

The *Betsey* of Portmadoc was wrecked at Howth on 19-2-1838. (177)

Mary Anne

The *Mary Ann* was wrecked at the West Pier at Dublin on 17-2-1838. The cargo of coffee washed out. (177)

Volusa, Raven

Two wrecks occurred at Skerries on 24-2-1839. They were *Volusa* of Salcombe whose master was Grant and the *Raven* of Belfast. All aboard both vessels were lost. A schooner was lost at Balbriggan at the same time she carried flour from Liverpool for Dundalk. (177)

MTB

The wreck of a motor torpedo boat has been reported not far off the East Pier at Dunlaoghaire. It is supposed to become covered with sand from time to time. The Irish Naval service ordered 6 motor torpedo boats in 1939. They were delivered in 1939-1940 and disposed to Colonel

Fitzmaurice in 1948 & 1950. The intention was to convert them to houseboats. One lies underwater in the Grand Canal Basin at Dublin. *MTB 5* was left to rot at moorings in Haulbowline. There is an unconfirmed view that another was swamped at sea in Dublin Bay.

Mary

The *Mary* was wrecked during the great storm of 1861 at the foot of Burdett Avenue at Sandycove. (95)

La Virtue

The *La Virtue* was wrecked near Skerries on 6-8-1771. Captain Christian Hall and his crew were saved. (90)

Unknown

A vessel owned by Mr Moffat was lost at the back of Howth on 15-10 -1765. She carried rum and sugar bound for Newry. (90)

Penelope

The *Penelope* was lost near Dalkey on 22-10-1768. The 200 ton vessel carried a cargo of pitch. The master John Ashe, and crew were saved. (90)

Europe

The *Snow*, Europe, was wrecked on the lands of Bremore, Dublin on 18-2-1766. She carried coal from Workington. (90) There were two further wrecks around the same time on the islands near Skerries.

True Love

The *True Love* of Whitehaven sank at Aston's Quay on 6-3-1764. She carried coal and was Captained by Williamson. (90)

Somerton

Two tugboats lay on the sands at Malahide Island for some twenty years. They had been beached when a thriving boatyard operation occupied the site of the current marina and apartments.They were described as former Belfast harbour tugs built in 1897. They were classic steam tugs as frequently photographed alongside the Titanic and at the launch of ships from Harland and Wolfe. The Sir Milne was taken to Clougherhead where she was beached on rocks because she had begun to leak. The Somerton was towed to Howth on 24-8-2000.

Willing Maid

A letter on 28-3-1764 from the owners Clibborn Robert & Son thanked Colonel Cobb and Mr Talbot for their help in rescuing the crew and cargo of the *Willing Maid* when she was wrecked at the Island of Donabate on 28-2-1764. Henry Haylor was master (90)

Coasters

A gabbard with coal and five coasters with herring and barley were wrecked in a gale at the South Wall on 8-2-1770. A sloop from Wales with slates was wrecked at Poolbeg on 17-2-1770. (90)

Speedwell, William

The *Speedwell* from Whitehaven to Dublin with coal was wrecked near the platters at Dublin Port on 11-12-1770. Captain Moore was in command. The William (Captain Thompson) was swamped at the Harbour mouth in the same storm. (90)

Somerton at Howth 30-9-2000

Photo: Author

Charlotte
The *Charlotte* of Rotterdam was wrecked at Merrion on 12-1-1771. Captain Saunders, his son and a crewman were lost. (90)

Unknown
An unnamed ship went onto the rocks at Skerries on 10-4-1764 and was wrecked. Two more were ashore. (90)

Providence
The *Providence* was wrecked at the South Bull piles on 12-1-1771. She was from London for Dublin captained by Mayne. (90)

Alexander
The *Alexander* of Irwin was wrecked near Skerries on 22-2-1766. She carried coal. Captain Ferris and all aboard were lost. (90)

Lady Forbes
The *Lady Forbes* of Glasgow was wrecked at Sutton on 19-1-1768. She carried rum bound for Waterford. William Glasgow was the master. (90)

Younart
The *Younart* from Whitehaven was wrecked at the North Bull on 3-5-1768. The master was Bowes. (90)

Globe
The *Globe* was wrecked at Baldoyle on 17-11-1842. Captain Thompson and crew were saved. The voyage was Demerera to the Clyde. (177)

Henry
The *Henry* of London stranded at the piles at Dublin on 14-4-1767. She carries porter and hops. The owner thanked the High Sheriff for saving the crew. Captain Thomas Rathbournes body was recovered and buried at St Marks. (177)

Enterprise
The *Enterprise* of London was wrecked at the second perch at Poolbeg on 31-3-1767. (177)

Sally
The *Sally* sank at the North Bull on 13-1-1767. She carried beef bound for Jamaica. In the same storm the sloop used to quarantine fevered sailors sank at Poolbeg. (90)

Dublin wrecks
On 13-12-1767 a Wexford sloop captained by Floyd sank in Dublin Bay. A sloop bound for Newry was wrecked at the piles. (90)

Polly
The *Polly* of Ross capsized at the Bar on 8-2-1766. The crew were saved by the men on the lightship. She was bound for Whitehaven Captained by Power. (90)

James
The *James* was wrecked outside Howth pier on 11-2-1842. Captain Metcalfe and crew were saved. (177)

British Queen
The *British Queen* was wrecked at Baldoyle on 17-11-1842. The Captain was Dixon. (177)

Unnamed
A vessel from Irwin was wrecked on the North side of the new lighthouse at Dublin on 20-9-1768. The passengers and crew were saved by the lighthouse men. (90)

WICKLOW

Lyneburn
The *Lyneburn* of Workington was mined near the Arklow Light vessel on 29-8-1917. The lifeboat went out and continued the search bravely into the minefield. A mass of floating wreckage was found and three men of a crew of eleven were rescued. The vessel was en route from Cork to Whitehaven with timber.

Trusty
The large sloop, *Trusty* stranded at Ardinary, six miles South of Wicklow on 29-3-1782. She had carried copper and coal from Swansea bound for Dublin. A later report indicated that she had sunk on the banks of Arklow. There was a proposal to "fish for the copper" and two customs officers were delegated to supervise the operation. (115)

Savage
The *Savage* of Portaferry was wrecked in Skerries Harbour on 12-2-1756. There are memorials in Holmpatrick graveyard to the captain William Murehead and to Thomas McClery aged 16 of Portaferry. (121)

Lennox
The Motor schooner *Lennox* with a cargo of bricks struck the Arklow Bank on 28-12-1921. The position was four miles South of the Arklow lightship. The vessel broke in two and sank quickly.

Eumaeus
The *Eumaeus* ran onto the Bank near the no 3 Kish buoy on 11-12-1939. She was outward bound from Liverpool.

Sloop
An unnamed Carnavon sloop was wrecked between Bray Head and Wicklow on 18-11-1840. One of the crew was lost.

Dublin Bay
In February 1944 the *Hill* renamed as the *Dublin Bay* got into distress and took water. She was beached at Brittas Bay and the crew saved by lifeboat. The 494 ton ship had been bought at Cardiff and was on her first voyage with new owners. The shipping shortage was severe at the time and any type of vessel was pressed into service.

Asian Parade
Many of the wrecks mentioned in these pages occurred many years ago. By contrast the *Asian Parade* ran ashore at 19 knots on the Codling Bank on 4-2-00. The 55,000 ton vessel had landed 1,700 cars at Dublin and was en route to Rotterdam when she went off course and grounded like many earlier ships on the Codling Bank. The initial fear was that her oil tanks would rupture as the Bank has many boulders. The oil was unloaded with some difficulty into a barge and

initial efforts by three tugs failed to release her. At Midnight on 6-2-00 there was a high tide and she was freed and towed to Dublin Port for inspection. It was not a moment too soon as by the afternoon of 6th a strong gale blew which would have damaged the vessel further.

British Tar

The *British Tar* was lost on Arklow Bank on 7-8-1840. She had sailed from St John New Brunswick captained by Blenkhorn. (177)

French Smuggler

On 27-11-1838 a vessel was seen in distress of the Wicklow coast. A skiff put out to reach her three miles offshore and lead her to safety. The skiff was upset near the shore and two of those aboard were drowned.
Mr Jones of the coastguard rescued the crew when the vessel came ashore at Six Mile Point. The vessel was French with a cargo of brandy and rum. (42)

Perthshire

The *Perthshire* was wrecked on Codling Bank on 10-12-1840. She was from Liverpool for Havannah captained by Jones. The crew were saved. (177)

Criterion

On 4-2-1841 the *Criterion* was stranded at Arklow. Part of the cargo was saved. The Captain was Fry.

Hale

The *Hale* went onto rocks South of Wicklow Head on 1-3-1841. Captain Evans and crew were saved. She had come from Runcorn. (177)

Kate

The ***Kate*** also from Runcorn was wrecked two days later on 3-3-1841 at rocks South of Black Castle.

Reliance

On 25-6-1841 the *Reliance* went to pieces at Mizen Head, Arklow. She was from Wicklow for Newcastle. The Captain was Bayne. (177)

Peace

The *Peace* was ashore North of Arklow and expected to go to Pieces on 18-12-1841. She was bound for Wexford from Dublin. The Captain was Corrier. (177)

Mary

The *Mary* was wrecked at Wicklow pier on 2-4-1771. She was from St Michael bound for Dublin. (90)

Charming Nancy

The *Charming Nancy* was wrecked on the Arklow Bank on 22-11-1766. She was from Dublin bound for Barbados. One of the crew was drowned and the others were saved by a fishing boat. (90)

Anne

The *Anne* was lost on the Arklow Bank in 1786. (125)

Darnall & Mersey

The *Darnall* & the *Mersey* were lost on the Arklow Bank in 1787 (125)

Smack

A smack Captained by Nicholson was lost on 13-12-1767 off Bray. (90)

Catherine Porter

The *Catherine Porter*, a brigantine from Chester, struck the Kish Bank "near Arklow" on 2-1-1867. The master John Jones and three others were lost. A crewman named Fennessy of Liverpool and a boy McKeon of Bray drifted on a raft for 36 hours. The men of the Wicklow SWASH (meaning unclear) lightship saw their plight and rescued them. The Irish Times and Daily advertiser of 8-1-1867 attributed the loss to the inadequate lighting of the sandbanks.

Betsey

The *Betsey* of Maryport was lost at Kilcoole on 3-12-1872. Her master was drowned. (177)

Fanny Palmer

On 3-12-1872 the *Fanny Palmer* was lost on the Wicklow coast. (177)

Kilvington

On 18-1-1840 the *Kilvington* was wrecked on the Arklow Banks. The voyage was Liverpool to Wexford. Captain Melhuish and crew were saved. (177)

Town of Ross

The *Town of Ross* was wrecked on Wicklow Beach on 31-10- 1839. She was from Quebec. The master was Holmes. (177)

Lord Huntley

The *Lord Huntley* from Chepstow was wrecked on the North Bar at Wicklow on 4-10-1839. Captain Prout and crew were saved. (177)

Myrtle

The *Myrtle* was wrecked near Wicklow on 4-10-1839. Captain Devine and crew were saved. (177)

Vigilant

The sloop *Vigilant* was lost near the Kish light vessel on 8-4-1839. She was from Aberystwyth. (177)

Jan a Stat

The Dutch Galliot *Jean a Stat* was wrecked at Bray on 24-2-1838. (177)

Jessie

The *Jessie* was wrecked on the Arklow Bank on 1-9-1837. She was en route from Wick to Cork. (177)

General De Gaul

In April 1957, the French trawler, *General De Gaul* was lost off Arklow. There was no distress signal nor any news of the vessel until two bodies of crewmen were washed ashore. No trace of the trawler was found.

Dagali

The bell of the *Dagali*, a First World War loss, was trawled up in 1968 by Michael O'Brien in the *Hetty Ann* The Maritime Museum at Arklow has the bell, marked 1909. The Dagali was shelled by a submarine 28-3-1917 at the Arklow Bank. The 742 ton vessel was Norwegian owned. She was en route from Hennebout to Glasgow in ballast.

Arklow Light Vessel

On 28-3-1917 after a German U boat sank the Norwegian steamer *Delgali*, the *Ardglass* and the *Wychwood.* Captain Rossiter signalled the Wexford schooner Harvest Home from the light vessel to warn her of the danger. However the schooner was sunk. Then the U boat commander ordered the crew of the lightship to take to their boats and then placed bombs on board. These failed to blow up and the light vessel was sunk by gunfire. The crew were picked up by the Annan. (7)

French Brig
An unnamed French Brig was seen in distress off Wicklow on 28-11-1838. Five locals went out in a rowboat despite the storm. The brig moved to seaward chased by the boat until she was three miles offshore. The brig was then driven ashore at Six Mile Point. However the skiff was upset in the surf and two were lost. The brig was supposed to be a smuggler with brandy and rum. The coastguard saved her crew of six. (124)

Kilvington
The schooner *Kilvington* was wrecked on Arklow Bank 24-1-1840 (1)

Jane & Harriet
The *Jane and Harriet* struck Wicklow Bar and became stuck there on 18-1-1830. She was from Milford for Wicklow. The Captain was Reid. (177)

Sloop
On 25-10-1830 an unnnamed sloop was wrecked at Five Mile Point. She carried ore from Arklow for the smelters at Swansea. (177)

Bess
The *Bess* of Wexford foundered off Wicklow Head on 25-1-1831. The Captain was Hayes. (177)

Foundly
The *Foundly* went ashore 5 miles North of Arklow. It thought that the vessel would not be salvaged. Most of the cargo was removed. The vessel was from Demerera for the Clyde Captained by McKechnie.

Emperor Alexander
The *Emperor Alexander* was feared wrecked on the Arklow Bank on 22-11-1832. The crew were saved. She was from Quebec for Dublin, captained by McKinnon. The fears were unfounded, later the ship was towed into Kingstown. (177)

Unknown French ship
The first prisoners in Wicklow Jail on opening in 1709 were French. There was speculation that they were shipwrecked. The Wicklow Borough minutes record the purchase of food for the prisoners but no ship name is mentioned. No other source of French prisoners can be imagined but no explanation is offered on why they were imprisoned.

Wasp
The sloop *Wasp* from Wexford foundered off Arklow Bank on 6-3-1784. Captain Abraham Hill and the crew escaped into their boat and were taken off by a brig from Arklow to Dublin. (155)

Onyx
The 400 ton, steamer *Onyx* foundered about 12 miles ENE of the South Arklow Light on 3-11-1898. The vessel was en route from Neath to Dublin. The master was William O'Kane from Carnlough. The report said "The steamer Onyx, Captain Evans from Glasgow (A newspaper error), coal laden for Dublin foundered on Thursday night in the Bristol channel. This steamer was only recently built and belonged to Mr William Robinson (correct name Robertson) of Glasgow. She left the Bristol Channel on Tuesday night

getting into Caldy Roads the following morning and was compelled to remain there for 24 hours in consequence of the heavy weather experienced there by a strong SW wind. On Thursday morning she took her departure from Caldy Roads at 8.00, a strong NW gale blowing. She cleared the Bishops at 1.30 on that day and had covered some 30 miles when the vessel was observed to have sprung a leak. The water made its appearance in the vicinity of engineroom. The pumps were set in motion and rockets fired which attracted the attention of the watch on board the steamer Bishop's Rock of Liverpool the time being 7.30 p.m. The steamer stood by until 11.30 when the inrush of water increased in volume. The crew, 11 all told, were taken on board the Bishop's Rock and brought to Cork. The captain and crew are in the sailor's Home. They are unable to assign any reason which would account for the sudden appearance of water in the place indicated." The inaccuracies in the contemporary newspaper account emphasise the importance of checking an event in several sources. In this case the captain's name in Lloyds list agrees with family information. (124)

WEXFORD

St Barbara
The schooner *St Barbara* from Lisbon to Dublin was lost on a Bank between Tuskar and Hook on 29-1-1784. She carried a cargo of fruit and cork. She had been trying to work up the channel but had been caught by a storm. The crew survived by clinging to the rigging in icy conditions. Captain John Fernandez de Silva and eight men were rescued by a wherry. (155)

Francis & Mary
The *Francis & Mary* of Wexford sank off the banks near the Forth on 11-8-1784. Thomas English, the master and two were lost while a third man swam to safety. The cargo was coal. (155)

Anna Christina
The Swedish vessel *Anna Christina* was wrecked at St Patrick's bridge, Crossfarnogue on 28-3-1782. S. Adolpho Halden was master. The cargo was 260 tons of potash. (115)

Brig
A brig was ashore on 25-2-1782 at the Hill of Clover according to Mr Trimble the excise Collector at Wexford. She carried a cargo of Portuguese wine but there were no papers aboard to give her name. A dog was reported to have survived and was still alive. The mention of the dog was significant as under old salvage rules if any man or animal survived the goods remained the property of the owner. If there were no survivors the goods were forfeit to the King. (115)

Minorca
The *Minorca* stranded in January 1955 at Cahore beach in the same place where 240 ton Pioneer was lost in 1914. The Pioneer's winch remains at the site and is uncovered at low tide. The *Minorca* was refloated by two Dutch tugs despite the Captain's fears that she would be a total loss. A wicker basket which contained a stone jar of rum remains in the Strand Bar. Captain van der Mollen and his crew all survived.

Greyhound
The *Greyhound* of Liverpool stranded at Wexford in September 1743. She was bound for Guinea with bale goods. Some of the cargo was salvaged. (115)

Prince Augusta
The *Prince Augusta* was wrecked at Wexford on 29-11-1743. Goods were salvaged. (115)

Vulcan
The *Vulcan* stranded at Tacumshane on 12-12-1831 She was from Sweden for New York Captained by Bunker. Only some cargo was saved. On 19-2-1832 Lloyds List reported that iron was saved from the Vulcan wrecked near Wexford on 5-12-1831. (177)

The iron ship Calcutta was wrecked at Kilmore in Ballyteigue Bay on 17-1-1874. She was bound for Surinam from Liverpool. The legend at the back of the photo suggests that she had loaded pyrites ore at Avoca and was wrecked in 1873.

Photo: George Morrisson Collection

St Patrick

The steamer *St Patrick* was wrecked at Hook Tower on 25-11-1831. She was bound for Waterford from Dublin The machinery and boiler were expected to be saved. The Captain was Forrest. (177)

St Patrick

On 29-11-1838 the *St Patrick* was wrecked at the Hook Tower. She had sailed from Liverpool. Four of the crew were drowned. (177)

Calcutta

The iron ship *Calcutta* was wrecked at Kilmore in Ballyteigue Bay on 17-1-1874. Data in the Board of Trade wreck register records that she was bound for Surinam from Liverpool. The legend at the back of the photo suggests that she had loaded pyrites ore at Avoca and was wrecked in 1873.

Arran

The *Arran* was wrecked at the Hook light on 21-2-1838. She had sailed from Wexford bound for Glouster. The crew all survived. (177)

Aedicia

The *Aedicia* was wrecked on 11-6-1838. The wreckage was found of Wexford Harbour. Her Captain was Johns. She had sailed from Fethard for Llanelly. (177)

Phoenix

The *Phoenix* went on shore on rocks at Bonmahon on 1-2-1839. She had been at anchor off shore loading copper ore. The Captain was Galway. (177)

Alert

The *Alert* was lost off Wexford on 21-2-1839. The crew were lost and the boats were washed ashore at the Harbour entrance. She was from Cardiff for Wexford. (177)

Robert Noble

The *Robert Noble* was wrecked at Carnafaraige on 29-11-1838. (177)

Thistle

The *Thistle* was wrecked at Kilmore on 28-11-1838. She was from St Andrews New Brunswick bound for Liverpool. (177)

Thistle

The *Thistle* was wrecked on Cawmeen banks at Wexford on 1-2-1839. (177)

Lord Ebrington

On 29-11-1838 the *Lord Ebrington* was lost off Ballyteigue. (177)

Frances

In the same gale on 29-11-1838 the *Frances* was wrecked on the small Saltee. Four of her crew were lost. (177)

Paragon

The *Paragon* commanded by Captain Watt was wrecked at Wexford on 24-2-1838. She was from Liverpool for Pernambuco. (177)

Belina

On 29-11-1838 the *Belina* was wrecked at Ballyteigue. She was bound for Strangford from Quebec. The mate was lost. (177)

Figurehead at Enniscorthy Museum.
Photo: Author

Ariadne

On 28-11-1838 the *Ariadne* of Belfast was damaged when she struck Tuskar. The wreck washed ashore on rocks at Raven Point. Lieutenant Lett of the coastguard rescued seven of the crew. There were six lost. (177)

Elizabeth & Alida

On 11-3-1839 the *Elizabeth and Alida* was wrecked at Wexford. She was from Amsterdam bound for Liverpool. The crew were saved. (177)

The 1892 ton, *Earl Beaconsfield* was abandoned off Hook head on 13-2-1884 The *SS Lara* towed her into Waterford harbour where she beached at Buttermilk Castle. The crew of 33 were saved.

Photo: Jacob Collection, Waterford Library

Brenton
The *Brenton* was wrecked at the Bar of Bannow on 8-9-1839. She was from Halifax bound for Liverpool. (177)

Mercury
The *Mercury* was lost off Morriscastle on 5-2-1840. She was from Wexford. The crew were saved. (177)

Eagle
The Eagle was lost on Wexford Bar on 14-2-1840. She was from Yarmouth bound for Wexford. The crew survived. (177)

Molly Moore
The *Molly Moore* was lost at Tacumshane on 17-12-1837. She was from Waterford. (177)

Glasgow
The *Glasgow* captained by Robinson sank at Tuskar Rock on 10-2-1837. She was from London bound for New York. The mate a seaman and seven passengers were lost. (177)

Maria
On 6-2-1837 the *Maria* was lost at Ballyteigue. She was bound for Dublin from the Cape of Good Hope. Captain Doyle and crew were safe. (177)

Betsey
The same day on 6-2-1837 the *Betsey* was also wrecked at Ballyteigue. She was from Catania bound for Glasgow. Captain Miller and crew were safe. (177)

Lincolnshire
The 3,965 ton ship *Lincolnshire* was torpedoed and sunk on 29-3-1917 8 miles SW of Hook. The ship carried non ferrous metal cargo for the French Government. The manifest included

1,500 tons copper, 525 tons zinc, 47 tons brass, 2,500 tons wagons, 415 tons machinery. Sorima worked on the wreck in the 1930s and recovered the bulk of the material. (152)

James Hadden

On 15-1-1837 the *James Hadden* was wrecked at Ballyteigue. She was from Campeachy bound for Liverpool. Captain Beatty managed to save his cargo. (177)

Perseverance

The *Perseverance* was lost at Blackwater on 15-1-1837. She was from Liverpool for Wexford. Captain Beatty and crew except for a boy were saved. (177)

Sultana

The *Sultana* was lost at Wexford on 26-1-1837. She was from New Orleans bound for Liverpool. Three of the crew were drowned. A small portion of the cargo of cotton was saved. (177)

Water Witch

On 18-1-1838 the *Water Witch* was lost on the Blackwater Bank. Her cargo of timber, turpentine and geneva was washed ashore between Wicklow, Greystones and Bray. Remarkably another vessel of the same name was lost at St Patricks Bridge in 1833 (33)

Water Witch

A severe gale on 28-11-1838 caused the loss of several ships. The *Water Witch* of Glasgow was wrecked at Carnsore. She was bound for Leghorn with coal and bales of goods. The crew were all saved with the help of Dr Wady. (17)

Bonne Julie

The *Bonne Julie* or *Julien* was ashore, abandoned at Bannow on 16-12-1831. She was from Dunkirk for Bordeaux Captained by Berton. (177)

Hopewell

The *Hopewell* was wrecked on the Saltee Islands on 23-7-1643. The Cromwellian wars were in progress and big plans had been made for the relief of Ireland and ships sent from Dublin. The Hopewell was part of the expedition and was en route for the fort of Duncannon. The report was made from the Lords Justiciary to Leicester and cited in the Ormond manuscripts. (58)

Loves Increase

During the Confederation of Kilkenny wars with Parliament, the Government sent ships and pinnaces to their representative Ormond at New Ross in Spring 1643 under Captains Hawood and Beatty. The *Loves Increase* under Captain Moody sank at New Ross. The report is from the Lords Justiciary to the Speaker on 3-4-1643. (59)

Recovery

On 30-11-1767 the *Recovery* of Weatherhead was wrecked on rocks at Wexford. He carried a cargo of merchant goods which were insured at Dublin and London. In addition a collection of rich and rare articles of nature collected on the coast of Europe was lost. The collection belonged to John La Touche the late governor of St Helena. (60)

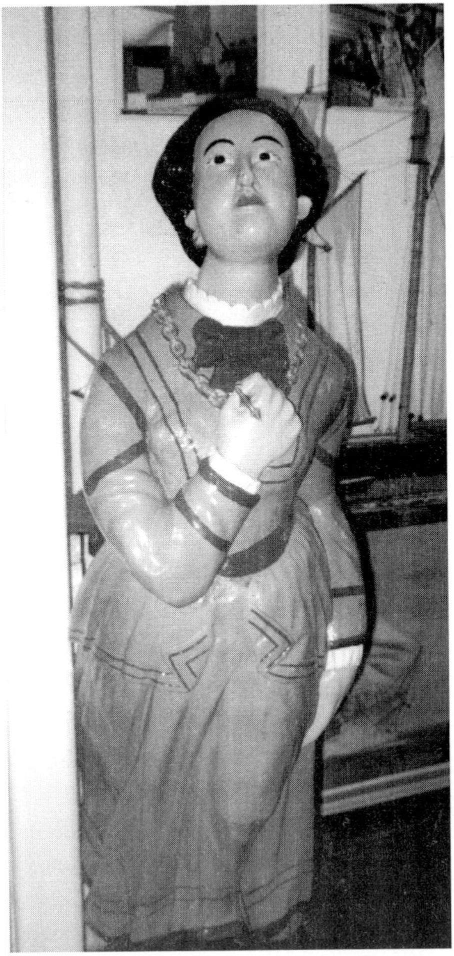

Figurehead at Kilmore Quay Maritime Museum.

Photo: Author

Malta

The *Malta* was wrecked on Wexford Bar on 22-11-1832. She was from Mirimichi for Wexford. The ship could not be saved but the cargo was taken off. (177)

Newcastle

The *Newcastle*, a 710 ton Windsor, Nova Scotia barque, was lost on 5-9-1872 at Tuskar. She was en route from Liverpool to Savannah with coal. All 13 crew were lost.

Amelia

On 23-12-1872 the 91 ton, Lancaster schooner, *Amelia* sank a mile South of Cahore Point. She was en route from Cardiff for Dublin with coal. Two of those aboard were lost.

Fanny

On 31-10-1878 the yacht *Fanny* was sunk in collision with the steamer *Helvetia*. The yacht was being used as a patrol craft by the coastguard.

Sam, Favourite, Macedonia, Ann

In a great SE gale on 1-12-1825 five ships went ashore near Tacumshane. They had sailed from Newport with cargoes of iron bound for Glasgow and Liverpool. Four were named as *Sam, Favourite Macedonia* and *Ann*. The fifth was unnamed and struck St Patrick's Bridge. Three were lost from one vessel but the other crews were saved. (65)

Rose D'Ivoire

The *Rose D'Ivoire* was holed when she struck a Rock at Hook lighthouse in the early 1980s. Despite the damage she reached the Harbour at Dunmore East and keeled over and sank in 20 feet. The skipper and crew got off into boats. The fire brigade tried to pump out the vessel but a rising tide hampered their efforts. She was a new vessel launched Lorient only 4 months before. The damage was beyond repair beyond repair and the loss was calculated at £200,000.

Grainville

The 1700 ton, *Grainville*, was en route from Belfast to Spain with a cargo of pig iron on 15-12-1981. She was only hours at sea when she began to take water. A bucket chain was organised to bale her out but the coaster took on 10 tons water when a porthole broke. Despite a serious list to port the Captain would not shelter and the radio officer was not allowed to send a mayday. When eventually help was called the ship was near sinking. Several ships joined the rescue effort. The ship was found drifting 10 miles SW of Tuskar without lights because the generator had failed. By the time the lifeboat reached the scene the ship had gone down. Wreckage was found by the Sten about 9 miles SSW of Tuskar Rock and 8 miles South of Carnsore. The *Pampero* and three French trawlers joined the search. A crewman was rescued by the Espoir and two more by the *Aurora* while two Sea King helicopters from Brawdy lifted five men by winch. The Captain, an officer and two crew were lost out of a total of twelve aboard. (16)

Akne Pahl

The 499 ton coaster, *Akne Pahl*, was ashore at Raven Point on 3-1-1972. Captain Cahl hoped to refloat the ship on a high tide after 12 days ashore. However on 20-12-1971 hopes to refloat her were considered poor because she was in ballast and came ashore at top of a spring tide. There was no further mention of the operation but it is presumed she was towed off.

Lode Star, Castle Bay, Glenmalure

On 8-12-1971 two trawlers sank off Hook Head. They were the 65 foot *Lode Star*, Captain Kelly Rogers and the 62 foot *Castle Bay*. The two vessels had collided while fishing and the Castle Bay sank at once. The Load Star picked up the crew of the first and the *Ingaro* of Dun Laoghaire attempted to tow the *Lode Star* to Slade. While en route the *Lode Star* filled and sank. Another trawler the *Glenmalure* sank near the Hook on 27-11-1970

Glasgow

On 8-11-1978, the *Glasgow*, a coaster, was lost 35 miles South of Carnsore. Four crewmen escaped onto liferaft and were saved.

Emily

The 227 ton collier, *Emily,* was sunk in collision with the Palatine 30 miles N of Tuskar on 30-3-1910. She was bound for Rosslare from Point Of Ayr with a cargo of coal. The vessel was owned by Coppacks of Connahs Quay. She was built in 1893 by Fullerton of Paisley, her yard number was 111. (120)

Notre Dame De Sacre Coeur

The 48 foot, Cornish trawler, *Notre Dame De Sacre Coeur* encountered a gale on 8-12-1978 and was blown across the Irish Sea. The engine room flooded and a Sea King helicopter from Brawdey responded to the distress message. Lightkeepers at Tuskar located the vessel. The helicopter took two survivors off picked up by a Swedish ship and Rosslare life boat took off the others.

"Shakespeare" a ships figurehead washed ashore at Ballyconigar preserved on a pub at Blackwater described as having come from the Thames wrecked on the Blackwater Bank.

Photo: Author

Urania

The Maltese ship *Urania* bound for Liverpool was wrecked on the Saltees on 8-2-1840. Six of the crew were lost. (1)

Urania

The *Urania* was wrecked on the Saltees on 26-1-1842. She was from Malta bound for Liverpool. Six of Captain Marengo's crew were lost. Despite the similarity of circumstances the different dates suggest that there were two ships called *Urania* wrecked on the Saltees. (177)

Naomh Seosamh

The trawler *Naomh Seosamh* went down in rough seas barely 100 yards off the Hook on 26-2-1957. She was returning to her home port of Dunmore East with a catch of herring when she began to make water. The skipper/owner John Hearne and two others were drowned. One survivor Liam McGarry swam to the rocks and was pulled ashore by the lightkeepers.

Sparkling Wave

The 50 foot, trawler, *Sparkling Wave* ran ashore on rocks at Bawnbeg half a mile North of the Hook light on 9-10- 1962.

There was thick fog at the time and it was thought that she was grounded by a 15 foot wave. The vessel had been purchased in Arklow that year for £3000 and was based in Kilmore Quay. The trawler was made fast to the rocks by a rope thrown to the lightkeepers but was badly damaged. Though the radio gear which proved valuable in summoning assistance was saved the vessel was smashed by the next tide. The crew were all taken ashore and driven to Duncannon.

Brooklands

The *Brooklands* formerly the *Susan Vittery* was lost off Tuskar in 1953. The *Brooklands* was the last of the working sailing vessels in Ireland to carry a figurehead. (147)

Phoenix

The *Phoenix* was wrecked on 22-8-1639 at Ballyteigue (19)

Hope

The *Hope* foundered on 4-4-1830 about 7 leagues ESE Tuskar. The master Mr Phillips, a seaman and two boys were saved. She was en route from Swansea for Chester. (177)

Aranci

The 129 ton steamer, *Aranci*, foundered 22 miles SbyW of Tuskar on 7-9-1932. She was in tow by the tug Strongbow from Newry to Portsmouth. The Aranci was owned by Coppacks of Connahs Quay. She was built in 1882 by Walker of Deptford. (120)

Sloop

A sloop was wrecked at the Bar at Wexford on 19-4-1786. Six of the crew were lost. In addition four rescuers who went to their assistance were also lost. (177)

Ranger

The *Ranger* went ashore on the Burrow at Ballyteigue on 22-10-1830. The master Mr Holt and crew were saved. She had come from Marseilles bound for Liverpool.

Horatio

The *Horatio* beat over the Blackwater Bank on 2-12-1831. She ran ashore at Cahore. The master Mr Gotham and crew were saved. She was from Liverpool for Newfoundland. (177)

Aid

The *Aid* was wrecked on the Blackwater Bank on 2-12-1831. Captain Stubb and the crew were saved.

Sarah

The *Sarah* of Cork captained by Beaze was wrecked on the Small Saltee on 21-12-1844. The crew were saved. (177)

Anne

The *Anne* of Barmouth went ashore at St Patrick's Bridge on 17-2-1819. The crew were all saved. The cargo was saved by the Lloyds agents Mssrs Samuel & Sandham Elly. 167 carloads of teas, wine hops sugar and spices valued at £10,000 were saved. The goods were lodged in the custom house of Wexford. Captain R Williams and his crew all survived. (93)

King George

The *King George* of Cork bound from Clonakilty to Liverpool with wheat was wrecked on the Saltees on 5-12-1818. Most of the cargo was saved. (93)

The *Mexico* was wrecked on the South Keeragh Island Wexford on 20-2-1914. The Fethard lifeboat was wrecked with the loss of eight of her crew during the attempt to save the crew of the *Mexico*. Eight of the Mexico crew were saved by the five lifeboat survivors and all but one were rescued with great difficulty from the barren islet the next day by Rosslare lifeboat.

Photo: Pat O'Connell Collection

Collier

A large collier went ashore in Wexford Bay on 16-12-1818. It was feared that she would be a total loss. (93)

Thorne

The *Thorne* of Weymouth was wrecked at Sandeel Bay on 26-11-1814. She was bound for Chester from London with military stores Captained by Ludlow. A party from the Cork regiment stationed at Duncannon fort and lead by Lieut. Atkins was dispatched by Capt. Reardon. They lodged the cargo consisting of 9800 stand of arms safely in the fort. (93)

Earl of Leicester

The Milford packet *Earl of Leicester* was wrecked between Slade and Wexford on 14-6-1819. The crew passengers and mail was landed safely at Slade. The ship is stove in but the mails were forwarded by the postmaster of Arthurstown. By great exertion of Messrs Ely & Sons Lloyds agents at Wexford, the ship was taken in to Slade bottom up with her masts gone. The wreck was sold but when an attempt was made to move her she sank on 14-7-1819. (93)

Sloop
A letter from Waterford reported on the 23-6-1785 that a sloop from Dublin to Waterford had been wrecked near the Harbour of Wexford. Only a boy survived. (155)

Shitelak
The *Shitelak* was wrecked on the Bar of Wexford on 11-4-1818. Captain Steele and the crew were saved. She was bound from London to Belfast with a cargo of wines and teas, rum sugar and bale goods. (93)

Caledonia
The *Caledonia* was wrecked at the burrow of Ballyteigue on 18-4-1818. She was bound from Liverpool for the Prince Edward islands in ballast and commanded by Captain Hingstone. Three of the twenty persons aboard were lost. Edward Meadows of Ballyteigue was prominent among the rescuers. (93)

Hero
The *Hero* of Banff reached Ballyteigue Bay with her masts badly damaged on 24-10-1822. The gale increased and the vessel was driven on a reef called Forlorn Point at Crossparkocue. She had come from New Orleans bound for Liverpool with a cargo of cotton wool. Captain James Hudson and crew landed safely. The cargo was mostly landed. (93)

Mary
The *Mary* of Glasgow sank 10 miles South East of Tuskar on 19-6-1820. She was bound for Gibraltar and Leghorn with general cargo. Captain Andrew McLachan and crew were landed safely. (93)

Hawk
The *Hawk* was wrecked on the Blackwater Bank on 13-4-1832. The ship was from Belfast Captained by McEntire. (177)

St Patrick
The paddle steamer *St Patrick* operated by the St George Steam Packet Company was wrecked at Churchtown inside the Hook Tower on 28-11-1838. Captain Sclute and 20 crew and passengers were saved. In all, six were lost. One man, supposed from America, escaped but finding that his wife was still aboard returned. At that stage the stern gave way from the paddles and both were lost. She was from Liverpool for Waterford. (17)

HMS Wolverine
The 16 gun brigantine *HMS Wolverine* was stranded on the Courtown Bank on 8-11-1855. It appears that she was refloated without loss. (171)

Spanish Packet
The *Spanish Packet* was wrecked at Black Rock, Wexford on 10-2-1837. She was from Genoa for Liverpool commanded by Wooton. (177)

Margarette
The *Margarette* was lost inside the Saltees on 18-2-1840. She had come from Bangor bound for New Ross.

Anne
The *Anne* of Barmouth went ashore on St Patrick's Bridge on 16-2-1819. She was from London bound for Dublin with a valuable cargo. The crew were

The *Manchester Market* owned by Manchester Liners was lost on the on the reef at Tuskar on 26-4-1903

Photo: Jacob Collection, Waterford Library

all saved. Through great exertion the Lloyds agents, Samuel and Sandham Elly salved 167 carloads of teas, sugar, wine, hops and spices valued at £10,000. These were taken to the custom house at Wexford. The extent of the cargo may be judged from the remark that there was yet more to come into the safe storage. (93)

Unknown

A letter in the Freeman's Journal on 2-10-1764 complimented Philip Palaliser for his noble act. He forgave all salvage due to him when a ship was cast on his Strand in Co Wexford. The letter proceeds to encourage other landowners with wreck rights to follow his example and have pity on poor merchants who were at a loss of their goods. The letter is signed "an Englishman".

Welcome

The *Welcome* captained by Crosstead, was wrecked at Blackwater or Castle Talbot also described as Ballivaldin on the estate of the Earl of Anglsea on 18-2-1766. Two boats drove ashore on land but no hands were found. The ship was pillaged and the crew murdered on coming ashore. Three suspects were arrested and lodged in Wexford jail. She had come from Virginia bound for Whitehaven with rum and tobacco. (90)

Coal ship

A coal ship bound for Cork was wrecked on Wexford Bar on 18-2-1766. (90)

Nancy

The brig *Nancy* was wrecked on Black Rock at the Saltees on 25-7-1769. She carried tar, cotton and Manchester goods. (90)

Favourite
The yacht, *Favourite* was wrecked at Ballystraw Bay, Duncannon on 29-8-1769. She was from Bristol bound for Cork Captained by Bastable. The cargo was mahogany, oil and planks. (90)

Theseus
On 16-10-1841 the *Theseus* was wrecked at Tacumshane. Captain Renell and crew were saved. The vessel had come from St John New Brunswick. (177)

Commerce
The *Commerce* was wrecked at Blackwater Hill, Wexford on 23-3-1771. She was commanded by Captain Smith. (90)

Unknown
Mr Curran master of the *Goodwill* reported on arrival that he had seen three ships wrecked at Wexford on 22-1-1765. (90)

Exchange
On 13-2-1768 the *Exchange* was wrecked near Wexford. She carried wine and brandy from Bordeaux for Dublin. The Captain was Merniagh. (90)

Diligence
The *Diligence* stranded near Wexford on 8-3-1768. She was bound for Boston from Liverpool. The Captain was Pearson. (90)

Mary
The *Mary* was wrecked on the Saltees on 26-2-1784. The cargo was boxes of fruit and 65 cwt of iron. Rich and Bryan was master and he was bound for Waterford. (115)

Mary
The sloop *Mary* from Guernsey was wrecked at Castletown on 24-2-1782. Wine was salvaged from the cargo. (115)

Perthshire
The *Perthshire* was aground on the Codling Bank on 2-12-1840 and expected to go to pieces. She was bound from Liverpool for Havannah. Captain Jones and crew were saved. (177)

Vermont
The *Vermont* was wrecked on Ballyteigue Bar on 15-12-1842. She was from Savannah for Liverpool. (177)

Palace
Pieces floating 2 miles North of Wexford were identified as from the *Palace* of London. This was the only trace found on 28-8-1841. (177)

Honor
On the 22-1-1842 the *Honor* was wrecked at Wexford. She was en route for Messina to Liverpool. The cargo of 700 boxes of fruit was saved. Captain Rouz and his crew survived. (177)

Cannon
Three large cannon lie at a wreck site at Rostoonstown near Kilmore. They are iron and measure about seven and a half feet long.

Unknown sloop
A sloop with coal bound from Liverpool to Larne sank nine leagues from Blackhead on 9-10-1784. The master Mr Stewart and crew were saved by the cock boat. Another vessel bound for Dungarvan was lost with all hands near the Blackwater. (155)

The *Crest* was wrecked at Rosslare on 1-3-1936. She carried a cargo of salt from Wexford to Dublin. She was owned by Mr Rochford of Kilmore.

Photo: Jim Maddock Collection

WATERFORD

Alfred D Snow

The American sailing ship, *Alfred D Snow* was wrecked off Waterford on 4-1-1888. The ship rounded the Hook and grounded abreast of Templetown Bay close to Broomhill shoals. The SSE wind quickly dismasted the ship and she went over on her side. The crew boarded their boat and remained attached by the painter. Meantime Captain Cotter of the tug Dauntless approached within half a mile of the wreck but could not get closer. The Dunmore lifeboat crew refused to launch though they would have has an easy approach from windward. The crew chose to drift to shore rather than row out to the tug. Their boat was swamped in the surf and the crew of 28 drowned. The *Alfred D Snow* carried wheat from San Francisco for Liverpool. The 232 foot, 1987 ton ship, was built in 1877 at S Watts and owned by Watts. (11) (12)

Elizabeth

Between 1803 and 1814 a Baltimore based sloop, possibly called *Elisabeth*, sailed from Waterford for Dublin with a cargo of potatoes. No further trace was found of the vessel. The captain was John Swanton (Captain Jack) Evans who lived at Ardrally on the Ilen near Skibbereen. The tale is related from family records and is typical of the smaller boat losses of the time which were largely undocumented in official records.

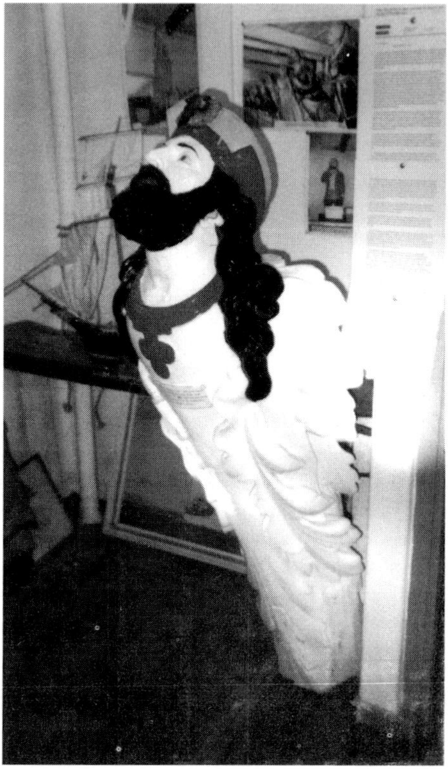

Figurehead of the American sailing ship, Alfred D Snow which was wrecked off Waterford on 4-1-1888.

Photo: Author

Tressnass

The schooner *Tressnass* was wrecked in the 1930s a mile and a half upstream on the Barrow from where it joins the Nore. The vessel carried coal for the creamery at Ballyneil or Roches, the general merchants at Ballyander.

The *Pembroke* went aground on the Little Saltee in February 1899 but was refloated and brought to Waterford.
Photo: Jacob Collection, Waterford Library

In the early 1920s the *Treasnass* sank above New Ross, she carried coal for Graves merchants of New Ross.
Photo: Patrick Shortall Collection

The *Nina Mendl* went ashore at the Furo on the Siur.
Photo: Jacob Collection, Waterford Library

George
On 3-1-1842 the *George* was wrecked on rocks at Clonea, Dungarvan. She was bound for Glasgow from Lisbon. (177)

Mary
The *Mary* went ashore at Clonea, Dungarvan on 7-8-1841. She was bound for Dungarvan from St John, New Brunswick. The Captain was Nichols. (177)

Serviceable
The *Serviceable* of Liverpool was wrecked at King's Bay, Waterford on 23-3-1769. Mr Terry was master. (90)

Providential Friends
The *Providential Friends* of Liverpool was lost at Tramore on 7-1-1764. (90)

St Henrick
The Stockholm ship *St Henrick* went aground near the smelting house at Waterford on 11-10-1770. She carried a cargo of iron. John Selinen was master. (90)

Unknown
The hull of a vessel was washed ashore on the lands of Lord Mount Florence at Bonmahon near Tramore on 31-12-1768. (90)**Glencoe**
The *Glencoe* was wrecked West of Waterford on 1-12-1840. She was bound for Calcutta from Glasgow. Her Captain was Keith. (177)

Two Friends
The *Two Friends* of Waterford was wrecked at Tramore Bay on 14-3-1769. John Henry was master. She carried sugar, hops and tobacco from London for Waterford. (90)

Unnamed
An unnamed Dungarvan boat was lost at Waterford Harbour mouth on 28-3-1767. Five of the crew were lost. The cargo was barley. (90)

Duchess of Leinster
The brig *Duchess of Leinster* was wrecked opposite the Hook Tower on

The 1200 ton, Italian barque, *Hansa* was wrecked in November 1899. She struck the ground outside Credan Head and came ashore between Credan and Western Bay. After being towed off she took ground again on the bar, but refloated during a storm and went on Drumroe bank a mile and a half below Passage. She had sailed from New Brunswick with timber for Waterford

Photo: Bernie Coakley Collection

21-1-1769. She was bound for Liverpool from Waterford with rum consigned by Newport, Long & Bull merchants. Captain McCarthy and the pilot were lost. (90)

Ellen

The Schooner *Ellen* was driven ashore at Ardmore on 7-4-1882. A strong Easterly gale prevented the ship's lifeboat from being used by the crew. The three aboard were saved by the coastguard rocket apparatus. (92)

Unknown

An unnamed ship from London sank going into Waterford on 22-12-1764. Captain Hogan and crew were lost. (90)

Unknown

A ship from Cadiz for Cork was wrecked at Island of Cain (Islandkeane) on 30-11-1765. She carried fruit and wine. Sloop. (90)

Harmony

The *Harmony* was sunk by the Cockburn on 12-2-1841 off Dungarvan. The vessel was en route

Detail of a bronze cannon trawled from the sea off Waterford.
Photo: Robin Leigh

from Wicklow to Bristol. (177)

Swift

The *Swift* was lost off Tramore on 17-1-1840. Some of the wreckage came ashore. (177)

Ellen Pope

The *Ellen Pope* was lost at Bonmahon on 19-1-1839. She was from Newport for Waterford. (177)

Medora

On 23-2-1840 the *Medora* was lost at Ardmore Bay. (177)

Jane

The *Jane* was wrecked in Dungarvan Bay on 10-2-1837 She was from Newport bound for Waterford. The Captain was Wakeham. (177)

Isabella

The barque *Isabella* went ashore at Waterford 28-11-1838. She was commanded by Captain Raymond and was en route from Pernambuco to Liverpool. It was hoped that she could be got off. There were 60 vessels windbound between Ballygar and Passage. (177)

Olive Branch

The *Olive Branch* was wrecked at the Bar at Dungarvan on 20-1-1838. Her master was Adams. The crew were saved. (177)

Jubilee

The *Jubilee* was wrecked at Dungarvan on 16-2-1838. She was bound for Liverpool from Mobile. The master was Edwards. (177)

Sir Francis Burton Linsay

The *Sir Francis Burton Linsay* was wrecked at Ardmore Bay on 16-2-1838. She was bound for Demerera from Liverpool. A boat from the Sir Howard Douglas which was aboard and some stores were all that were saved. The crew were lost. (177)

The *Moresby* was wrecked at Dungarvan on 24-12-1895. The 1259 ton vessel followed the schooner *Mary Sinclair* into the bay thinking it was Cork harbour. The crew anchored but not realising the danger the refused to abandon ship when the Balinacourty lifeboat offered assistance. The wind arose and distress signals were fired. This time the lifeboat crew refused to go out and twenty lives were lost.

Photo: Wigham Collection

A Hooker wrecked on the wreck of the *Moresby* at Dungarvan.

Photo: Andrew Kelly Collection

The *Peri* was lost at Seaview near Ring on 2-11-1907 She was owned by Moloneys of Dungarvan. Two of the crew of four were lost.

Photo: Andrew Kelly Collection

Brothers

The *Brothers* was lost in Tramore Bay on 24-10-1838. She was from Maryport for Ross. The Captain was Evans. (177)

Comala

The *Comala* also described as Comallo was lost at Dungarvan on 29-11-1838 She was from Singapore for Liverpool. This is likely the Camilla of Glasgow listed above. The 500 ton ship carried coffee, cloves, pepper, teas and tin worth a total of £30,000. The location was described as Corrignaman opposite Helvick. Fourteen of the crew were saved and three Kinsale pilots who had boarded the ship. The wreck was described as in the same place as the St John lost a few days before. (124)

Isabella

The *Isabella* was wrecked at Waterford on 28-11-1838. This truly remarkable vessel first beached on the Hook side but refloated and crossed the river beaching again upstream carried by the tide. Though assisted by a steamer an attempt to refloat her failed. However she refloated of her own accord and drifted downriver to sink in the channel. Despite sinking she rose again and an effort was made to bring her to the town pier. (177)

Providence

The *Providence* was wrecked at Tramore on 20-11-1830. The master was Mr James and she was bound for Cork from Newport. (177)

Unity

The *Unity* was wrecked between Waterford and Dungarvan on 2-12-1830. The master, Mr Power and three crew were lost. (177)

Picton

The *Picton* was wrecked at Waterford on 6-12-1830. She had come from Oporto Captained by Crystal. (177)

Eliza

The *Eliza* foundered off Waterford on 30-9-1831. She was en route from Cork to London. The master was Williams. (177)

Lusitania

The *Lusitania* stranded at Ardmore. She was from Liverpool to Oporto. The cargo was saved but the vessel broke up on 23-10-1831. (177)

Christian

A headboard with the name *Christian* was washed ashore on the Waterford coast on 3-5-1830. About 150 pieces of American timber were also washed ashore at the same time. (177)

Elizabeth & Anne

The *Elizabeth and Anne* foundered leaving Waterford on 7-10-1832. The master Mr Lewis and all the crew were lost. (177)

Shamrock

The river steamer *Shamrock* sank on 3-6-1854 near Waterford. The vessel carried pigs from the market at Ross. It was the custom to make two journeys on a fair day. As the craft neared the pier the pigs rushed to one side and the Shamrock took in water and sank. The crew and drovers were all saved. (27)

Barge

On 4-10-1960, two barges which had been sheltering at Dunmore sailed. The weather deteriorated and a gale was forecast. The life boat authorities anticipated trouble due to a strong ebb tide and a heavy ground sea. The Dunmore East lifeboat had only passed the pier Head when flares were seen from one of the barges. The engine had failed and she was lying close to shore exposed to the wind and seas. She was being driven rapidly onto Laweesh Rock. The lifeboat went in to rescue the only man aboard by placing her bow into the barge amidships. At the third attempt and guided by a searchlight the men on the lifeboat hauled the bargeman aboard. This was difficult as the barge had no freeboard nor rails and the man had only the tiller to hold. The second barge which had been on tow by the first had been cut adrift but had not drifted as much because she carried 40 tons of ballast. The drifting barge was saved by being taken to Dunmore. (35)

French East Indiaman

A French East Indiaman sank off Credan Head, Waterford, prior to 1758. An obstruction due to the wreck was mentioned in connection with a Royal Naval ship which visited Waterford in 1758. (3). The Captain of the *Duke of William* recounted the story in connection with previous history of his voyage prior to loss of the *Duke of William* in America. The ship went into Waterford, the pilot came out and the pilot boat was lost at high rocks. The pilot said that the channel had been made very narrow because a large

The *Tyne* of North Shields ashore at Ballinacourty Dungarvan in 1909.
Photo: Jacob Collection, Waterford Library

French East Indiaman was lost on the Bar and he did not know the marks to clear the wreck, this happened in 1758.

Grinder

In 1811 the schooner *Grinder* out of London bound for Lisbon with a cargo of wool blew off course and went aground on Tramore beach. (8).

Edward

The *Edward* was wrecked at Ballymacaw on 19-12-1837. She had come from Cork bound for Waterford. Captain Buckley and his crew were saved. (177)

Favourite

The *Favourite* was wrecked on rocks at Dogs nose on 5-1-1838. She had come from Cork bound for Waterford. The crew were saved. (177)

Harmony

The *Harmony* of Belfast foundered off Dungarvan 16-2-1841. The crew were saved (1)

Commerce

In 1811 the sloop *Commerce* out of Plymouth with a cargo of bacon bound for Waterford was lost in Tramore Bay. (8)

Kate

The *Kate* of Bristol captained by Collings discharged and then capsized at Waterford on 21-12-1844. She sank in deep water with the loss of four lives. (177)

Elizabeth.

The *Elizabeth* went to pieces on going ashore in "Tramond", Tramore Bay on 11-1-1844. She was from Newport bound for Kinsale captained by Travers. (177)

Draper

There was more wreckage half a mile from Waterford on 25-9-1783. This included staves of brandy pipes and hogsheads, claret hogsheads and vinegar tierces. The cargo also included reeds, almonds, gloves. The ensign which came ashore was English and from the cargo she must have been from Bordeaux. One of the stern boards had letters which could be *Draper* but the bottom portion was missing. There were no survivors and it was not evident until late in the day that a second vessel had been lost. (121)

Clareen

The *Clareen* was stranded at Waterford in 1924 (vol. 1) further information came to light in ref. 144. The Clareen was salvaged and repaired and reregistered at Waterford. This became apparent when she was reported as having collided with the jetty at Aberystwyth in March 1927. The auxiliary schooner Industry was also reported (1440 to have been lost on the Irish Coast.

Dutch vessel

A report from Waterford described the remains of a Dutch vessel wrecked to the West of Waterford Harbour on 25-9-1783. Four crew were lost and three saved. Half of the cargo which drove ashore was saved. (121)

Foreign ship

A large square rigged vessel was observed three leagues from Tramore Bay in great distress on the afternoon of 9-9-1783. Guns were heard during the night and in the morning there were no tidings of her. She seemed to be foreign with white sides but because of high seas there was no possibility of affording her any assistance. (121)

The following was prepared by Brian Mac Alister of Moorings marine noting wrecks which can be dived on the Waterford coast

Wreck	Tons	Depth (metres)	Type
Marguerite	1500	10	Steam Ship
Grogham	499	10	MV
UC 44	150	10	U boat
Shaninsay	100	18	trawler
Kerrick	110	18	trawler
Oasis	2000	12	iron sailing ship
George Milburn	235	21	mine sweeper
Alfred D Snow	1987	32	Sailing ship
Lismore	2130	38	Ss
Trafford	215	52	Ss
Ethal Manor	1875	58	Collier
Anthony	6445	59	Liner
Feltrea	5254	61	Ss
Coordy	2470	62	sailing ship
Ary	642	46	Ss
Carlow	1770	65	merchantman
Lincolnshire	3965	66	Ss
Ardmore	2500	68	Ss
Karina	2300	70	Ss
Manchester Engineer	6300	74	liner

CORK

Betty
The *Betty* foundered off Youghal 13-8-1784. The 200 ton ship was en route from Boston to Dublin with a cargo of flax seed and rum. Captain John Williams and his crew of sixteen perished except for one man and a boy. (155)

Abbett
The *Abbett* sank off Ballycotton after contact with the Royal Saxon on 13-3-1841. The vessel was en route from Neath to Cork. The crew were saved. (177)

Clemenson
The *Clemenson* of Whitehaven was wrecked at Ballycotton on 28-11-1838. Her master was John Newby. She carried a valuable cargo of copper ore, cotton and indigo. The vessel was bound for Liverpool from Port Cabello, La Guyra. Cotton bales were picked up at Cove. The coastguard called out the military to assist in protecting the wreck. There is no mention of survivors. (124)

Mary
The 568 ton, *Mary* of Liverpool was wrecked at Ring, Clonakilty on 28-11-1838. She had come from Marenham in South America with 400 bales of sarsaparilla, 50 casks of India rubber, 50 barrels of balsam capivi. Local gentlemen Msrs Lucas, Gallway and Crofts organised the rescue of captain George Smith and the 17 crew.

Large vessel
A large vessel was wrecked at Reanny Head near Rocky Bay in a gale on 8-3-1783. Every individual aboard perished. It is supposed she was in ballast as no cargo was driven ashore. (121)

Catherine
The hooker, *Catherine* of Youghal owned by Davis & Cox sailed for Cork from Youghal with 100 barrels of herrings. She reached the Fanwick river but ran on shore at Greenland house inside cable Island. The surf on the beach threatened to drown all but the two crewmen were saved by seven men put out in a yawl and saved them. (93)

Unknown
A square rigged vessel was seen two leagues from shore labouring in an extraordinary manner on 6-3-1785. A boat put out to make inquiries but no answer was made from on board. Repeated attempts were made to board but proved ineffectual due to the heavy swell. Before morning she sunk and vessel and cargo were lost. The boatmen supposed that she was a foreigner and had been deserted when she sprung a leak. (155)

Briget
The *Briget* sank at Cable Island, Youghal on 21-10-1830. The crew abandoned the vessel. However the coastguard managed to tow her to the beach. (177)

The *Three Brothers*, a sailing ketch was wrecked in 1961 at Youghal.
Photo: Andrew Kelly Collection

Unknown
On 7-1-1832 masts and casks were washed ashore at Whiting Bay, Youghal. They came from a ship which had foundered recently. (177)

Matilda
The *Matilda* went ashore at Ballycotton Bay near Youghal on 20-11-1830. She was from Neath for Cork captained by Matthews. (177)

Examination boat No 3
The *Irish Poplar* was entering Cork Harbour during a severe gale on 12-12-1942. The pilot boat was to transfer the pilot and the examination boat transfer the Harbour Control Officer. His function was to reveal the correct signal for entering through the Harbour defences and check contraband wartime cargoes. This left the two launches alongside the *Irish Poplar* which began to move up the Lee channel bound for Rushbrook Dockyard. The ship was light and very high in the water so that her propeller was not fully submerged. As the launches passed along the side of the ship obstructing each others escape they were driven against the ship by the seas. Disaster struck as both launches were hit repeatedly and sank. One survivor made shore on

Haulbowline but all the rest aboard were lost, four on the Examination boat and two on the pilot boat. (41)

John

The *John* was wrecked at Ringabella in November 1781. The cargo was saved (115)

Gunhole Bay

A reef at the Northern end of Holeopen Bay East at the Old Head of Kinsale is close to a location known as Gunhole Bay. Three cannon were found here in 14 metres between the reef and the land. And also on the seaward side of the reef. They imply that a ship was lost on the reef. (177)

Anchor

An anchor was raised from a sandy bottom inside High Island at the SW entrance to Union Hall

It was 20.5 feet long and weighed five and a half tons. Some canvas remained adhered but the wooden cross piece had disappeared. It was thought to be about 1700 and of French style. It is intended to place at the pier at Union Hall. The anchor was located when a local vessel became impaled on it. (177)

Matthews Adventure

The *Matthews Adventure* was reported lost on 10-12-1766 at Crosshaven. She carried rum, hops, sugar and porter from London for Londonderry. A rebate of duty of £220 was allowed by the Customs for the dutiable goods lost. In January of the next year Lane Bensons and Vaughan merchants of Cork petitioned that the goods saved might be sent to their destination without payment of duty until they arrived. Some confusion is introduced when mention is made that this wreck stranded at Crookhaven. These include 65 puncheons of rum, 25 hogsheads of porter. Wool, bundles of cask hoops. Goods to the value of £1780 had been salvaged. The Commissioners gave permission to proceed so long as the vessel carried a "trusty officer to ensure that the duty would be paid on arrival at Derry" (115)

Another report mentions that two vessels were wrecked at Cork and that there was not enough space in the King's Cellar to accommodate all the goods salvaged. Storage had to be rented. Further correspondence in March 1767 indicated that the wreck was at Crookhaven and that the sum for the salvage of £1104 was in error and should read £114. However the vessel is called Martha's Adventure. The cargo is detailed as 2000 weight of hops, 173 watch movements and 45 ounces of plate.

Elizabeth

The *Elizabeth* was wrecked at Crookhaven on 25-8-1767. Mr French, a customs boatman, claimed for his salvage services. (115)

Adventure

Mention was made of the salvage of goods worth £610 from the *Adventure* at Youghal on 15-4-1767 (115)

Liberty

On 8-11-1877 the 10 ton smack *Liberty* was lost threequarters of a mile

The 82 ton steam collier *Rover* of Cardiff went ashore at Whiting Bay, Youghal on 7-7-1899. The collier was badly damaged.

Photo: Andrew Kelly Collection

NW of Mizen Head, Co Cork. The Liberty was 19 years old and owned by W. Roan of Arklow.

Louise de Castile

A small Island South of Whiddy is known today as Lousy Island. However old Admiralty charts call it Louise Island. Bill O'Donnell of the Anchor Hotel at Bantry suggests that it may have been called Louise de Castile Island and may be so named after a wreck. A small timber part of a rib with a brass pin was found nearby.

Lady Harriet

The *Lady Harriet* took shelter in Long Island Sound on 20-12-1795. She was bound for Dublin from Cadiz with a cargo of fruit. The vessel was plundered by a mob of people who took the cargo and destroyed the hull. Not an atom was left afloat. All was cut away with hatchets brought for the purpose. The remains of the vessel were later salvaged by Richard Hull of Leamcon and his brother. The brig was owned in Cork and captained by Colt. (120)

Priscilla

The *Priscilla* was accidentally burned with her cargo of coal at Reenadona in the Ilen river on 24-12-1926. The 84 ton 2 masted schooner was built in Hylton in 1871. Her captain was James Poden of Sherkin Island. (120)

Four X

The 80 foot puffer type vessel *Four X* was used to service oil tankers at the Whiddy Terminal. The vessel was about 100 years old when she was abandoned as a derelict at Bantry Pier.

In a tidy up operation she was sunk East of League Point in 10 fathoms.

Wreckage

The tiny Harbour of Puleen just West of Castletownbere is a noted spot where currents meet and drive wreckage ashore.

Kerry Head

The *Kerry Head* was sunk by a German FW Condor long range patrol plane which crashed just after the attack. It is believed that the plane was damaged in the explosion of the Kerry Head or it tipped the mast. Though no crew survived the sinking, some cattle were found ashore and thought to have come from the wreck. The wreck lies in 37 fathoms and from the substantial mass detected it must be in good condition. On a sonal screen the vessel is at the edge of an area of rough ground to its West.

Paris

The *Paris* was en route from Holland to Fenit with a cargo of basic slag. While six miles South of Fastnet a seacock in the engine room burst and flooded the ship. Skipper Wagner was banking on the bulkheads holding until a tug arrived to the rescue. Meanwhile the Baltimore lifeboat took off the crew from a dingy while the *LE Grainne* stood by. There was no subsequent report so she is assumed to have been saved.

Holmfield

The 600 ton *MV Holmfield* went aground in 1963 at North end of Whiddy Island.

Submarine

The mystery submarine which was seen to run up on Dhulic Rock was observed by Mr Hosford former owner of a supermarket in Skibbereen. A group were standing on Galley Head during World War II and saw the sub rear out of the water on striking the Rock. An unidentified echo and rust stains indicate a wreck at 63 metres just inside the Ludgate. This might be the sub as no other wreck is known at this site. There is no record of a submarine loss around this location.

Inis Arkin

The 58 foot 45 ton *Inis Arkin* caught fire on 22-6-1930 and sank. The crew were picked up by the liner Scythia bound for Cobh from New York. She lies at 51.39.813N 9.40.591 W.

Carbery King

The *Carbery King* was sunk 14 miles South of the Stags by a submarine. On the 3-5-1917 the *Sir Edward, Birkbeck, Hibernia, Fastnet, Lucky Lass, North Star* were all sunk nearby in similar circumstances. A submarine came alongside and placed bombs aboard or scuttled them all between 13 and 16 miles South of the Stags.

Advocate

On 15-4-1852, the *Advocate*, a 296 ton barque was wrecked on the cliffs at the East side of Roberts Cove. The 15 crew were rescued by the Roberts cove coastguards. She carried a cargo of teak from Moulmein for London. (177)

The *City of Chicago* wreck occurred at 190 foot high cliffs at the Old Head of Kinsale. The 360 passengers were lucky to be transferred to the ship's boats or helped up the cliffs by coastguards. The view to the deck from the cliff above gives an idea of the heights to be scaled.

Photo: courtesy Subsea

Spanish trawler

A Spanish trawler lies 1.1 miles North of Sheep Head. The position is 51.33.93 N, 9 51 39.9 W.

Alma

On 25-2-1923 the *Alma* was driven ashore in a NW gale at Reen, Skehanore near Ballydehob. She was a 32 ton lugger engaged in coastal trade. The cargo was salvaged by the National army who occupied Balllydehob in 1923 during the Civil War.

Brass cannon

A "brass" cannon was found on a diving trip near Mizen Head. It is not clear what ship it may have come from. It is unlikely that L'Impatiente carried bronze guns as her cannon were iron. The location of the gun or any accurate description are unavailable. (120)

Andreas G

The Spanish trawler *Andreas G* sank at the Sav estuary in January 1960 at Bantry Bay (see vol 1) though of little monetary value the owners raised her and towed the wreck back to Spain. She was their first boat and had established their fortune which explains the attachment.

Maso 19
The wooden Spanish trawler was wrecked at Donovan's Point West of Gearies in October 1954. The crew were rescued by locals in hazardous conditions. (120)

Hope
On 4-1-1788 the *Hope* of Waterford was stranded at Youghal. She was bound for London with a cargo of provisions captained by Thomas Walsh. Though the cargo was saved it was expected that the vessel would be lost. (30)

Aranci
The *Aranci* sank 22 miles S by W of Tuskar on 7-3-1932. The ship was being towed by the tug Strongbow from Newry to Portsmouth. The 179 ton, Aranci was built by Walker at Devonport in 1882 and lengthened in 1884. She was owned by Copax of Connahs Quay.

Alison
On 22-10-1928 the *Alison* was sunk in a collision with the collier Zillah, owned by Zillah Shipping and Carrying Co Ltd. The wreck of the Alison was raised by Palmer of Ringaskiddy. They used two liner tenders as lifting vessels to raise and beach the Alison.

Rosses Morn
The trawler *Rosses Morn* was abandoned after she struck a rock and was holed on 4-2-99. The trawler had been fishing for herring with six men aboard. Four had landed at Cobh and the remaining two took the vessel on to Castletownbere. As they neared Courtmacsharry they were hit by heavy seas, driven on rocks and holed. Both Mr Murphy and Mr O'Driscoll evacuated the vessel using life rafts but Mr Murphy was missing when a helicopter winched the owner Mr David O'Driscoll to safety. (73)

Abet
The schooner *Abet* foundered on 23-3-1841 at Cove after striking an emigrant ship (1)

Medora
The brig *Medora* went to pieces at Youghal on 22-2-1840. She was en route from Yarmouth to Swansea. (177)

Havre
A buoy was being placed over the wreck of the *Havre,* an American vessel sunk off the pierhead at Cork on 24-4-1840. (1)

Eliza Anne
The *Eliza Anne* was wrecked on 30-11-1830 at Roche's Bay. The owner and 3 passengers were lost. She was en route from Bordeaux for new Providence captained by Miller. (177)

George McCausland
The *George McCausland* was lost off Youghal on 18-1-1831 she was identified by bits of timber washed ashore. (177)

Shaw Stewart
The *Shaw Stewart* was wrecked near Oysterhaven on 26-11-1831. Her master was Sinclair. The voyage was Greenock to Limerick. (177)

The *Assaye* went aground on 28-1-1865 in Ross Bay near Galley Head during fog. The ship was built as a paddle frigate in Bombay for the East India Company in 1854.

Etching: Illustrated London News

Unknown

On 16-12-1831 a hooker encountered wreckage and casks floating off Barry's Head. Two pipes of brandy and casks were brought into Kinsale. One was marked James Henessy, Cognac and another Violet & Co.

John Campbell

The John Campbell was wrecked at the entrance to Crookhaven on 15-12-1831. She was bound for Cork from Quebec. The crew were saved. Her captain was Campbell. (177)

Economy

The Economy was driven out of Castletownsend and wrecked on 7-12-1830 She was from Limerick for Bristol captained by James. The crew were lost. On 2-4-1831 she was raised with little damage, even the cargo had not been washed out. The Jupiter from Hamboro for Cardiff was wrecked at the same time. (177)

Star of the Sea

The *Cork pilot boat* a 41 ton yawl was lost in a collision in 1920. A claim was made against the Admiralty according to a Cork Harbour Commissioners letter.

Lady Flora Hastings

The *Lady Flora Hastings* was wrecked near Schull about 1845. (9)

La Soldida

It is attractive to associate Spanish Point near Crookhaven with the frigate La Soldida recorded as lost at

The French oil tanker *Betelgeuse* broke in two and caught fire at the Whiddy island oil terminal in Bantry Bay on 8-1-1979.

Photo: courtesy James Murphy

Crookhaven but nothing has been found underwater at the site. The Spanish frigate sank 25-1-1780. One local story said that a ship had beached near Spanish Point for repairs.

Sirius

The *Sirius* was lost in June 1847. She was famous for making the first transatlantic crossing under steam. Several salvage efforts were made and many souvenirs survive. A pump rod was raised after 51 years and bought by Masons of Birmingham who cut it up to make medallions. The black dog figurehead from the Sirius is in Hull Maritime Museum.

Mary Lorraine

Six fishermen were picked up from a liferaft at the entrance to Kinsale Harbour on 7-4-1994. Their trawler had run aground on the rocks. A local sea angling boat performed the rescue.

Maria

The 50 ton smack *Maria* foundered in a gale off Rocky Island on 31-12-1900. (178)

Claudia

On 29-9-1994, the 140 foot fishing boat, *Claudia*, sank 12 miles East of Ballycotton. The two fishermen aboard escaped.

Carraig Liur

A French three masted fishing boat was wrecked on Carraig Liur beneath the old lighthouse on Cape Clear The date is not clear (10) This may be the *Hourtien* wrecked on 15-9-1931 described in volume one.

Pescalanza

The 120 foot, Spanish trawler, *Pescalanza* was lost in a gale on 2-11-1998 80 miles South West of Mizen Head. The British registered trawler had a crew of twelve. Five were rescued from a life raft by the French registered *Ategorreta* which had been fishing nearby. A sixth survivor was picked up from the vessel along with four bodies. It is thought that the trawler was capsized by four metre waves driven by a force nine gale. (16)

Vriendchap

The brig, *Vriendchap* from Effequito on Demerary was wrecked on the rocks near Galley Head on 8-12-1786. She was bound for Middleburg with a cargo of 156 hogsheads of sugar, 63 bags of cotton and 700 bags of coffee. Captain Adrian Laundiaz survived but the mate and one sailor were drowned. (121)

Zeclont

The galliot, *Zeclont* stranded at Red Strand near Galley Head on 8-12-1786. She was bound for Vaure in France from St Andre with 270 bags of Spanish wool and logs of dye woods. The master was Cornelius Derks. It is not clear if the stranded ship was freed. (121)

Amity / Lark

Cannon from either the *Amity* or the *Lark* wrecked in Dunworley Bay survive at Ballea Castle, Carraigaline the property of Robin Power. They would have been raised by the Collins brothers in the 1890s. (33)

Unknown

Glass beads and cylinders were found on the beach at Dunworley Bay. They were described as 15/16th century and of near eastern origin. It was presumed that a trading ship had been wrecked at the location. (164)

Fastnet

Mention was made in a display about the telegraphic connectors between Fastnet and Crookhaven that a wreck had been observed on the Fastnet Rock. There is no further information nor record of a wreck at that location. A member of the Circle Diving Group confirmed that they found no such wreck when they investigated the large brass "mushroom" connectors now on display at the Maritime Museum.

Sally

The 60 ton sloop Sally went down off Black Ball Head on 30-11-1830. Captain Roycroft and the three crew were lost. The sinking was seen by the coastguard. She was from Swansea for Castletownbere. (177)

Warrior

The Warrior was wrecked at Coolmain between Seven Heads and the Old Head of Kinsale on 19-1-1840. She was from Liverpool bound for Charlestown. The captain was Jones. (177)

Pompey
The sloop *Pompey* of Cork was wrecked at Dunany cove near Clonakilty on 6-4-1768. Her master was James Sangster. She had come from Antigua with a cargo of rum and logwood. (90)

Helen & Mary
The *Helen and Mary* was en route from St Ubes to Limerick with a cargo of salt. She was wrecked at Coles Point on 6-12-1768 entering Cork Harbour. The captain was Michael Burke. (90)

Saga
On 16-2-1895 the Swedish brig *Saga* was lost between Ballycotton and Poor Head. She had been abandoned and newspaper accounts said that there was no information on the reasons why the crew left the ship. The cargo was white powder and she had sailed from Burnt Island, Leith for Nickerbie in Central America. A similar named ship was described in "Cork" by Daphne Pouchin Mould as ashore in February 1883 with bloody evidence of mutiny. There is no newspaper account associated with February 1883. It would seem that the two ships were the same but whatever about the mutiny the bloodstains were unfounded (122)

Sloop
An unnamed sloop was wrecked at the Old Head of Kinsale on 22-12-1767. She was from Padstow for Cork. (90)

Thomas
The *Thomas* of Dublin was wrecked at Rocky Bay, Cork Harbour on 26-8-1766. Two of captain Steward's crew were lost. She carried rum from Barbados. (90)

Unknown
An unnamed Stockholm ship was wrecked at Youghal on 24-6-1766. She carried iron bound for Waterford. (90)

Unknown
An unnamed ship from Dublin bound for Jamaica with beef was wrecked at Donnamore near Timoleague on 24-6-1766. (90)

Revenue barge
The Seven Heads revenue barge was lost at Kinsale on 26-4-1766. Five boatmen and three women were lost. Two more had returned to the station on horseback. (90)

Hampton
The *Hampton* of Lancaster was stranded at Dunworley on the East side of Clonakilty Bay on 22-12-1767. She had sailed from Barbados bound for Bristol. The master was Richard Lethbarrow. (177)

Hampden
The *Hampden* was wrecked at Sandy Cove, Kinsale on 13-11-1770. Her captain was Dudley. (90)

Sloop
An unnamed sloop was wrecked at Clay Castle Bay near Youghal on 15-11-1768. She carried rum and fruit bound for Waterford from Cork. John Mackey was master. (90)

Industry
The *Industry* was upset between Passage and Cove on 28-1-1769. (90)

Union

The *Union* of Bristol was lost at Kilbritain on 27-12-1763. She was bound for Limerick from her home port. (90)

Collier

A collier was lost off Ballycotton on 27-12-1763. Mr Vernon was her master. (90)

Lord Clare

The *Lord Clare* of Bristol was wrecked at Castlehaven on 24-12-1768. She was bound for Malaga from Cork. Captain Phelps and his crew were saved. (90)

Unknown

A ship from Dominico bound for Liverpool was wrecked in Bantry Bay on 28-4-1770. She carried a cargo of coffee, cocoa and cotton. The master was henry Guyon. (90)

Rose

The *Rose* of Cork was wrecked at Castlehaven on 24-12-1768. She carried wine, brandy and vinegar from Bordeaux to Waterford. The cargo was saved and lodged in the cellars of Richard Townsend. William Dowlan was master. (90)

Charming Susannah

The snow, *Charming Susannah* of Cork was driven ashore at Haulbowline on 1-9-1764. She was bound for the West Indies. Captain Terence Connor and the crew were assisted by the men from HMS Hussar commanded by Captain Such. (90)

Tempter

A trawler *Tempter* is marked on a shipwreck chart as lost near the Old Head of Kinsale. The date is however ambiguously given as 1961 or 1956.

Dronning Sophie

The coal hulk *Dronning Sophie* was raised on 19-11-1930 by Palmers. The vessel had sunk in a storm at Monkstown drowning the two watchmen aboard. Dronning Sophie was built of teak at Moulmein in Burma in 1847 as the Sir George Pollock. Originally she was fully rigged and measured 630 tons.

Boat

A boat was lost on 15-11-1825 on a rock between Cape Clear and Skibbereen. It was market day and a group were en route for the event at Skibbereen. They also had a purpose to change English silver coinage for Irish in accordance with the regulations. Seven lives were lost though initial reports indicated that some 50 people had perished. (17)

Sarah

The *Sarah* foundered off Ballycotton Island on 5-11-1842. She was en route from Swansea to Waterford. Her captain was Tedball. (177)

Speedwell

The *Speedwell* was en route from Clonakilty to Dublin. She was wrecked at Poor Head on 1-2-1830. The crew and 180 bags of flour were saved. (177)

Unknown

An unknown vessel was wrecked off Youghal on 30-1-1837. Wreckage was washed ashore which included a seaman's chest marked "Christopher O'Connell, Philadelphia". (177)

A study of newspaper accounts between 1800 and 1840 provides a further example of the differences between a local list and the information recorded in Lloyds list. This is an interesting comparison of data from the newspapers collated by Tim Cadogan and published in Mizen Historical Journal. Lloyds List mentions only a few of the wrecks

Name	Date Lost	Master	Location	Home Port /voyage	Comment
Albion	3-12-1828	Glanville	Grays Point Baltimore	Cove to Lisbon	Mentioned in Lloyds list
Argo	21-4-1822	Unknown		Whitehaven	Mentioned in Lloyds list
Bacchus	1-11-1835	Martin			
Barbara	25-11-1829	Denis Casey	South side of Crookhaven	Berehaven	
Baring	10-10-1814			troop transport	Mentioned in Lloyds list
Betsey	6-11-1800		off Garnish	Liverpool	
Boaunis	11-12-1802				
Canada	17-6-1811		Dunboy Berehaven		
Charles	9-5-1836		Off Cape Clear	Charleston	
Confiance	21-4-1822	Morgan	Dunlough Bay	Amsterdam	
Darthulla	11-10-1822	Blenkinsop	Crookhaven	Newfoundland	
Earl of Leicester	24-6-1835	Dorning	Berehaven	Liverpool Limerick	
Economy	5-12-1830			Newport	
Effort	17-10-1831	Shaxton	SW Dursey Is	Bideford	
Emmeline	21-1-1840	Hoyt	Glengarriff	St John NB	
Europa	13-1-1834	Hill	Rosscarbery	Liverpool - Bahia	
Fitzroy	1-6-1835		Dunkelly Dunmanus Bay	Quebec- London	
Grace	28-11-1838	Reed	Roaringwater Bay	Got off	
Guardian	31-3-1805	Duplex	Toe Head	New York	
Hannah	17-10-1823		Long Island	South Shields	auctioned
Hope	13-2-1823	Middleton	Ballerisard Crookhaven	Newry	
John Campbell	1-12-1831	Patterson	Crookhaven	Cork	auctioned
Josias	25-11- 1830		Black Ball Head	Kinsale	
Jupiter	5-12-1830	Behniko	Castletownsend	Hamburg	
Kitty	1-8-1830			Cape Clear	
Lady Charlotte	23-10-1838	Bettingall	Long Is Sound	Liverpool	

Name	Date Lost	Master	Location	Home Port /voyage	Comment
Maria	15-3-1810		Castlefreake	Plymouth	
Martin	9-5-1827		Berehaven		
Mary	1-5-1833	Morris	Barrels Rock	Demerera-Dublin	
Mary	1-1-1804		Glandore	Boston	
Melchbourn	1-6-1827		unknown	Bristol	
Messenger	1-11-1835			Sunderland	towed to Cork
Oralia	27-11-1837	Rowland	Bere Island	Plymouth	
Prince Kutousoff	13-12-1829		Castlefreake	Whitby	
Providence	17-12-1813	Roberts	Mizen Head	Carnavon	
Robert & Edward	22-4-1822	Readfearn	Castlehaven	Whitehaven	
Rood Rech	31-12-1807	Daw	Newfoundland - Waterford	Poole	
Sally	27-11-1830	Roycroft	Black Ball Head	Swansea	
Thomas Tucker	28-11-1838	Moore	Carthy Island	Liverpool	
Thomas Worthington	26-11-1835		Crookhaven	St John NB	
Trial	20-1-1834		West end Cape Clear	London	
Trio	25-2-1827	Bexfield	Dunlough Bay	Derry	
Try Again	11-9-1828		Crookhaven	Quebec	auctioned
Triphena	20-1-1838	Roberts	Castletownbere	Nidbear - London	
Unity	30-4-1822		Berehaven	Glasgow	
Argo	30-4-1822		Berehaven		
Vittoria	17-12-1831	Forster	Berehaven	London	saved

Alessandra
The *Alessandra* went to pieces at Cork on 10-2-1837. (177)

Albion
The *Albion* was abandoned at sea on 25-12-1836. She went ashore at Galley Head on 10-2-1837. The cargo of timber for London was saved. (177)

Oxford
The *Oxford* was wrecked at Clonakilty on 28-2-1837. The figurehead and timbers were washed ashore. (177)

John George Elphinstone
The Newcastle schooner, *John George Elphinstone* was lost off Ballycotton on 13-9-1837. The vessel sank leaving the masts showing above water. She carried butter and bacon from Cork to London. Seven crew were lost. (177)

Laurel
The Brig *Laurel* was lost at Robert's Head on 20-9-1837. She carried staves from Kinsale for Cork. (177)

Jane
The brig *Jane* was wrecked at Fish Island, Richmond Bay, Cork on 31-10-1837. She was bound for Waterford from Miramichi. The captain was Whelan. (177)

Thomas Halburton

On 14-8-1839 the *Thomas Halburton* was run down by a barque off Cork Harbour. The crew were saved. (177)

Mary

The *Mary* was wrecked at the Old Head of Kinsale 0n 14-2-1839. Captain Fudge and his crew were safe. She was from Liverpool for Limerick. (177)

John Lambert

The *John Lambert* was wrecked at Ballyshane rocks at Ring in Clonakilty Bay on 14-10-1839. She was from Archangel bound for Cork. The crew were saved when the ship went to pieces. (177)

Spartan

The *Spartan* heeled over and stove in at Cork on 24-8-1837. She was from Civia Vechia captained by Cornish. (177)

Fanny Voose, Friends

The *Fanny Voose* and the *Friends* were both wrecked off the lighthouse at Cork on 18-2-1838. The Fanny Voose was from Hull. (177)

John & Eliza

The *John & Eliza* was wrecked at Cable Island, Youghal on 16-2-1838. She was from Carnavon bound for London. The were saved except for a boy. (177)

Unknown

An unnamed Spanish brig was wrecked at the Old Head of Kinsale on 20-1-1838. (177)

Commerce

The *Commerce* was wrecked on rocks at Youghal on 29-12-1837. She was from Swansea. The captain was McGrath. (177)

Tryphena

The *Tryphena* was wrecked at Castletownbere on 20-1-1838. The 60 ton vessel carried a cargo of oats from Nidbear to London. (177)

Havre

The *Havre* sank in 12 fathoms off Cork Harbour on 10-2-1838. She was from New Orleans for Liverpool. The captain was Vernon. (177)

Rona

An unnamed wreck was found on the Stags Rocks off Toe Head. There was a pintail from a large sailing ship, maybe from *Rona* a 638 ton sailing ship owned by W Clifford & Son, Liverpool Built by A Stephen & Sons Glasgow in 1867. She was wrecked on the Stags off Toe Head on 14-10-1893. A sextant was found and remains of pottery. The pottery had a border in the design of a rope with a central emblem possibly that of a shipping line. The emblem was surrounded by the remains of letters ......e s.... This could be a name like White Star. No ship of that line was known to have been lost on the Stags. The possibility of second hand pottery from the White Star Line cannot be discounted. (33)

Mary

The *Mary of Jersey* was wrecked at Baltimore on 19-4-1751. She carried a cargo of wine. (177)

Santa Theresa

The French ship *Santa Theresa* whose master was Jacques Guerrin went ashore at Horse Island, Castlehaven in Summer 1751. Three boats went to her

The wreck of the *Killarney,* 26-1-1838 at Rennie Bay.
A contemporary etching, artist unknown.

assistance and saved the cargo of indigo. The authorities were suspicious because three boats and crews were able to put to sea so quickly. Enquiries were also made as to whether the pilot had put her into danger deliberately. (115)

Society

The *Society*, a sloop, of Youghal, sank a league off Castletown near Skibbereen in 1751. The cargo was discharged into a sloop before she sank and concealed ashore. Many watched all night in the expectation that wreckage would be washed ashore, Butter branded "Youghal" was seized. There was no account of the master and crew. As the cargo was insured, the Commissioners of Customs and Excise gave direction that the insurers should be told of the strange circumstances of the loss. (115)

Lucy Ann

The *Lucy Ann* was wrecked on rocks at Charles Fort, Kinsale on 13-1-1844. She was from Ichiboe to Bristol. (177)

Govenor Orckbut

The *Govenor Orckbut* foundered near Cape Clear on 23-1-1844. A boat was washed ashore at Cape Clear. A further boat and the ship's figurehead came ashore at Castletownsend. The captain was John Harwood. (177)

Prince Albert

The *Prince Albert* of Bantry became a total loss when she struck Ballycotton

The *Tadorna* was wrecked on 15-11-1911at Ballycrenane strand East of Ballycotton. She had only been built in 1910 at Swan Hunter on Tyneside.

Photo: History of Cork shipping, Barry

Island on 11-3-1844. She had come from Liverpool with a cargo of salt. The crew survived. (177)

Clifton

The *Clifton* caught fire in Cork on 25-3-1844. She was scuttled in deep water. The ship was outward bound for St John's. the captain was Carroll. (177)

Unknown

Wreckage from an unnamed ship was cast ashore at Kinsale on 18-10-1844. (177)

Latona

On 7-2-1842 the *Latona* went ashore between Courtmacsharry and Kinsale and was expected to be wrecked. She had come from Alexandria Captained by Sutton. (177)

Unknown

Wreckage was cast ashore at Rabbit Island, Glandore on 8-11-1844. Papers in a chest referred to three different ships. Cargo had been transferred to a *Shamrock* captained by Duncan and this may have been the wreck. (177)

KERRY

Cleopatra

On 27-4-1844 the *Cleopatra* was wrecked at Ventry Harbour. She was from Sunderland bound for Richibuto. Captain Harisson and crew were saved. (177)

Wild Goose

The sloop, *Wild Goose* was seized by the excisemen and sunk at Kenmare about 25-11-1751. The local MP Daniel O'Connell petitioned that she be raised as she was an obstruction to navigation and herring fishing. The Commissioners of Customs and Excise agreed to allow him to have her raised if one third of the value was paid to the seizing officer. (115)

Unknown

A ship from the West Indies was lost on the Kerry coast near the mouth of the Shannon on 31-12-1768. She carried sugar and rum. Another vessel was lost nearby. She carried wine from Oporto for Cork. (90)

La Asturiana

The stern frame of a vessel was washed up at Dingle on 21-3-1842. A box was marked *La Asturiana* ARC Navera. (177)

Sarah

The *Sarah* bound for Newfoundland was wrecked on the West coast of Kerry on 19-12-1767. Captain Thompson was in command. Twenty five passengers and crew perished. (90)

East Indiaman

On 27-7-1841 Captain Evans of the *Loadstone* reported that an East Indiaman was seen bottom up 9 miles off the Scelligs. One of the characteristics which identified her as an important ship was the coppered bottom which even then was unusual. (177)

Unknown

On 10-10-1785 a vessel supposed to be foreign was wrecked on the rocky islands called Blosques (Blaskets) off the coast of Kerry. Every soul perished. There were 14 chests driven ashore containing wearing apparel, plate, watches and other valuable articles. It was imagined that the ship was Spanish and bound from some port in the Americas, or the islands bound for old Spain. (155)

Lemon Rock

An Admiralty pattern anchor was found by divers on a ledge at Lemon Rock off the Blaskets. It was 5 feet long with the letters OTTOMH inscribed. The anchor lies on the on the sheltered side of the Rock. This may be the only trace of an otherwise unknown wreck.

Lochar

Near the wreck of the *Quebra* lies an Admiralty pattern anchor. It is likely to be the only remains of the sailing ship *Lochar* after which the Rock is named. Little is known about the *Lochar* except through Folklore.

French Trawler
The wreck of a French trawler lies just North of Smerwick Harbour at a depth of about 40 metres. Local fishermen indicate that she was wrecked about 1960.

Eliza
On 25-3-1839 the bulwark and other wreckage from the *Eliza* was picked up at Dingle. (177)

Vigilant
The *Vigilant* was wrecked on rocks at Sybil Head on 11-2-1840. She carried a cargo of fish oil from Newfoundland for Aloa. The captain was Strong. (177)

Brilliant
The *Brilliant* was abandoned off Hags Head on 20-8-1837 because she had 10 feet of water in the hold. She was from Newport bound for Quebec. The captain was Figg. (177)

Venus
The *Venus* was wrecked at Inch on 7-1-1839. She had come to the West of Ireland from Glasgow. Another Dublin vessel was wrecked at the same place and time during the Big Wind. The master was Fern but his mate was lost. (177)

Union
The *Union* was wrecked at Inch on 21-2-1839 She was bound for Limerick from Sligo captained by McAlister.

Integrity
The *Integrity* foundered off Brandon Head on 13-3-1837. She was en route from Tarbert to the Clyde. Captain Fallon and the crew were saved. (177)

Paddy Carey
The Paddy Carey was lost at Inch Bar on 14-3-1831. She was bound from Charlestown for Liverpool with Mr McKesser as captain. The masts were cut down as the ship approached the beach but the vessel broke up after 12 days. The crew were saved. (177)

Conceicao da Crux
The *Conceicao da Crux* struck rocks in the Kenmare River and was went to pieces on 15-3-1831. She was bound for Lisbon from Cork. (177)

Gestrickand
The crew of the *Gestrickland* of Gelfe were picked up off the Blaskets on 3-1-1832. Their vessel had been bound for Gibraltar captained by Watherbord. (177)

Aid
The *Aid* went ashore during a gale at Rosbeigh Point, Tralee on 21-12-1831. The Master Mr Chapman and the crew were drowned. She was from Mirimichi for New Ross.

Isabella
The *Isabella* went ashore at Ballinascelligs Bay on 21-12-1830 and was totally wrecked on 4-1-1831. The coastguard assisted by country people took the mate and 13 crew from the shrouds. She had come from Mirimichi bound for Liverpool. (177)

Gertrude
The *Gertrude* sprung a leak and sank off Minard on 12-1-1832. The crew were saved. The vessel was en route from Galway to Cork with Mr McDonnell as master. (177)

Audrey Anne
The 65 foot fishing trawler *Audrey Anne* sank off Brandon Head on 5-12-1998. The trawler began taking water and was abandoned by the two crewmen before she sank. Fenit lifeboat made attempts to pump the water but to no avail. (177)

Unknown
An unnamed ship was wrecked at Brandon Bay on 7-11-1838. She had come from Newfoundland. A further unnamed wreck occurred on 1-2-1839 at Smerwick. (177)

Sloop
On 10-1-1788 a sloop drove on a Rock in Dingle Harbour and went to pieces. All the crew were lost. Empty casks marked "butter Cork" were washed ashore. (30)

Trawler
On 24-11-1998 a trawler began sinking off Valentia. The crew were taken off by another trawler. (177)

Roche
The brig *Roche* McEvars was driven ashore at Valentia Harbour on 26-3-1841. She was from Demerera for Glasgow. (1)

Brothers
The Dingle hooker, *Brothers*, was wrecked at Ballyheigue Bay on 4-5-1841. She carried potatoes for the Protestant colony at Dingle. (1)

Unknown
An unnamed waterlogged vessel went to pieces off Sybil Head on 21-2-1840. (1)

St Lawrence
The barque *St Lawrence* went ashore at Ballyheigue Bay on 7-2-1840. (1)

Salus
The *Salus* bound for the West Indies was lost with all hands on the Kerry coast on 21-2-1843. (1)

Ben Nevis
An auction notice on 13-1-1852 advertised the sale of the cargo of the *Ben Nevis*, a 950 ton ship, which stranded at "Fuonagh's" Strand Ballydavid Head near Dingle. (1)

Princess Royal
The *Princess Royal* was wrecked at Inch Island on 13-10-1844. She was from St Andrews bound for Cork. (177)

CLARE

Lucy
On 27-3-1845, the *Lucy* was wrecked on the Malbay coast near the Cliffs of Moher. She was from Limerick to Preston with wheat. (177)

Maria
The trawler *Maria* sank off Kilkee on 27-5-1994. The Doonbeg based vessel was lobster fishing near the rocks at Donegal Point. She began to take in water and her difficulties were noticed from the shore. A pump was brought out by helicopter but failed to control the inflow. The five fishermen aboard along with a helicopter winchman were taken ashore by the Kilkee rescue boat just before the Maria sank.

Aircraft
A Dutch aircraft crashed in the Shannon in 1957. An RAF recovery team used inflatable bags to lift the wreck and salvage diamonds and a box of Rolex watches from the airliner. The boats were supplied by the Board of Works to assist in the operation.

Windsor Castle
The *Windsor Castle* went ashore on Scattery Island (Date unknown). The cargo was salvaged with the assistance of the islanders.

Mars
The *Mars* was damaged after striking Whelp Rock in the Shannon on 6-10-1842. The Captain was Morgan. The account is not clear on whether the vessel sank. (177)

N S de Solidada
The *Nostra Senora de Solidida* of Lisbon was wrecked near Kilrush on 26-2-1782. She was plundered of her cargo of salt, fruit and figs. Mr Sexton of Limerick claimed salvage expenses. (115)

Cicero
The *Cicero* struck Reeves rocks and fell over while going down the Shannon from Limerick on 22-9-1832. Part of the cargo was saved. The tide was washing in and out of the wreck. The vessel was bound for Quebec. (177)

Amity
The *Amity* was abandoned by her crew and went ashore at the Mouth of the Shannon on 20-10-1832. She was from Limerick for London Captained by Maylor. (177)

Iolan Chleire
The Schull trawler *Iolan Chleire* sank after a collision with a French trawler 67 miles West of Loop Head on 16-5-1999. The French trawler, Rohellian, was disabled in the incident when her propeller became fouled. The naval vessel *Ashling* arrested the French vessel under fisheries legislation because of the controversial circumstances of the incident. The Schull vessel was built in 1978 The crew of five aboard the *Iolan Chleire* were rescued by the French trawler.

Scotia

The *Scotia* struck Hogshead Rock and sank in the Shannon on 22-2-1830. She had been on route from Limerick to Glasgow. On 1-2-1830 the vessel was raised and taken for repair. (177)

Lady Landsdowne

The wreck of the lake steamer *Lady Landsdowne* lies off the hotel at Killaloe on Lough Derg. Several items from the wreck are in Liverpool Maritime Museum. They were recovered by a team from Liverpool University in 1967. The *Lady Landsdowne* was built by Lairds in Birkenhead in 1833 and was the first iron paddle steamer built there. After a career on the lake she sank at her moorings. (70)

Mountaineer

About 1826 the *Mountaineer* was lost on Mountaineer Rock off Dromineer. The paddle steamer was one of the first on the Shannon. The Rock was described as just below the surface. However the level of the lake was raised after the construction of the Ardnacrusha hydroelectric generation works in 1929. (70)

Barge 45M

On 1-12-1946 the Grand Canal Company barge *45M* was en route from Dublin to Limerick with a cargo of stout when she was struck by a gale. The buffeting caused the cargo to shift and the tow between the barge and the tug, St James, parted. The barge sank off Parkers Point on Lough Derg between Portroe and Killaloe with the loss of three lives, one survivor swam to shore. In 1971 the barge was bought for £20 from the owners, CIE. The barge was located using an echo sounder in 65 feet of water and raised by attaching 80 barrels to the submerged hull. The buoyancy was provided by filling the barrels with air and extra lift was provided by chain hoist cables from the surface. Finally the operation was completed by June 1975. The barge had surfaced in perfect condition and even the Swedish, 1912 built Bolinder engine started without an overhaul. The barge is now restored to its original condition and sails on the canal system. The slow water journey was reputed to bring the stout into perfect condition and the pint in that area of Limerick was eagerly sought after by connoisseurs. (118)

Neptune

The Portuguese collier *Neptune* was cast about at sea for 17 days before she came to anchor between Mutton Island and Seafield on 26-1-1854. She was directed to safety by three local men, Egan, Skillane and Boyle who ventured out in a canoe. The crew landed in their boat and said prayers for their safe deliverance. But while at their prayers they were set upon by local savages who attempted to rob them of all they had saved. The crew holed their longboat to prevent the mob from going out to pillage the ship. The thieves were driven off by William McMahon JP, Kilmurray assisted by a band of police. The compliment consisted of the Captain John Baptiste Roees, nine crew and another Captain Jessa Jos Silva. The *Neptune* carried coal from Liverpool to Lisbon. Despite the gale the anchors were barely holding the next day but it was expected that they could not outlast the storm and the ship's rudder was gone. (75)

Blucher

The fine barque *Blucher* from Venice with a cargo of Galetz Indian Corn bound for the firm of Balantynes, of Ennis went ashore in a gale in March 1863 in the River Fergus about half a mile below Clare village. She was lying on her side having her beams cracked, hatches torn up, and everything broken. She was built in the last year and cost £3000 but was insured for £1200. Her Captain and part owner is Mr D Bartets. At low water it was possible to discharge her cargo. (Clare Champion 13-3-1998)

Trinity

An auction notice on 9-4-1847 advertised the sale of the 131 ton brig, *Trinity* of Exeter. She lay damaged in the Shannon. (177)

John & Mary

The schooner *John & Mary* was driven into Liscannor Bay and was in a precarious position on 28-10-1842. She was from America bound for Galway. (1)

Grecian

On 8-3-1894, the brig, *Grecian* with a cargo of coals was driven ashore by bad weather. The 521 ton, cargo was auctioned at Cappa. (168)

Ciro, Caroline

On 19-2-1847 the hulls of two wrecked vessels were sold on the Strand at Kilrush. They were the *Ciro* and the *Caroline*. (177)

Eliza Ann

The *Eliza Ann* was wrecked on cliffs at "Ilvorn", (Islevaroo) Kilrush on 26-1-1842. She was bound for London from Limerick. (177)

William

On 17-4-1783 the *William* was wrecked at Mal Bay. She carried bark, bottles, and glass from Bristol for her home port of Galway. The crew except for two were lost. Assistance was rendered by Thomas Moroney on whose estate the wreck occurred. (1)

Unknown

An unnamed boat belonging to Mr Rose of Clarecastle going to Limerick with corn was reported wrecked in the Shannon 28-1-1806. The crew of 8 or 9 were lost. (5)

Haabet

On 4-2-1806 an auction was announced to be held at Kilrush to dispose of the hull and materials of the Danish brig *Haabet*. (5)

William

An auction of the remains of the *William* stranded at Liscannor was announced on 4-4-1806. (5)

Felicity

The *Felicity* went ashore under rocky cliffs near Kilrush on 20-11-1830. Her Captain was Johnstone. She was bound for Glasgow from Limerick. The *Tiffin*, *Dryden*, *Grunel* and *Baird* were in trouble during the same storm. (177)

Clare

The *Clare*, sloop from Limerick for Ennis with teas, sugars etc. foundered near Grass Island on 20-5-1806. The crew were saved. (5)

Wreckage

A stairs was washed ashore during a gale in 1997 opposite O'Looneys pub at Lahinch. It was broken up in the subsequent gales. It must have come from a ship which broke up underwater.

Milford Eagle

The 120 foot, 295 ton trawler *Milford Eagle* of Milford Haven caught fire 150 miles West of Shannon on 31-1-2000. Four of the crew were lifted to safety by a coastguard helicopter based at Shannon. The helicopter winchman, Noel Donnelly (who was subsequently awarded a medal) then joined the remaining 12 in the liferafts until they were picked up by the Irish trawler Alamar.

Lord Newboro

The *Lord Newboro* was wrecked at Liscannor Bay on 9-3-1838 She was from Sligo bound for London. The Captain was Pritchard. (177)

An Orient

The French trawler An Orient was swamped by a large wave 60 miles off Loop Head on 1-10-2000. The trawler sank with the loss of six of her crew. Three men were rescued by the Irish Coastguard helicopter based at Shannon.

GALWAY

Lancashire Witch
Walter Bourke, a merchant of Galway petitioned for his expenses in the salvage of the *Lancashire Witch* of Liverpool. The ship was wrecked at Park, Galway on 30-12-1781. She was bound for Africa captained by James Potter. Most of the cargo had been lost. (115)

Richard of Lancaster
The *Richard of Lancaster* was wrecked on 23-2-1782 50 miles from Galway. (115)

Eugene
The *Eugene* went to pieces after striking Sline Head on 18-4-1841. The 200 ton vessel had come from St John NB with timber. She had been abandoned at sea on 24-12-1840. (177)

Cyclops
The *Cyclops* was abandoned off Dunbay and drove ashore at Mutton Island on 22-12-1831and went to pieces. The master fell overboard and the carpenter was dead. The coastguard saved the remainder of the crew. (177)

Wreckers
A note records that some nefarious fellows were lately apprehended in Connemara in the act of practising the stalking horse for the villainous purpose of deceiving a ship in distress when the wind blew hard on the coast. The stalking horse is a fellow with a lanthorn on a pole, who moves in the night near the rocky shore with a pace resembling that of a horse going slowly and which, to a vessel at a distance, appears like the motions of a ship with her lights up. This most infamous deception which has been practised in Connemara has been often the means of enticing ships upon shore and which when wrecked have been plundered by the villainous perpetrators. The item in the Dublin Chronicle of 5-1-1788 gives no further detail but comments that "This interesting custom was known to our forebears of the North of the country is far from unlikely". (30) While folklore on false lanterns is common, this vague account is the only contemporary mention of deliberate luring of ships ashore in Ireland. All other accounts of wreckers merely involve recovery of material from ships which came ashore by accident.

Philip Godby
The *Philip Godby* was sunk by gunfire from a German submarine on 11-2-1940. The incident was described as off the West coast of Ireland. The Philip Godby was formerly the Togimo and the Cisnesll.

Hercule

On 21-3-1854 the French ship *Hercule* was abandoned off Dingle and later towed into Galway. The vessel was spotted inside the Blaskets and could not clear Kerry Head. The crew took to their boat and made for Clogher Head. The coastguard could not launch their boat due to the bad weather. Mr George Hamilton chief boatman at Feritears cove CG saw their plight and knowing that there was no landing at Clogher Head he raised a flag on a staff from the old ruins on Sybil Head. The boat made for him and he led it to a safe landing place. His wife attended to the 10 rescued crewmen before they were taken to Dingle the next day on three cars. Here they were presented to the inspecting lieutenant of coastguards. A statement was taken by Mr Williams, droits of the Admiralty. Mr Sterne representing the Shipwrecked Mariners Society put them up in lodgings before they were sent to the French Consul at Cork. (27)

ABC 1

The fishing boat *ABC 1* sank after hitting rocks off Inisboffin on 1981. Three men drifted past another Achill trawler before they came ashore at Keem Bay. The skipper was Paddy Conroy. (169)

Seadog

The 125 ton, steel hulled trawler *Seadog* was abandoned before she sank 150 miles off Slyne Head on 16-12-1998. The crew of seven Spaniards and 11 Portuguese were picked up from liferafts by the *Caprichio* and landed at Valentia Island. The trawler began taking water on Tuesday morning but was abandoned before a rescue helicopter could take out a pump.

Orion

On 20-1-1840 the *Orion* was wrecked on the coast of Galway. She was bound for Liverpool from Newfoundland. There were no survivors. (1)

Ocean Queen

The *Ocean Queen* was driven ashore at Roundstone on 18-2-1842. She carried rum and sugar from Demerera. (1)

Lively Lady

The fishing trawler *Lively Lady* sank off Rosseval and two aboard were lost. The date was about 1970.

Unknown

The boatman of the *Naas,* revenue cruiser, based at Galway reported that a ship was wrecked at Benowen on 21-2-1782. She was from Jamaica bound for Liverpool with a cargo of sugar and rum. Four casks of rum, six casks of pimento and cotton were salvaged and taken to Galway. (115)

Queen Adelaide

The *Queen Adelaide* was en route from Limerick to London on 30-11-1830 when she was wrecked between Roundstone Bay and Slyne Head. (177)

Rival

The brig *Rival* sailed from the Clyde with troops for Oporto on 24-11-1832 and was wrecked off the West coast of Galway on 4-12-1832 Straw bedding and casks of rum were washed ashore. The Captain was John Wallace. (177)

Blackstone

The *Blackstone* of Whitby went on the rocks at the entrance to Loughataille on 20-11-1830. Her Captain was Easdale. The ship was on her beam ends. The storm damaged seven other vessels in Galway port but they were expected to be refloated. (177)

Lillas

The *Lillas* struck Black Rock in Galway Bay and went to pieces on 22-11-1830. The master Mr Chambers and four crew were saved. She was bound for Limerick from Troon. (177)

Kelly

The Kelly was wrecked in Connemara on 29-12-1831. She was from Plymouth for Galway. The master was Lime. (177)

Mashona

The destroyer *HMS Mashona* sank 50 miles West of Slyne Head on 28-5-1941. Forty six of the crew were lost. The loss occurred during the hunt for the Bismarck after she had sunk the battlecruiser *HMS Hood*.

Killigrene

The *Killigrene* was wrecked in Connemara on 27-10-1837. She carried wine for Falmouth. (177)

Hope

The *Hope* sank 10 leagues off Slyne Head on 5-1-1840. Her cargo was timber. A boat was picked up at Sligo. (177)

Consolation

The *Consolation* was wrecked at Clifden on 1-12-1840. All the crew were lost. (177)

Neptune

The *Neptune* was wrecked on the coast of Connemara 23-10-1841. She carried timber from Bjornberg for Marseilles. The wreck was identified by a cap floating among the debris. The Captain was Stenfoers. (177)

Unknown

An unnamed,400 ton, brig came ashore bottom up at Boffin Island, Clifden, on 8-2-1842. The cargo was staves. (177)

Eanach Dhuin

On 5-9-1828 a boat sank in Lough Corrib en route from one of the islands on the lake to Galway. The cause was that an animal bound for the fair at Galway had put its foot through the floor of the boat which was rotten. The story is commemorated in a poem attributed to Antoine O Reachtabhra or Raftery but thought by some scholars to be the work of another poet Sean O'Ceallaigh. The poem was translated by Douglas H yde into English but it looses much of the melody of the language in translation.

Ma fhaighimse slainte beidh caint is trachtadh
ar an meid a bathadh as Eanach Dhuin,
's mo thrua amarach gach athair is mathair
bean is paiste 'ta ag siladh sul.
A Ri na ngrasa cheap Neamh is Parthas,
nar bheag an tabhact duinn beirt no triur,
ach la chomh brea leis gan gaoth na baisteach
lan an bhaid acu a scuabadh ar siul.

While I keep my health, there'll be talk and discourse
on the number drowned out of Eanach Dhuin,
and my grief tomorrow, each father, mother,
child and woman with pouring eyes.
King, gracious Maker of Heaven and Paradise,
of small account, maybe two or three
but a day so fine, with no rain or tempest,
a full boatload to be swept away.

Great the wonder, before the people,
to see them stretched with their heads laid back,
screams and wailing to affright the people
combing hair and the ruin laid out.
The Height of Autumn and all these youngsters
waked and brought to their burial place,
dressed not for marriage, but for the coffin.
O King of Glory, was it not great wrong?

Baile Chlair, it was fast approaching,
but their luck prevented to get so far,
and Death was strong, that gives no quarter
to the woman's son that was ever born.
Unless 'twas fated that day to drown them
was it not wretched, O King of Grace,
to lose them all, on no lake or ocean,
in an old foul boat and they close to land?

Tomas O Fearail, God's blight upon you,
so many bright girls you have done to death
with your ancient vessel, decayed and brittle,
heading merrily for Cnoc an Dulain.
The boat dismembered, the people scattered,
and the sheep were loosed out to swim away.
Home all were taken and stretched together
of men eleven, and of women eight.

Sean Mac Coscair, great the pity
that you e'er set foot in a ship or boat,
and the many steps that you took with vigour
back to London, to Beal Tra.
When you decided that you'd try swimming
the young girls seized you on every size
and your mother thinking, if a hundred foundered
you'd be the winner that would swim ashore.

I arose myself on Friday early
and heard the wailing and the beating palms
of women jaded by the nightlong labour
with stretching corpses their only task.
O God, O Christ Who suffered slaughter,
O true redeemer of the naked poor,
to holy Paradise bring safely with you
all these poor creatures that were so despoiled

A bitter curse on that same location
may star not shine there, may sun not rise
to drown that number as they went together
on Thursday early to the Galway fair,
men who would settle their ploughs and harrows
and plough the stubble and shake the seed
and the women likewise, in all things expert,
for weaving homespun and the linen thin.

Heart-impaling and mountain-burning
on the place they died in, and hard reproach,
for the many creatures it left prostrated,
crying and mourning each Monday morn.
Not faulty knowledge it was that strayed them
but great misfortune at Caislean Nua.
My story's ending: that many drownings
left much affliction in Eanach Dhuin.

Arosa

The Spanish trawler, Arosa was wrecked on Inisgoodle near Slyne Head on 3-10-2000. There was just one survivor from her crew of 14.

MAYO

T.H. Haviland
Wreckage from the *T.H. Haviland* came ashore at Westport on 6-1-1844. (177)
Kate Nickelby
The *Kate Nickelby* of Glasgow was wrecked at Belmullet on 22-12-1844. The cargo was sugar and rum from the West Indies. (177)
Arrow
The revenue cutter, *Arrow* was wrecked on the Mayo coast on 20-9-1782. A crewman was awarded £17 for the loss of his clothing and bedding "in the naval service". (115)
Jamaica
The brig, *Jamaica* stranded at Killala on 12-3-1782. Several people were prosecuted for plunder as a result. (115)
Ann
The Ann went ashore at Broadhaven 26-10-1841. She was from Limerick bound for Glasgow. (177)
Sceptre
On 8-4-1841 bits of a vessel identified as the *Sceptre* came ashore at Belmullet. She was from Liverpool bound for Galway with oats. She left Cork on 14-2 and left Galway for Blacksod on 27th. There was no news of her crew. (177)
Neptune
The coastguard cutter *Neptune* was wrecked on Iniskea on 23-1-1837. The crew were saved. (177)
Douglas
The *Douglas* of Sunderland was wrecked on rocks at Blacksod. She floated, drifted off and came ashore again. She was from Limerick for London. The crew were saved. (177)
Betsey
The *Betsey* was wrecked at Killala on 4-2-1837. She was en route from Ballina to Sligo. (177)
Favourite
The *Favourite* was wrecked at Broadhaven on 30-10-1837. She had come from Dublin with stores for the lighthouse on Eagle Island. The Captain was Stone. (177)
Assistance
The *Assistance* struck a reef at Black Island Bay near Westport and was hogged on 16-4-1838. (177)
Maria Allesandre
The *Maria Alessandre* was wrecked near Erris on 24-9-1830. Three of the crew were drowned. She was en route from Bergen to Sicily. (177)
Thomas
The *Thomas* was en route from St John, New Brunswick bound for Galway struck a reef in Westport Bay on 14-12-1830. She was abandoned, drifted off and was not heard of afterwards. (177)
HMS Pylades
The 18 gun vessel *HMS Pylades* went ashore at Roona Point on 13-4-1831. She was reported on her side high and

dry. There is no account of a total loss in naval records. (177)

Thistle

The *Thistle* went ashore near the Quay at Westport on 4-3-1831. (177)

Lindifini

The *Lindifini* was lost on rocks in Killala Bay in 1980. The 60 foot trawler was spotted drifting at Kilcummin Head. Mr Ewing's trawler saw her strike rocks and go down but he could not find anyone when he reached the wreckage. There were three lost.

Christina

The *Christina* of Greenock Captained by Baxter stranded at Killala on 24-1-1830. The report said that she was not expected to be refloated. (177)

Hannah

The *Hannah* struck a Rock in Killala Bay on 23-4-1832. The crew were saved by the coastguard. The master was Bowen. (177)

Hibernian

The *Hibernian* was washed ashore at Blacksod on 30-1-1840. (177)

Aimwell

The *Aimwell* was wrecked at Blacksod Point on 13-1-1838. She was from Glasgow bound for Limerick. (177)

Greyhound

The *Greyhound* of Whitley and the *Mary,* a sloop of Galway were wrecked at Broadhaven on 1-1-1771. (90)

Sloop

A Sligo sloop Captained by Jones sank at Killala on 30-12-1766. (90)

Eagle

The goods and hull of the *Eagle* were auctioned at Killala on 7-3-1771. The material was salved by Andrew Kirkwood of Kilcommon and Company. Alex Cain was master and the ship came from Philadelphia. (90)

Brig

An unnamed brig was wrecked Northward from Blacksod Bay on 21-3-1842. All aboard were lost. (177)

Jas Richmond

The *Jas Richmond* foundered in deep water North of Eagle Island on 23-12-1842. The Whitby vessel had been abandoned on the 19th. (177)

Unknown

On 1-7-1840 masts, spars and timber from an unknown ship were washed ashore at Belmullet. (177)

Broad Oak

The *Broad Oak* was wrecked on the main at Knockbeggar on 16-1-1841. She sailed from Ballina. (177)

Dispatch

The *Dispatch* was wrecked on Iniskea on 2-11-1844. The captain was McDonagh. (177)

Shelldrake

The *Shelldrake* was wrecked on 8-5-1842 on "Inisquette" Island, Clew Bay Westport. She was en route from Liverpool to Westport. (177)

Pryde

The *Pryde* was wrecked at Belmullet on 28-11-1844. She was en route from London to Westport. (177)

Unknown

A 150 ton ship was wrecked at Cross, Erris on 28-11-1844. The cargo was tallow and sugar. (177)

SLIGO

Urania
The *Urania* was wrecked on rocks at Sligo on 21-4-1841. She was from Christainasund bound for Oporto. (177)

Tom
The *Tom* a sloop from Sligo was in government service and lay in the Pool at Sligo for the purpose of taking volunteers for the Royal Navy. She was wrecked on 23-1-1783 and one of the recruits was drowned. (121)

Superb
The *Superb* was wrecked at the entrance to Sligo Harbour on 26-11-1832. She had come to Sligo from Glasgow. All the crew were lost and 50 tons of coal were saved from the cargo. (177)

Unknown
In the late 1920s a barquentine was stranded on the stones on the Western end of Bartra Island opposite Enniscrone. A Mr Kelly considered salvage, but the auctioneer's description of refloatable was optimistic because the keelson was shattered and the vessel was a total wreck. The vessel had encountered trouble on the Bar and ended up on Bartra Island.

Unknown
A large brig reached Sligo Harbour on 20-4-1841. The vessel was bottom up and thought to be foreign. The cargo was timber. (177)

Acorn
The *Acorn* went ashore 20 miles from Sligo on 3-1-1832 and was feared to be a total loss. The vessel was wrecked on 7-1-1832. (177)

Barge
Large pieces of a 200 foot barge were spotted off Cloonagh Pier on 16-3-1994. It broke loose while on tow across the Atlantic.

Anchor
An anchor was found by divers at Brandy Point in Broadhaven Bay in August 2000. It is supposed to have come from an Armada wreck lost in the vicinity. The date was not clearly determined and the name Brandy Point could be associated with a later wreck. Since a chain was attached the anchor is almost certain to be of a later date.

Californian
The hull of the *Californian* was cast ashore in Sligo Bay in 1847 where she lay until 1853. The wreck was then purchased by Mr Delany a local merchant and fitted out to carry emigrants from Sligo to New York.

The 293 ton vessel set off with 52 aboard and a cargo of 300 tons of pig iron. The stowage of the cargo was poor as there were no sections and it became loose. Having sailed on 6-10-1853 she put back to Sligo on 21-10-1853. Many passengers left the ship and there were complaints when their passage money was forfeited. The inspector of coastguard at Westport attempted to inspect the ship but she had sailed on 3-11-1853. The *Californian* began to leak when 120 miles out and those aboard took to the boats. There were Mr Delany, the Captain, the mate Mr Nash, four sailors and one child in the gig. The lifeboat had four men 13 women and children while the longboat had seven men, 13 women and eight children. The provisions were inadequate and Mr Nash approached the longboat and took some of their water by force before casting them adrift again. The gig was picked up by a passing vessel. After many difficulties the two remaining boats reached Achill Island but 15 children and three adults had died from lack of water. The details were revealed at a court case where Delany and Nash were charged. (72)

Lady Hood

On 20-11-1830 the *Lady Hood* ran ashore at the pool of Sligo. Her Captain was McKenzie. The Martha and the Ballina were ashore also at Oyster Island. (177)

Ellanore

The *Ellanore* Captained by Pine was wrecked on a Bank at Ballysodare Harbour on 16-2-1832. She was outward bound for Liverpool. The cargo was being discharged. At the same time balks of timber and a handspike marked James were picked up off the coast. (177)

Armada chest, probably from Streedagh. Now at Hamilton's Brownhall, Ballintra.
Photo: Lucius Emerson

DONEGAL

Nephrite
The steamer, *Nephrite*, went ashore a mile North of Burtonport on 2-7-1927. She was owned by Robertsons of Glasgow. The cargo was coal from Ayr for Galway.

Argus
The *Argus* went ashore at Malinbeg on 15-12-1842. She had come from Greenock. (177)

James Cooke
The *James Cooke* was lost on Inisowen Head on 27-11-1841. Only one man was saved. She was from Sligo bound for Glasgow. (177)

Unknown
A ship from Leith with a cargo of salmon bound for the East Indies foundered in Donegal Bay on 18-2-1764. David Eagle was master. (177)

Unknown
Captain Hawthorn and all aboard were lost in a wreck at Sheephaven on 5-1-1771. (90)

Othello
The *Othello* Captained by John Cousins was wrecked at Malin on 5-1-1765. (177)

Albion
On 5-10-1840 the Albion was wrecked at Sheephaven between Milford and Ramelton. She was from Saltcoates captained by Thompson. (177)

Loyalist
The *Loyalist* was wrecked at St John's Point, Bruckless, Killybegs on 3-9-1840. A NE gale drove her ashore while en route from St John, NB to Sligo. The crew and cargo were saved. (177)

Britannia
On 9-7-1840 the *Britannia* was wrecked on Ballyshannon Bar. The cargo of timber from St John NB was saved. (177)

Henry Volant
On 12-10-1842 the *Henry Volant* went ashore at Ballyshannon Bar. She was from Quebec commanded by McEwing. (177)

Louisa Connolly
On 15-12-1842 the *Louisa Connolly* was wrecked on the Bar at Ballyshannon. Some material was saved. The Captain was Kirkpatrick. (177)

Emerald
The *Emerald* was scuttled in Lough Swilly to extinguish a fire aboard on 24-4-1840. Captain Wilson was bound for Derry. (177)

Emerald
The *Emerald* of Belfast was lost at Downings on 28-11-1837

Emerald
The Emerald was wrecked on a Rock near Letterkenny on 8-4-1839. She was from Bangor for Letterkenny. Her Captain was Sims.

Eller
The 243 ton steamer *Eller* foundered 6 miles SE of Rathlin O'Beirne Island on

28-4-1936. She carried coal from Birkenhead to Ballyshannon. She was built in 1896 by Fullerton of Paisley (yard no 129) and was owned by Coppacks of Connahs Quay. (120)

Miranda

The *Miranda* from Greenock was wrecked off Dunfanaghy on 28-11-1837. Only a punt, a keg, oranges and lemons from the cargo were washed ashore. (177)

Newry Vessel

A Dutch built vessel owned at Newry was lost near Inisowen Head on 11-8-1786. The crew were saved. The locals descended and seized every article belonging to the ship and crew. (121)

Jane & Thomas

The *Jane and Thomas* was wrecked in Downings Bay on 3-4-1838. She was bound for Ballyshannon from Liverpool Captained by Wally. (177)

Lion

The *Lion* went ashore at Bruckless on 21-2-1839. She was condemned but the crew and master, Forbes were safe. (177)

Greenock

The *Greenock* was lost at Inistrahull on 28-1-1839. Her voyage was Quebec to Hull. Captain White and crew were saved. (177)

Saldahana

Two 50 gallon casks and carronade survive in a farmyard near Ballymastoker Bay. They originated from the *Saldahana.* Recently an anchor believed to have been on the Saldahana was snagged by a trawler. The Saldahana was lost on 4-12-1811. (33)

Louisa

The *Louisa* was wrecked at Ballyshannon on 20-4-1840. She was bound for Liverpool captained by Robson. (177)

Resolution

The coastguard at Killybegs found 40 or 50 logs of timber and the stern of a ship marked *Resolution* on 2-4-1832. There was no trace of the crew. (177)

Lord Exmouth

A boat marked *Lord Exmouth* was washed ashore on the Donegal coast on 25-6-1832. It was presumed that the boat came from a vessel of that name lost at sea. (177)

Unknown

A lifeboat with a red star on each bow and a name terminating with the letters "field" was washed ashore at Burtonport on 30-1-1894. Cotton bales were also found on the beach. There was the suspicion that a large steamer had been lost offshore. No further information was discovered. (118)

Grassen

The *Grassen* was lost at Glencolmbcille on 30-11-1832. She was bound for Naples from Bergen. Both crew and cargo were saved by the coastguard. (177)

Fame

The Fame was destroyed by fire off Dunaff Head on 3-12-1832. The crew were saved. (177)

Huskisson

On 8-3-1830 the *Huskisson* was wrecked on Ballyshannon Bar. The vessel carried a cargo of oats of which 60 tons were saved. (177)

Robert & Isabella
The Maryport vessel *Robert & Isabella* was lost with all her crew at Boylagh Bay near Rutland Island on 12-3-1831. John Leabody was the master. (177)

Saladin
The *Saladin* of Belfast was towed into Ballyconnell, Falcaragh near Inisboffin,Co Donegal on 7-10-1830. She became a total wreck. Her Captain was Murray. (177)

Eliza
The *Eliza* of Liverpool was wrecked at Ballyconnell on 12-12-1831. She was bound for Ballyshannon Captained by Milne. (177)

Eleanor
The *Eleanor* was wrecked 3 miles East of Bloody Foreland on 24-3-1832. She was from Saltcoates with coal for Sligo. The Captain was McLoughlin. (177)

Brittany
The 2926 ton, *Brittany* sank after a collision on 5-2-1918. She was in a convoy on route from Liverpool to Montevideo. She sank 40 miles NNW of Tory.

Customs barge
The Sligo customs barge was lost at Arran (Arranmore) about 28-1-1767. The man in charge was a Mr Martin who, according to the report, was drunk and anchored in an unsafe place. The vessel carried salt bound for Killybegs. (115)

Bustle
In April 1765 the *Bustle*, of Killybegs was driven ashore after ten hours riding at anchor during a Westerly storm. She was apparently based at Killybegs and engaged in whaling. There was a whale industry there operated by Mr Nesbitt and the Bustle carried blubber between his Killybegs base and Liverpool. The *Bustle* was 90 tons and first appeared in Lloyds register in 1762. The remark was passed that when the stranding occurred large crowds assembled to save the ship and gear which was not the usual barbarous plunder. (4,160,161)

Pride of the Ocean
The half decker *Pride of the Ocean* sank at Burtonport on 18-2-1972. There was no crew aboard when the moorings broke and she was smashed on the nearby rocks.

Venus
The schooner *Venus* of Portaferry struck on Rotten Island at Killybegs Harbour. She sunk immediately on 19-7-1842. (1)

Montagnaise
The schooner *Montagnaise* of Belfast laden with barley was wrecked SW of Tory Island lighthouse on 21-1-1842. All aboard were lost. (1)

Empire Heritage
The oil tanker *Empire Heritage* was torpedoed by U 482 on 8-9-1944. She lies at a depth of 68 metres at position 55.27 n 8.01 W which is some 17 miles NW of Malin Head. She carried a deck cargo of Sherman tanks which lie on the seabed. The wreck has been visited by scuba divers and filmed.

Dove
In 1602 the *Dove* was wrecked at Malin. The Danish ship carried stockfish, ling and cod. All was pillaged and the Danes appealed for redress to the High Coutrt of admiralty in London. (19)

Ebeneezer
The *Ebenezer* was wrecked at Trabreaga Bay in 1778. The Harveys of Malin hall were presented with a cup by Lloyds for saving the crew and cargo. (19)

Horn Head wreck
A mystery wreck at Horn Head is believed to contain munitions. On 3-10-1918 a speech by John Leslie was censored from the Belfast Newsletter. It referred to an attempted German invasion which failed when destroyers intercepted a vessel and beat her off near Horn Head. It is possible that this otherwise undocumented vessel could relate to that incident. The volatile state of Ireland toward the end of WW 1 is illustrated by the declaration of martial law in Clare on 7-5-1918. The reason was that three men were arrested in the South of the country on suspicion of gun running. They were described as friends of Roger Casement. The Censorship records are in the national archives among the Chief Secretary's papers. Another censored item refers to a German submarine base on Tory during the First World War.

Cherokee
A wreck North of Horn Head at position 55 17 150, 008 01.600 is thought to be the *Cherokee.* There seems to be only one of this name with the following Lloyds data "Cherokee 1961 Gravenhurst SS Co 328t 120foot Built Canadian SB Co 1907" A steam whistle was salvaged from this wreck made by Hastie of Greenock now Brown Bros. Edinburgh. The makers had the serial number which showed that the steam whistle was sold in August 1945. It was placed in the *British Fern*, an 8640 ton tanker owned by the British Tanker Company, built by James Lang of Sunderland in 1946. The sister ships were the *Hally,* and the *Princess*, whose hull numbers were 771, 772, 773. The ship was broken at Hughes Bolckow of Blythe and parts used in 1961. There is no mention in Lloyds register or in Dictionary of Disasters at Sea of the *Cherokee* or any plausible wreck in that position. The presence of ammunition aboard suggests a wartime loss. The 200 foot remains are at 56 metres and flattened. Damage at the centre suggests that she was torpedoed or mined.

Unknown
A wreck was marked off Buncrana in 1923 at a depth of 6 fathoms. It lies on a line between Buncrana Castle and the fort on other shore. This may be a first world war wreck from the base aboard *HMS Hekla* moored at Buncrana.

Submarines
An Irish Navy video found two submarines during the search for the *Carrickatine*. One was believed to have been sunk during Operation Deadlight

the other is reckoned to be *U 482*, this lies between the *Empire Heritage* and the *Pinto*. Fishermen found an echo between Tulla and Glasheedy but this is confirmed as an aircraft. The captain of U 482 was the famous "ace",Count Metisco. His U boat was presumed lost of The Mull of Kyntire but is now believed to lie off Malin Head. The *U 482* may have struck a mine in the deep minefield off Malin.

Unknown

On a course between *Audacious* at 55 28 311, 07 45 157 and *Laurentic* a large object lies proud of seabed 7.2 miles from *Laurentic*. Some sources believed this to be the missing trawler *Carrickatine*. Another souce believe that this is an aircraft wreck.

Laurentic

By far the most extensive and successful salvage operation conducted in Irish waters was the recovery of the *Laurentic* gold. (165) The 14,950 ton armed merchant cruiser sailed from Buncrana on 23-1-1917. She had landed a sick seaman and was en route across the Atlantic from Liverpool with 3211 bars of gold worth £5M at the time but today they would be worth £300M. The ship was only an hour out into Lough Swilly when she struck a mine and sank with the loss of 350 lives. There are several extensive accounts of the six year struggle to recover the gold. The expedition was led by Commander Damant the pioneer of diving science who progressed the scientific diving decompression tables. It was due to his diligence that there were no serious accidents during the Laurentic work. Initially the work commenced The forty tons of gold was packed in boxes which weighed 160 pounds. The first few boxes were recovered quickly by the divers who were able to enter the passage to the storeroom and haul the boxes out through the side of the ship. However a gale arose and the ship was smashed beyond recognition despite the 40 metre depth of the water. The first season saw £500,000 worth of gold recovered. The next year explosives had to be used to open up the wreck but the work was difficult and slow. Only £10,000 worth was recovered. Damant and the *HMS Racer* were called away to investigate sunken submarines and they did not return to the work until the next season. Over seven years work, £4.7M worth of gold was recovered and the greatest treasure hunt of the time ceased in 1924. By then 3,186 of a total of 3,211 gold bars had been recovered. The eleven divers were awarded the OBE and Damant was made Captain. For every £100 recovered the divers were awarded a bonus of half a crown so they had £6739 to divide between them.

In 1960 a story was related concerning the theft of two of the gold bars from the *Laurentic*. During 1923 a Derry detective, James Dykes was on patrol when he received a tip off that there was a plot to steal the gold and that two bars had already been taken.

Gold retrieved from the Laurentic in a recompression chamber aboard the *HMS Racer.*

Photo: David Masters

It was common knowledge that gold worth £5,000,000 had been salvaged from the Laurentic and that the salvage ship *Racer* was heavily guarded by destroyers after shots had been exchanged with three boats which had approached the *Racer* at night. Two divers were bribed by a dealer in the East End of London to arrange the theft. The gold was checked carefully when it arrived at the surface but there was no possibility of supervision 40 metres below the surface. The divers fixed buoys to the gold bars and a fishing vessel put out at night when the *Racer* was anchored in Lough Foyle. The ingots were recovered and taken to London. Despite extensive searches of the dealer's premises no trace of the ingots was found. (139)

After Captain Damant and his crew of the Racer had salvaged the *Laurentic* gold in 1923 others tried their hand at finding the missing bars. Commander H Rivers Malet worked from the Estoy in the mid 1930s and Consortium Recovery visited the wreck with the *Holger Dane* in 1985. Among the material raised was one of the guns, now at Merseyside Maritime Museum.

Kate Crosbie

The 696 ton barque, *Kate Crosbie*, bound from Belfast to Miramichi in ballast, sank on 28-9-1890 3 miles NE of Horn Head. The vessel was built in 1867.

Caliope

The *Caliope* lies outside Downings Harbour (33) and recently two of her anchors have been raised and placed on display at Downings.

Chagford

The Q ship *Chagford* was formerly the 2,095 ton Admiralty collier *Bracondale*. She had been refitted to carry a four inch gun, two 12 pounders, a howitzer, two maxims and two torpedo tubes. She sailed from Buncrana on 5-8-1918. Two days later she was torpedoed by a submarine 125 miles North West of Tory. The damage causes the concealed guns to be exposed, and, as the panic party left the Q ship the submarine surfaced 750 yards away. The crew which had remained aboard after the "panic party" had departed opened fire and hit the submarine. A second and then a third torpedo struck the *Chagford* but she was kept afloat by her cargo of timber. Every hour or so the submarine returned and the party left on the *Chagford* anticipated that she would be boarded. The crew boarded a motor boat and were picked up by a trawler. They returned and took the *Chagford* in tow but she broke up and sank on 7-8-1918. A message from *U44* revealed her location and she was attacked and sunk by *HMS Oracle* off the Hebrides. (136)

Jamaica Merchant

The *Jamaica Merchant* was wrecked on Tory in 1744. She was from Barbados. (19)

Belfast

The *Belfast* stranded on Tory on 11-4-1811. Her cargo was coal from Harrington. The cargo was salvaged by the islanders on one low tide. At the next tide the ship was dismembered. The crew set off in the ships boat and travelled the 200 miles back to Cumberland. (19)

Osprey

On 1-3-1833 the *Osprey* was lost with all hands on Tory. (19)

Argo Delos on Torbeg Islet 22-11-1960.

Photo: Sunday Post

DERRY

Wolf

The *Wolf* sank near Derry on 3-2-1838. She was from Glasgow bound for Derry. The *Mary* of Cork took off the crew. (177)

Wolverine

The 914 ton destroyer, *HMS Wolverine* collided with the Flower class sloop *Rosemary* off Lough Foyle on 12-12-1917. (171)

William Mannell

The wreck of the *William Mannell* lies just off Culdaff. The circumstances are somewhat of a mystery. The story says that in 1946 a ship was abandoned by the crew after cook who was steering had bounced her off a rock. She began taking water and was abandoned.

Sloop

A sloop with merchandise bound for Coleraine drove ashore on Magilligan shore and was totally lost on 11-8-1786. All the crew were lost. Two pilots were aboard, a father and son, the son alone survived. (121)

Heckler

A wreck in Tramone Bay is described by folklore to be a frigate and is known as the *Heckler.* This might be a corruption of French name. Cannon were found at the spot. No further information was found about this wreck.

Hugh and James

A report from Captain Mackey said that the *Hugh and James* was burned at Derry on 13-1-1767. (90)

Armada chest in Culdaff House, Inishowen.

Photo: Lucius Emerson

SHIPWRECK RESEARCH

Many fishermen, surveyors or divers find a trace of a wreck and are interested in discovering more about the vessel, its cargo and its career. The item trawled up from the seabed is often a cannon or an anchor and these items can be dated approximately. Usually the only proof positive is finding an inscribed bell or the builders plate. Not all bells had the ship name inscribed and several ships had more than one bell. The makers plate affixed to most modern steamships will give the yard number and date as well as the name of the shipyard. Very few shipyards have survived and if you are lucky the records will have been transferred to a nearby museum or archive. Unfortunately a great deal of material has been lost. The directions in this section refer in particular to tracing shipwrecks using sources in Ireland.

Local history and folklore usually record an event if it was of relevance to the local community. Where foreigners are involved the detail is considerably more vague. Traditional storytellers have the tendency not to let the truth get in the way of a good story. The strength of folklore is that local tales are usually accurate about the location of a shipwreck. A ship's name can be corrupted in oral tradition and therefore can be quite misleading. Even newspapers can get the ship name wrong. This is especially the case where the name is in a foreign language. Many of the names in Wexford folklore are confusing because of the corruption of French names into anything sounding like a plausible name to the storyteller. Beware of the false historian, there has been more time expended on yarns that have gained credibility by repetition. Always seek evidence and contemporary references. This is what separates journalism where the sources are concealed with history where ample references and authorities are given in footnotes. This characteristic separates the better local histories from collections of pub yarns. Another time waster is the person who claims to know a great secret about some event but cannot reveal it for some complicated reason. They will use phrases like "tell me what you know and I will tell you whether you are correct or not." They are only fishing for real information, they rarely have facts that can be verified. In an air of secrecy and intrigue *Lusitania* rumours and unreliable yarns abound.

Lloyds Register
Any named ship registered with Lloyds may be traced in an annual publication called Lloyds Register of Shipping. Nowadays there are three large volumes but a single volume sufficed when the register commenced in 1764. The Maritime Institute Library in Dublin holds the registers from 1803. Earlier registers are held at the Guildhall Library (Aldermanbury, London EC2P 2EJ 0044 171 600 3384) and Maritime Museum in Liverpool. Liverpool has Lloyds registers from 1764. The register gives ship name, where built, tonnage, Captain's name and owners. There are often several ships of the same name and approximate tonnage registered. Without an accurate ship name the List can be of no help.

Lloyds List
Lloyd List is a newspaper which records shipping movements and news from 1741 to date. A section covers casualties. The early Lloyds lists from 1730-1839 were reprinted in 1969 by Gregg and are still on sale from Fisher Nautical in Sussex BN 6 8SD. Two publications have used the Lloyds List to assemble data on shipwrecks. These are Hocking's Dictionary of disasters at sea during the age of steam and Richard Larn's monumental works on Shipwreck Index of the British Isles. Local lists have shown that Lloyds list covers only about one third of the wrecks which have occurred in Ireland. The Reprint of Lloyds list may be consulted at Ulster Folk and Transport Museum, Cultra, Bangor N. Ireland. Full sets of Lloyds list are at The Merseyside Maritime Museum (Albert Dock, Liverpool. L3 4AA 0044 51 207 0001).

Admiralty Wreck Register
The Hydrographic office of the Admiralty maintains a wreck register of 60,000 items at Taunton. This records wartime losses especially of steel ships. The data has been augmented by the work of Admiralty survey ships. The data can be accessed from their computerised register for a modest fee. The Admiralty wreck section are always interested in obtaining information on shipwrecks from people who find them or discover the name of a wreck hitherto unknown. Write to Wrecks section, Hydrographic office Taunton, TA1 2DN. The Royal Navy also has semi classified lists of sonar contacts whether Rock, wreck or shoal. The Irish Navy has similar lists especially in the North Donegal area where many contacts were recorded in the unsuccessful search for the trawler Carrickatine.

Irish Lights
If a wreck was lighted or buoyed as a danger to shipping there may be a mention in the records of the Commissioners of Irish Lights. Their archive is not open to the public and the information is limited often to terse minutes. Irish Lights are at Pembroke St., Dublin 2.

Charts

Many wrecks were marked on old charts and some even remain marked on the modern Admiralty charts. Start with the current chart and then check an old fathom chart. It is worth going back as many of the wrecks mentioned at one time were subsequently deleted. The old charts are a work of art and the engraving and illustration are well worth a look for their artistic merit alone. There are several chart symbols for a wreck.

Reference Books

There are several reference books which are indispensable to any ship wreck researcher. The first is Hocking's Dictionary of Disasters at Sea During the Age of Steam. Volume one covers 1860 to 1963 and volume two covers 1963 to 1980s. This work catalogues wrecks but selects British ships, larger ships and incidents where the loss of life was significant. It is published by Lloyds. Paul Kemp's U Boats Destroyed, published by Arms and Armour, is a useful start for German submarines but excludes the U boats scuttled after both world wars. British vessels lost at Sea republished by Patrick Stephens is another shipwreck essential. The Shipwreck Index works by Richard Larn published by Lloyds are an immense body of work and cover UK in seven volumes. (163)

National Maritime Museum, Greenwich

The resources of the library at the National Maritime Museum in Greenwich are incredible. The staff are helpful and a written query to the museum accompanied by a photograph of an item from a wreck will identify it if identification is possible. Even if you do not have a lot of material to search, the visit to Greenwich is well worth the trouble to see the Maritime Museum and Cutty Sark. Access is by Underground, Jubilee Line, Docklands Light Railway, or more appropriately ferry from Westminster pier. The address is Trafalgar Road, Greenwich, London SE10 9NF phone 0044 181858 4422.

Navy ship

A naval ship wrecked or lost in recent years (since 1773) will have a court martial record. A quick reference is in Gosset's Lost Ships of the Royal Navy. The full story in the original record of the court martial is held at the Public Records Office. Digests of courts martial are available from 1755 to 1806. Letters to the Admiralty may cover a loss from 1698. One incredible set of archives are the logs of naval ships held in a monthly format for each named ship. Not all the logs have survived but material like the dispositions of navy ships base by base for the First World War have survived. There is a fine Admiralty Library at Portsmouth

(Royal Naval Museum, HM Naval base PP66, Portsmouth PO1 3NH) 0044 1705 727577) Colledge, Ships of the Royal Navy, volumes one & two lists all the ships and their career whether broken sunk or wrecked. Many merchant ships carried a gun for defence against submarines during both world wars. If a diver finds a gun or ammunition aboard a wreck then there is a probability that the ship was lost during wartime. The lists of war losses are documented in Admiralty publications British Ships Lost at Sea Due to Enemy Action. This consists of four HMSO publications, covering warships and merchant ships lost in WW 1 and WW2 assembled and republished in 1978 by Patrick Stephens publishers. It is important to remember that only British losses are recorded in this work. A ship could have been French, Norwegian, Greek or even American. A list of foreign ships lost during the war is held at Kew. German submarines are listed by Paul Kemp in U boats Destroyed. This is the most modern and comprehensive account of the submarines sunk during the wars. One exception to the listings were the Q or Mystery ships which tended not to be listed among the Fleet nor among the merchant ships. These were disguised merchant ships with heavy guns and torpedo tubes concealed aboard. A naval crew manned the guns while "panic party" lured the submarine closer by abandoning the ship. There are several publications dealing specifically with these vessels. (136, 149). Specialist books also deal with cannon (167).

Society for Nautical Research

The Society for Nautical Research (Stowell House, Heathfield, East Sussex, TN1 OLX) has studied the history of ships and the sea since 1910. It publishes the quarterly journal Mariner's Mirror which is a treasure house of information. They also provide timbers and rigging for the *HMS Victory* preserved at Portsmouth as well as paintings for the National Maritime Museum at Greenwich. The Mariners Mirror may be consulted by members at the Maritime Institute Library at Dun Laoghaire.

Trinity College Dublin

While the National Library and the main university libraries are copyright deposit libraries for Ireland and are entitled to receive all books published in Ireland, Trinity College Dublin is a UK copyright Library and is entitled to receive a copy of all books published in Britain or Ireland. This gives the collection a unique comprehensiveness. This is a source for all difficult to obtain books and the staff are very obliging to a researcher. In theory no book published in Britain or Ireland should be missing from the Trinity library.

Bookdealers

In the UK there are several book dealers which trade exclusively in maritime books. Their catalogues are huge and their knowledge is truly encyclopaedic. Do not hesitate to consult their catalogues for even the most obscure books which might carry information on your wreck. Among the most prominent are:

Anthony Cooke, Unit 202, Station House, 49 Greenwich High Road SE10 8JL. 181 694 1178

Frank Smith Aviation & Maritime Books, 100Heaton Rd, Newcastle on Tyne, NE6 5HL 0191 2656333 fax 224 2620,

Motor Books, St Martins Court, London.

Mainmast Books, 251 Copnor Rd., Portsmouth Hampshire PO3 5EE 1705 645555

Underwater Books, JA Barak, The Retreat, 18 Town Hall Rd, Havant, Hampshire PO9 1AN

Underwater Books 104 High St Hastings, TN34 3ES 0044 1424 435905)

Fisher Nautical, Huntswood, St Helena Lane, Streat Near Hassocks Sussex BN 6 8SD

Robert Humm, Station House, Stamford, Lincolnshire, PE3 2 JN. phone0044 1780 66266

Anthony J Simmonds, 23 Nelson Rd., Greenwich, London SE 10 9JB phone 0044 181 8531727

World Treasure Books, PO box 5, Newport, Isle of Wight, PO 30 5QE.

Local sources

The value of local sources must not be ignored. The local pub is not a bad place to start because some tales about a wreck often reveal vital information. The pub may even contain a photograph of a nearby wreck. Small museums may retain press cuttings of a local event or even artefacts from the wreck. Similarly the local library can have a closed section where research material by local historians and historical societies is retained. The local historical society is often based at the library and the librarian may be able to give a contact address for the secretary or if you are lucky the shipwreck expert. Even graveyards have a tale to tell. If people were lost in the wreck then they are possibly buried in the nearby cemetery. Headstones will have names and a date for the event. Unfortunately few sailors' burials were in marked graves. They were often interred in a "strangers plot" used for the burial of transient visitors whose bodies were not claimed. The tendency of the coastguard was to bury shipwreck victims in the Church of Ireland cemetery which was usually their own church. Burial records are sketchy before 1850. Church of Ireland burial records are frequently held at their central library at the Representative Body offices, Rathgar Dublin 6.

Public Records Office

The Public Records Office (Ruskin Ave., Kew London TW9 4DU 0044 181 392 5200) is the most incredible storehouse of information. Situated in beautiful surroundings it is the finest place in which to work of all the libraries and archives. It is amazingly well organised and provides a wealth of pre prepared information. Even accommodation in the area is listed in information leaflet 26. Take the 15 minutes for the guided tour to getting started. It will pay dividends. Most records of maritime interest are in the ADM series.

Newspapers

If a date is available for the wreck then a newspaper is probably the most accessible source of information. In the absence of a precise date the search through newspapers is tedious and it is easy to miss a small item in a badly copied microfilm. Wartime newspapers were censored and therefore contain no wreck information. No matter how old the newspaper there is a chance that it has survived in some repository. The Report of the Newsplan project in Ireland contains a list of the newspapers held in various locations throughout Ireland and Britain. The British Library repository at Colindale Avenue, London NW9 5HE 0044 171 323 7377) holds the most extensive collection of British and Irish newspapers. Many county libraries have copies of the local papers on microfilm. In Dublin the Gilbert library of Dublin Corporation (138 Pearse Street, Dublin, 2, 01 677 7662) has a very extensive collection of the Dublin papers. The National Library, Kildare Street, Dublin. 2 has papers from around the country. An index to the holdings in all Libraries had been prepared in recent years. Palmer's Index to the London Times can be a very quick way to search material. It has been computerised lately and the Gilbert Library has the disc. If you are lucky and the event was sufficiently significant to reach the London papers, the index will find the ship name and therefore lead you to the date of the wreck. A limited index to the Freeman's Journal was prepared by a group of prisoners working in Mountjoy Prison, Dublin. It covers the period 1783 to 1792 though it is described as covering 1700-1799. There also exists a Belfast newsletter index 1737-1800.

Board of Trade

The Board of Trade published their summary of wrecks of British ships and ships lost on the coast of Britain each year in the British Parliamentary Papers between 1850 and 1919. The basic details are given. These include location, captain's name, voyage, cargo, wind conditions and of course date. Most larger libraries e.g. The Trinity library and the National Library have the bound sets of the British Parliamentary Papers. There is a three volume index accompanying the set.

Submarines

The German U boat archive at Cuxhaven contains information on U boats of both world wars. Contact Horst Bredlow, U Boot Archiv, Bahnhofstrasse 57, 27478 Cuxhaven, Altenbruch, Germany 0049 4722 322. A good starting Point is Paul Kemp's book, U Boats Destroyed published by Putnam, 1997, ISBN 1 85409 321 5. Unfortunately U boats are one of the subjects which attract mystery stories and fables. Many of the stories are repeated so often that they gain credibility by their widespread circulation.

Fishermen

Fishermen's charts have been a rich source of wreck locations. Fishermen do not like to have their nets torn by sharp objects on the seabed. As a result they note obstructions, these can be rocks or wreckage. By experience they can sometimes distinguish the obstruction especially if rust particles are adhered to the nets. Many artefacts have been dragged to the surface by nets. The most noted item of this nature in Irish waters was a bronze cannon found off Waterford. An Armada cannon was found in the 1890s in Blasket Sound by netting. Anchors are the item most frequently snagged. Identification of this material can help identify a vessel.

Ballads & Songs

Many shipwrecks are mentioned in songs and ballads. The information often includes the day of the wreck but frequently ignores the year. Songs of the Wexford Coast collated by Fr Ransome in 1948 is probably the most recent collection but a large collection of ballad sheets was assembled by Joly and forms part of the National Library collection. Among the Joly ballads there are some which refer to shipwrecks near Ireland. The loss of the *Volunteer* probably refers to the wreckage of the *Rival* washed ashore at Galway on 4-12-1832. Another ballad refers to the *Union* lost on Rathlin on 14 May but the year is not described but is before 1836. The story of the *Francis Spaight* on 22 November, again year unknown before 1836, describes cannibalism of the cabin boy Patrick O'Brien and eventual rescue of fourteen of the eighteen survivors by Captain Tillard. Another ballad refers to the loss of the *Belfast Lark* bound from America to Ireland with only four surviving from 200 aboard.

Archaeological research

Both Duchas and the Northern Ireland Department of Environment hold databases of shipwrecks as part of the National Monuments Register.

Customs & Excise

Where material was salvaged from a wreck the Customs and Excise took charge of the goods and disposed of them to meet the cost of salvage. Then the owners would be paid the value less salvage and storage. The minute books of the commissioners of customs and excise for Ireland have survived. The minutes refer solely to protection of the revenue and usually the only data mentioned is the nature and value of the cargo. Tobacco, wine, and wool were taxed goods and were especially carefully guarded. The minutes for 1767 to 1830 are at the National Archives in Dublin. The original minute books may be consulted from 1730 to 1830 at the Public Records Office at Ruskin Avenue, Kew, London.

Professional researchers

Many libraries and institutions have a list of professional researchers who will try to answer your query for a fee. These individuals are not part of the institution and you make a private arrangement with them to find out information for a fee of approximately £20 per hour. Some specialise in maritime affairs and are therefore very effective, others give a disappointing service. In all cases the more precise the data the more satisfactory will be the outcome. Using a researcher is an inexpensive alternative to making the trip yourself. For the PRO at Kew a list can be provided, request information leaflet 20.

Computerised and internet information

The Divernet site has a question and answer forum and the Canadian site Northern Maritime Research based in Nova Scotia has world wide data on 100,000 shipwrecks. Http://www.chebucto.ns.ca Roy Stokes has a database of Irish Shipwrecks. The University of Newcastle is working on a universal shipping register at the Department of Marine Technology, Newcastle on Tyne NE1 7RU, (0044 191 222 6712). This project proposes to use a Global Ship Number to help distinguish between the 800 ships called Ann for example. Based in the Armstrong Building (having association with the Tyne shipbuilders of that name) the department is working on a British shipbuilding database covering 100,000 ships and 5000 shipbuilders. The University of Ulster Centre for Maritime Archaeology has a database on 3000 Northern Ireland shipwrecks. Duchas also has a database as part of the National Monuments Register.

Something written??

If you suspect that a book or article may exist on your wreck there exists a database for that too. David Dillingham and Associates are assembling a book on shipwreck books. This book will cover all the books written on shipwrecks world wide. Write to 2a Sudley Terrace, High St, Bognor Regis, Sussex, PO 21 1EU 0044 1243 822984.

Purchasing a wreck

All wrecks are owned by someone. The Irish State has taken over ownership of all wrecks over 100 years old under the National Monuments Act. The Liverpool and War Risks Insurance covered wartime ships and own most British wartime wrecks.. This was a consortium of insurance people which came together to administer the Government insurance schemes for the duration of the war. The Salvage Association covers the interests of shipowners. (Bankside House, 107 112 Leadenhall St., London EC 3A 4AP. 0044 171 623 1299). The Admiralty also sell wrecks so long as they are not war graves. The Liverpool and War Risks Insurance company still operates as a residual entity. They carried the insurance on British ships during the war. The situation with Norwegian and Greek vessels is similar but dealt with in the country of ownership.

SALVAGE

Port Yarrock

The Port Yarrock was lost in Brandon Bay with all her crew on 29-1-1894. The events are detailed (97) by Sile Mulcahy. Because the copper ore in the cargo was quite valuable and the wreck was not too deep as well as being sheltered from the South West salvage commenced almost immediately. WJB Moncas, a Liverpool firm commenced salvage in 1895. Mr Waterson an English engineer was involved, he was related to a Moncas of Wexford. Their technique was to use an 8 inch salvage pump to lift the ore. There is little known about their efforts. They must have left a considerable amount of the cargo untouched.

In 1912 Ensor took over the salvage of the *Port Yarrock* but Ensor used a 12" pump and succeeded in lifting a considerable amount of the copper between 1912 and 1916. (141) The work ceased during the First World War when U boat activity became intense off the South coast and all salvage effort was applied to saving torpedoed ships.

A standard patch shown on the *Alison*. The standard patch was made to fit almost any vessel by means of rubber gaskets. It was invaluable in saving torpedoed ships during the First World War.

Photo: Dr. Palmer

The Puffin

The Daunt Rock Lightship, *Puffin*, sank when her bows were torn out by her anchor chain during a storm on 8-10-1896. There was immediate interest by the Commissioners of Irish Lights to determine the cause of the disaster. The Firm of TH Ensor were at work promptly. The *Puffin* was raised and the damage assessed (see photo in Volume I) but during the work a diver was lost:

The sunken Lightship - Sudden death of a diver (Cork Examiner Monday 7 June 1897 p6)

The tug *Mayflower* brought the body of Henry Judson to Cobh on Saturday. Saturday was his first dive, he went down with Pat Collins but the tide was strong and both ascended and dived again at slack water. Both remained down for 45 minutes. After a rest Judson went down with John Collins. They were working to attach wires and slings to the Puffin. Collins surfaced first as there was no room for the two to work together at the position where they were working. Judson surfaced 10 minutes later. Ensor saw no necessity to continue and they were proceeding in their small boat to the tug *Mayflower*. Judson was observed breathing heavily and died en route to Queenstown. Dr Bricknell declared the cause of death as apoplexy. Judson had been recommended to Ensor by Siebe Gorman in whose employ he was. Though from Whitstable, he had recently lived at Ramsgate. He left a wife and two children. Ensor was a careful employer and Saturday was the third day's work on the Puffin.

There were two wires already attached and they were working on a third. He was buried at Queenstown. Pat and John Collins were Cork divers and are mentioned in many accounts of diving in the area.

Ensor's wartime salvage

No mention was made of salvage on the South coast by Ensor in Keeble Chatterton's Danger Zone (26) though there were accounts of the work done by the Admiralty in saving ships. The omission of his salvage work was a mystery in what must have been his busiest period. It can only be concluded that the author of Danger Zone in his anxiety to project the Navy salvage work in as favourable a light as possible deliberately did not even mention the contracted work. In some of the work Ensor co-operated with the Cork firm, Palmer's of Ringaskiddy. Newspapers carried no information on shipping affairs due to censorship which meant that there was not even casual mention of salvage work. It was clear that a resource such as Ensor's salvage company would not be ignored. Recently a paper came to light which described the activity. (2) Dublin Port records also contained some material on the famous salvor. It was the practice when torpedoed to make all possible speed towards the nearest beach so that the ship could be run ashore on a sandy bottom with minimum damage. This explains why so many ships described as sunk were recovered. Then the ship could be patched, pumped out and refloated. The following ships were attended to and saved. The date of the event has not been traced in every case.

Wayfarer

After torpedo damage on 11-4-1915 the 9599 ton *Wayfarer* was patched, pumped out and refloated. She was taken to Liverpool in April 1915.

Q5 Farnborough

The Q5, *Farnborough* fought and sank a German submarine U83 on 17-2-1916. The Farnborough, disguised as the Loderer, was damaged in the attack and brought in to Bantry Bay by destroyers, tugs and sloops. She sank in shallow water and was refloated by Ensor.

Huronian

The 8766 ton *Huronian* was attacked by torpedo on 28-12-1915 some 8 miles S by E of Fastnet. Despite the damage she reached Bantry Bay where she was patched and repaired before resuming her journey.

Baltzer

The Russian barquentine Baltzer was also attacked by submarine and salvaged by Ensor.

WT Lewis

On 2-9-1915 the 2166 ton sailing vessel, *W.T Lewis* was attacked by gunfire from a submarine 95 miles West of Fastnet Rock after being captured. She did not sink and was towed in for repair.

Alexandrian

The 4467 ton, *Alexandrian* was attacked by torpedo off SW Ireland on 23-10-1916, that time the torpedo missed. Then on 9-1-1917 she was attacked by gunfire and torpedo 20 miles SW of Fastnet Rock. She was beached at Berehaven and repaired.

Hundvaage

The *Hundvage* was torpedoed and beached patched and pumped out.

Quantock

The 4470 tons *Quantock* was torpedoed on 26-4-1917 off Fastnet Rock. Two of the crew were lost but the ship was saved.

Rathlin Head

The 7378 ton, *Rathlin Head*, was torpedoed South West of Ireland on 25-5-1918, twice in the engine room and stokehold and also in the fore end. After beaching she was pumped out and refloated by Ensor. She was taken to Belfast for repair. Three of those aboard were lost.

Rathmore

The *Rathmore* was saved on an unknown date during the war. She was partly flooded after a collision, patched and pumped out. While ships lost due to enemy action are easilty traced, those lost by collision or grounding are particularly difficult to find because of censorship of all shipping news.

Grainton

The 6042 ton, *Grainton* was torpedoed and sunk in the Irish Sea on 18-3-1918. The ship was refloated and taken to Dublin for repair.

The 5242 ton *Berwinvale* was torpedoed on 16-3-1916 about 30 miles West of Fastnet Rock. She was taken to Bantry and salvaged by Ensor and Palmer's.

Photo: Dr. Palmer

Berwindvale

The 5242 ton *Berwindvale* was torpedoed and captured on 16-3-1916 about 30 miles West of Fastnet Rock. The submarine was driven off. The ship was taken to shore where she sank, a patch was fitted and she was refloated and taken to Liverpool. The cargo of 3000 tons of wheat was pumped over the side as there were no buyers for the damaged goods. The Berwindvale was built in 1911 at Sir Rayloton Dixon's yard at Middlesboro for the Berwindvale SS Company.

Kotka

This barque *Kotka* was sunk by gunfire, patched and refloated

Reddam

The *Reddam* suffered collision damage on the South coast in circumstances which are not clear. The ship was patched by Ensors and pumped out.

Kelvinbrae

The *Kelvinbrae* was sunk by collision. A shield was fitted and the ship patched and refloated before being taken to port for repair.

Legane
After a collision the damaged bow was cut off by gelignite. The scrap was cleared away and the bulkhead shored before the Legane was taken to port for repair.

Fishpool
The *Fishpool* was saved from fire by flooding the hold. Then she was saved from wreck by being pumped out by Ensors.

Bay Nyassa
On 25-7-1917 the 4973 ton, *Bay Nyassa* was attacked by a submarine in the Atlantic. The gunfire set the 4937 ton ship on fire. To put out the flames she was flooded and pumped out by the Ensor salvage company.

Luciline
On 13-3-1917 the 3765 ton, *Luciline* was torpedoed 40 miles WNW from Tearaght. She was beached before being patched and patched and pumped out. Fifteen of the crew were killed.

Dominge de Larenga
The *Dominge de Larenga* went ashore on rocks in Valentia district. The bottom was damaged and a timber shield fitted underneath before the water was pumped out.

Taff
The stranded *Taff* was taken off Wexford sands in 1920 by Ensor's salvage team.

El Zorro
Salvage continued on the Wartime wrecks after the First World War. The *El Zorro* remained ashore at Rennies Bay where she had gone ashore on 28-12-1915. (photo in volume 1). In 1921 her three 70 ton boilers were salvaged and floated into Queenstown.

Hermonie
The wreck of the *Hermione* was blown up and the scrap lifted at entrance to Waterford Harbour. No date is given for this but because it was not picked up in newspaper reports it is presumed to have been during the First World War censorship period.

DIVING BELL
The description (129) of a diving bell used at Howth was typical of such apparatus in the early years of the 19th century. This was just about the time of the introduction of the early helmet diving apparatus.

Dr Colladon (of Geneva) being in Ireland in September 1820 had an opportunity of going down in a diving bell then in use at Howth Harbour. The bell was attached to a vessel. The workmen were employed in clearing the entrance to the Harbour. The bell was an oblong iron chest 6 feet by four feet and five feet high. The bell was cast in London, weighed four tons and cost £200. The roof had eight or ten holes covered with thick glass to admit light. The air entered through a leather pipe and was supplied from the surface under pressure.

MODERN SALVAGE OPERATIONS

Current diving operations in Ireland are conducted by firms such as Celtic Salvage and Towing of Cobh. They have worked on many smaller vessels raised around the coast. Larger work such as removal of the wrecks of the *Kilkenny* and *Betelgeuse* were by Smit Tak of Rotterdam. The latter firm lost a Dutch diving supervisor Jaap Pols killed during Betelgeuse salvage. The removal of the wreck of the Betelgeuse was one of the largest ships ever raised anywhere. The work was completed in Summer 1979. Most of the deep saturation diving operations in Irish waters have been carried out by oilrig support vessels who have this capability. Often during idle periods these vessels will attempt salvage work when they have suitable resources in the area. Deep Water Recovery and Exploration of Fife, Scotland also investigated Irish waters looking for the *Laconia*. They operate the 116 ton, *Redeemer* in the style of Sorima using a grab but directed by a camera instead of the famous observation chamber. The importance of the Redeemer type of salvage is that the cost of operating a grab vessel with a crew of six, is very small by comparison with the expense of a saturation diving support ship. A grab vessel can also operate in 1800 metre deep waters with a surprising degree of precision. Some modern innovations have

The salvage ship *Redeemer* showing her lifting gear.

Photo: courtesy of Deepwater Recovery

improved the technique of Beasley and Sorima. The underwater camera and especially improved hydraulic control of the grab give improved results. The use of GPS for four point location finding also allows more precise work. The key to the deep water salvage is the cable to the grab. It consists of an inner core with the power cable and a coaxial data cable surrounded by three weight bearing layers of steel wire. Deep Water Recovery hold the record for depth for deep water salvage on the *Francois Viljeux*. She was lost on 14-2-1979 45 miles off Cape Finisterre with cargo of copper. The demonstra-

The salvage ship *Redeemer* on a four point mooring over a wreck.
Photo: courtesy of Deepwater Recovery

tion of effective work in 1250 metres of water brings a huge number of wartime wrecks into the grasp of the salvor.

A new design of grab cable using lighter carbon fibre allows depths of 6000 metres to be accessed. This opens up the possibility of economical salvage from immense depths. The French company IFREMER operate at the other end of the spectrum using the *Deepsea Worker.* Their technique involves 10 metre sections of rigid pipe to carry the grab. The grab is more powerful and they have had success in the Mediterranean, near Oman and off Spain. The cost of the operations with a 37 man crew makes most salvage uneconomic. (154)

LOSS OF LIFE IN IRISH SHIPWRECKS

A question frequently posed is what was the worst shipwreck on the coast of Ireland. There were many disasters where the number of victims is unclear. This is especially so in the case of the Armada wrecks. Often correct data on passengers is not available. Even the number of victims on the *Tayleur* in 1854 is disputed. A revision of the figures in this case suggests a toll of 355. A list of the *Lusitania* victims was published by Cunard in 1917. (143) There is also an accurate list of the Leinster victims. (21) The *Norge* lost on Rockall is one of the great forgotten disasters and unremarked in Britain or Ireland because the emigrants were Scandinavian. Because of the large numbers aboard emigrant ships frequently suffered large loss of life. The worst cases were the *Pomona* and the *Tayleur.* This table lists wrecks in order number of lives lost.

Ship	Number Lost	Location	Date
Lusitania	1200	Kinsale	7-5-1915
Norge	632	Rockall	1904
L'Impatiente	552	Mizen	1796
Leinster	501	Kish	1918
Pomona	388	Off Ballyconigar Co Wexford	1859
Tayleur	355	Lambay	1854
Laurentic	350	Lough Swilly	1917
Seahorse	338	Tramore	1816
Great Lewis	300	Hook	1645
Rochdale	265	Seapoint	1807
Boadecia	250	Old Head of Kinsale	1816
Two Brothers	211	Kinsale	1656
Saldahna	200	Donegal	1811
Spanish Armada 26 ships	250 average	West Coast	1588

EMIGRANT SHIP LOSSES

Tayleur

One of the best known shipwrecks in Ireland is the *Tayleur* lost on 28-1-1854 at Lambay. (22.23) The White Star Line sailing ship was on her maiden voyage from Liverpool to Melbourne with emigrants when she struck the rocks at Lambay in an easterly wind. Of the 560 aboard some 360 were lost including nearly all the women and children. The cause of the disaster was variously blamed on compass error due to the magnetism of the ship. Some foreigners in the crew were considered incompetent and the crew was thought to be inadequate to wear ship and manage the sails. It was clear that the ship was not properly tried out and had been rushed into service to cater for the mass of emigrants heading for Australia for the Kalgoorlie goldrush.

Pomona

The emigrant ship *Pomona* was lost on 28-4-1859 off Ballyconigar. There were 388 persons lost in the disaster. (vol 1) After the *Pomona* disaster local merchants William Armstrong, Main Street, Wexford along with Mr Carty, Curracloe and Frank Hore of Wexford engaged divers to recover the bodies. Jack Allen an English diver worked on the job for the Liverpool and Glasgow Salvage Association. Bodies were recovered and buried at St Mary's Churchyard Wexford. Fearing plague from the decomposed bodies no more were allowed at Wexford, then improvised burials occurred at Morriscastle, Ballyconnigar, Curracloe and Rosslare. The figurehead is in Wexford county Museum. The anchor is on display at Kilmore Quay.

Robert Kelly

The emigrant ship *Robert Kelly,* from Liverpool for New York with 690 passengers, went ashore at Jack's Hole on 6-3-1854. Fishermen saved all aboard and took them to Wicklow whence they re-embarked in the *Iron Duke*. A report on March 9th indicated that the Arklow fishermen had stayed aboard the *Robert Kelly* to enforce their claim of salvage. When the tide surveyor went aboard found that the fishermen had committed great depredations on the cargo. By midnight the seals on all the casks had been broken off and brandy was spilling about the deck. He fishermen would not allow anyone aboard not even the commander. They threatened to sink any boat which approached. A small boat alongside was filled with tea and clothing and he was informed that an effort was being made to lighten the ship. About 150 aboard were claiming salvage. The Harbour master was not allowed within pistol shot of the ship. On the 10th Mr Wade, the tide surveyor, resealed the stores but some had been made away with. He found the Arklow men still aboard making great havoc with the possessions of the unfortunate emigrants, boxes were open and goods a scattered. Cabin doors were smashed and even the medicine chest from which they were mixing seidlitz powders to cool their stomachs after their bout at the brandy casks. The commander of the ship went to Dublin and had a word with the American consul, Colonel Brown at Dublin Castle sent down a large body of police and turned all the Arklow men ashore. The fishermen looted the stranded ship and 150 of them were drunk about the town, 45 were fined and 21 sent to Kilmainham jail. The *Robert Kelly* was refloated and towed by two steamers to Kingstown.

Wild Deer

The *Wild Deer* struck the reef at North Rock near Cloughey. Luckily she held together for a few days until she broke her back on 17-1-1883. She had sailed from Glasgow for Otago with 209 emigrants, 40 crew and 900 tons of cargo. All aboard were saved by a flotilla of boats from Cloughey organised by the coastguards.

Unknown

During the Cromwellian plantation of Ireland wholesale transportation wa semployed to remove suspected tories. Most were sent to the West Indies at the behest of British merchants. In July 1653 an unnamed ship was pressed into service at Limerick by the Comissioners in Ireland to carry 600 "tories" to Spain. By the account of Captain Armiger Warner the tories abused his men ran the ship on a rock which split her to pieces and robbed all the goods and seamen's clothes. He petitioned the Lord Protector for his damages amounting to £1600. (175) The account does not describe the location of the wreck and the petition was made on 26-6-1654.

Exmouth

Emigrant ships were lost on other shores apart from Ireland. The *Exmouth* of Newcastle sailed from Derry on 24-4-1847. The 248 emigrants were escaping the Famine by heading for Quebec. The ship hit a terrible storm and three days after leaving Derry the *Exmouth* was driven ashore on Islay. The alarm was raised but the islanders could not put to sea because of the swell. Men were lowered down cliffs but only three seamen survived and 108 bodies were recovered. They were buried on the Island and a cairn was erected 150 years later. Some emigrant ships were lost at sea and on the North American shore. The most famous of these were the *Titanic* and the *Empress of Ireland*.

TROOPSHIPS

Several troopships were lost on the coast of Ireland. Troopships frequently travelled in convoy as in the case of the *Prince of Wales* and *Rochdale* which were accompanied by seven other ships when the left Dublin. The ships themselves were usually larger than average for the time and were often retired East India ships. This might suggest that they were in poor condition after several voyages to the East. The ships tended to remain at anchor in tropical waters while the difficult negotiations were pursued with the Orientals. During this time weed accumulated on the ship's bottom and the ship worm bored into the planks thereby weakening the structure. The losses tended to occur in phases relating to wars and the movement of armies. The Great Lewis was during the Cromwellian wars, The *Rockingham* during the American War of Independence, *Prince of Wales, Rochdale, Lord Melville, Boadecia and Seahorse* during the Napoleonic period, *Lusitania*, *Laurentic and Leinster* during the First World War.

Lochgarry

On 21-1-1942 the David McBrayne Ltd. ship *Lochgarry* sank a mile East of Rue Point on Rathlin. She was bound from Glasgow for Oban to pick up soldiers for the Faroes. Initially she struck rocks off Torr Point and the ship could only reverse. As she was sinking fast the lifeboats were lowered, flares fired and two boats made for shore with 30 aboard. The third boat struck a Rock and 29 were drowned. The 1670 ton ship was formerly called the *Lairdstock* and the *Vulture.*

Georgetown Victory

The 7604 ton, liberty ship, *Georgetown Victory* was wrecked at Killard Point, Co Down on 30-4-1946. She carried 1400 sailors and marines from Freemantle bound for Glasgow to be demobbed at the end of the war. All aboard escaped before the ship broke in two. Most of the wreck was removed as scrap but considerable remains lie underwater. The *Georgetown Victory* was built in 1945. (33, 34)

L'Impatiente

Not all the troop ships lost were British. The French frigate bombardiere *L'Impatiente* was lost at Mizen on 30-12-1796. She was one of 43 ships which accompanied Wolf Tone from Brest to Bantry. The French expedition was commanded by vice admiral Morard de Galle and had been storm bound at Bantry. The fleet abandoned their landing attempt and was returning to France when *L'Impatiente* was wrecked. There were only seven survivors from the 560 aboard. The victims were buried in the sands at Barley cove. A further

The liberty ship *Georgetown Victory* was wrecked at Killard point on 30-4-1946. The 1400 demobbed sailors and marines aboard escaped before the ship broke in two.

Photo: Jim Blaney

French frigate *La Surveillante* was scuttled in Bantry Bay because she was not fit to make the return voyage. The ship of the line *Scevola* also foundered out to sea from Mizen Head but accounts do not relate how many were lost. (33)

Amite

The French frigate *Amite* of Brest was lost off Ardglass in 1797. Apparently she was to deliver guns to the United Irishmen. The rendezvous failed and the *Amite* was driven ashore in a SE gale at Sheepland Harbour just North of Ardglass. There was only one survivor from a crew of 104.

Swan

The 18 gun, 272 to naval sloop *HMS Swan* capsized off Waterford on 16-8-1782. The vessel formerly called the *Bonelta* was purchased in November 1781 and named Roebuck. She was renamed *Swan* on 2-3-1782. The ship sailed from Waterford for Plymouth with the *HMS Artois* and ten transports carrying troops. During a squall the ship was overturned and foundered in under three minutes. Captain McBride and sixteen of the 110 aboard escaped in a boat with few oars and were saved when they came ashore at Castletown, Co Wexford after fourteen hours afloat. (33)

Seahorse

The *Seahorse* was lost at Tramore on 30-1-1816. She sailed from Ramsgate for Cork carrying 15 sailors, 74 women and children and 279 soldiers of the 2nd/59th regiment. The troops were recently returned from the Napoleonic wars in the Peninsula and the Continent. An easterly gale arose while the ships crossed the Irish sea and the only sailor who knew the coast fell from the rigging and broke his legs The ship was unable to weather Brownstown Head and soon the *Seahorse* lost her masts and rudder. Though her anchors were let out she grounded a mile out in Tramore Bay. There is a memorial in Christ Church Drumcannon and a plaque is set in the cliff face on the Doneraile walk opposite the wreck site. Some material from the Seahorse survives in the Waterford area including a belt buckle and a musket which were washed ashore. One of the survivors Henry Hartford wrote a letter to his father from Tramore, which was published in the local newspaper.

"My dear father, I lose not a moment tho hardly able to write, to acquaint you of our dreadful shipwreck in this Bay yesterday two o'clock. Thanks to the Almighty for my marvellous escape. I feel too much at present to attempt giving you a description of so dreadful an occurrence. I will only tell you out of 304 men of the Regiment, 34 women, 33 children and about 20 sailors and 16 officers, only 4 officers

Headstone raised above the grave of the Seahorse victims

Photo: Tony Caulfield

and 25 rank and file and 32 sailors have escaped yesterday. I will now give you a correct list of the officers saved and those lost. Officers lost Captain J MacGregor, Lt William Neal, Major C.W. Douglas, Lt Abraham Dent, Adj. Edward Scott, Lt James Ceddes, Lt W. Gillespie, Ensign A.C. Ross. Ensign W.F. Hill, Surgeon James Hagan, Ass Surgeon P.R. Lambe, Master William Baird, Mr Allen of the navy. Officers saved Lt J Cowper, A Mc Pherson, henry Hartford, Ensign W Seward.

Since I was born I never witnessed such a sight, the screams and prayers of all. The sea sweeping off numbers

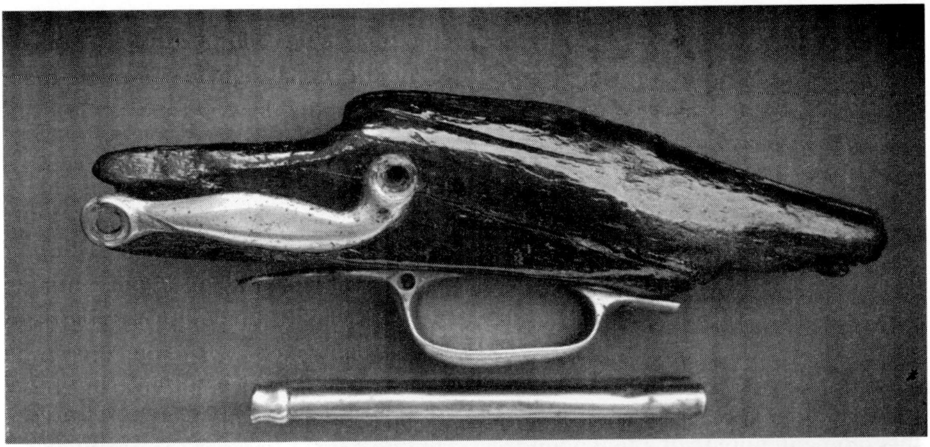

The *Seahorse* was lost at Tramore on 30-1-1816. She sailed from Ramsgate for Cork carrying 15 sailors, 74 women and children and 279 soldiers of the 2nd/59th regiment. The troops were recently returned from the Napoleonic wars in the Peninsula and the Continent. These were among the items from the washed ashore at Tramore. The Lord Melville and the Boadecia of the same convoy were lost the same day near the Old Head of Kinsale.

Photo: Tony Caulfield

at a time, picture to yourself our situation, the beach crowded with people who could render no assistance: no boat could live in such a sea, or put out for the surf. God only knows how I was saved. I stuck to the wreck until she went to pieces, and then took hold of a plank which was washed from me four or five times and I by look got hold of others. All I recalled was being completely exhausted, and from the cold could hold the plank no longer. I was then washed on shore, and taken up apparently dead. I don't know how I recovered, but when I did, I found myself before a large fire. Every bit of our baggage is lost; I am this moment with a parcel of borrowed clothes. I have nothing in the world except what was on me when I left the ship. The great part of the baggage was washed on shore but all plundered last night by the inhabitants. The boxes and chests that were not opened were broken open by the people about here. I am told that it would take upwards of a thousand men to keep the baggage from being plundered. I have not at this moment more than a few pounds, and I will therefore have to draw upon the agents for some money. I was obliged to get some from them when I was in England and buy some clothes. I had three dozen of new shirts, that I bought at Deal and got a good bargain of, and intended to bring with me to India, also some new Regimentals and boots. I am told Government will allow money for the loss of our baggage, if so I can keep some of that, for the purpose I got it from you for. I understand they will allow us for what we value our loss at. Tell my mother, Annie and Beck, I had some presents of silk shawls and handkerchiefs I brought from France, all of which are lost. I will feel much obliged to my mother, if she send me a few shirts and a few pairs of stockings, as I have this moment nothing in the world, but the battered clothes I came on shore with. I am afraid this will not leave Waterford till tomorrow as no post leaves this today. If my mother can send the things to me I will receive them at Waterford where we intend going this evening or tomorrow. She can send them as a parcel direct to the coach office, as we must stop at Waterford for some days to get some clothes, and shirts and stockings are not things to be bought in a hurry.

My shins and thighs are black and blue with striking against the wreck, and my hands and one of my legs cut with some of the nails. I feel this moment very stiff in the limbs and tho before a large fire, perishing with the cold. I hope tomorrow to be much stouter, let me have a line from you, I don't know where I will put up, but you direct me at the Post Office. I now conclude this letter and again return my thanks to the Great God for my providential escape, and I will ever feel grateful for his goodness. Never could there be such a horrible sight this morning, and I fancy this morning, I fancy I see the agonised countenances of the unfortunate sufferers on the wreck. I know my dear father, how happy my dear family will feel at my escape and remember me to all and believe me, dear father. Yr ever dutiful son, Henry Hartford.

There is this moment a brig in distress in the same place we were wrecked in. The sea is washing over her decks: everyone says she will be lost: my God, what misfortunes there are in this world." (The brig was the Appolonia, J Parry, master from London to Cork with tea, sugar etc., crew of seven saved by locals.)

The sailors lost on the Leinster are buried at the military cemetery at Blackhorse Avenue, Dublin.

Photo: Author

Leinster

The mailboat *Leinster* was essentially a troop ship and among the 501 lost when she was torpedoed were some 326 troops. The majority of the military, those whose bodies were found, are buried in the military cemetery at Blackhorse Avenue in Dublin. The date 10-10-1918 is the only indication that the graves belong to Leinster victims. The ship name was not mentioned on most of the standard War Graves commission headstones. Only a few markers erected privately reveal the ship name. There were many regiments and nationalities represented including Australians, Canadians New Zealanders British and Irish. The units included Navy, RAF, USN, engineers, lancers, machine gun corps. In total there were 757 aboard, 680 civilians and troops, 22 post office mail sorters and 56 crew. (21)

Lord Melville

The troopships *Lord Melville* and *Boadecia* were lost near Kinsale on 30-1-1816. The bodies of the victims were buried on the beach near Coakleys Hotel. The 818 ton *Lord Melville* also of the same ill fated convoy carrying the 82nd regiment struck the rocks 300 yards off the Old Head on the evening of 30-1-1816. The vessel remained intact and a boat was launched but swamped and the crew of twelve drowned. Eventually the shipwrecked were saved by the men of Kinsale Head lighthouse. The *Lord Melville* was a former East Indiaman. (33)

Boadecia

The brig *Boadecia* which accompanied the *Seahorse* lost at Tramore was herself lost on Curlane rocks on 30-1-1816. The rocks separate Garretstown and Garrylucas beaches just West of the Old Head of Kinsale. The gale forced the ship into the deadly lee shore of Courtmacsharry Bay. The vessel carried the 2/59 Regiment returning from the Battle of Waterloo to garrison duty at Cork. Most of the crew and compliment numbering 255 were drowned. They buried in a mound on the beach. In 1900 the remains were reinterred in Old Court cemetery. A photograph was recently unearthed showing a cart carrying the skeletons for reburial. (33)

Thorne

Though the *Thorne* wrecked at Sandeel Bay, Slade in 1814 was not strictly a troopship the cargo was 9,800 stand of arms. They were taken to Duncannon Fort.

Rochdale & The Prince of Wales

On 19-11-1807 several troopships left the Pigeon House Harbour at Ringsend near Dublin with troops bound for Liverpool. The *Prince of Wales*, packet of Parkgate, captained by Edwards had the 97th regiment aboard along with recruits from the South Cork and South Mayo regiments of militia. The 97th was also known as the Queen's Germans. The next day the ships were seen working about the Bay and trying to stand into the Harbour. There was a very heavy fall of sleet and snow. Towards evening gun signals were fired indicating distress. Captain Edwards described the events thus: Having arrived opposite Bray Head the sea began to swell and the wind blow a hurricane. He threw all his anchors out but the ship dragged them all along impetuously. She drove without a rag of sail towards Dunleary Point and he expected to be dashed against the rocks there. He repeatedly told the officers of the danger before she struck about 6 or 7 in the evening. (150)

The accounts describe the ships getting six leagues off shore when the storm forced them back. The anchors were cast out at Man O War roads between Dalkey and Dun Laoghaire. The master of the Prince of Wales with Robert Jones, nine seamen, two soldiers, two sailors, passengers, two women and children, took to the long boat when the vessel struck off Sir John Lees house at Blackrock. The boat party got safely to Mr St George's house at Blackrock.

The losses from *Prince of Wales* were Lieutenant Maclean of the 18th foot, with 61 volunteers from the South Mayo militia. Lieutenant Foley 58th foot, Captain Gregory and Lieutenant Kilkelly of the 32nd foot, Sergeant of

Loss of the Prince of Wales Packet

The troopship *Rochdale* was wrecked at the Martello tower at Seapoint on 18-9-1807. Another ship of the same convoy the *Prince of Wales* was wrecked at Blackrock house nearby. They had sailed from the Pigeon House harbour in Dublin with the 97th West Kent regiment bound for the continent. Some 100 men women & children were lost on the *Prince of Wales* and 265 on the *Rochdale*.

Illustration: Walker's Hibernian Magazine

the 25 Rgt, Ensign Beaven of the 10th foot, Ensign Baggot of 85th foot Ensign Kidd of 85th foot, Lieut. Wasey of 2nd foot, Lieutenant Brown of 62 foot. Each officer had a party of soldiers and servants The total 120 officers and men lost. There was a report that the hatches were battened down but Mr Moss, the coroner deputed a party of four gentlemen to visited the wreck site and ascertained that there was no substance in the story. An immense amount of baggage was washed ashore and a large party of troops were put on guard. Looters gathered as was usual at the time and one from Dun Laoghaire was drowned. All the weekend was spent in collecting the bodies for burial at Monkstown and Merrion cemeteries. A memorial was also placed at St Begnet's graveyard, Dalkey. The account (132) is somewhat confusing as the numbers aboard do not seem to include crew and the detail is predominantly regarding the military aboard. Captain Edwards was subsequently tried but acquitted.

The *Rochdale* was wrecked on th erocks at the Martello tower at Seapoint. It was observed that no pilot could have steered her alongside at the Martello as neatly as she lay. The *Rochdale* had aboard the staff of the 97th regiment In all two hundred and sixty five perished in the *Rochdale* including major Gormocan, lieutenants Long and Power, ensign Way, 8 sergeants, 9 corporals, 173 rank and file, 44 women, 29 children. There were no survivors from the *Rochdale*.

The same night a collier was lost with all hands at the South Bull, A trader belonging to a Dublin Broker was also lost. The Liverpool Packet was feared lost as a vessel fitting her description was seen bottom up off Bray.

The Lark another transport from Dublin reached Holyhead in safety according to one report but a later report indicated that she too was lost.

Unknown Canadian Troopship

The official censor removed a story from the Freeman's Journal of 15-10-1917. It related a report from America that a native of Tory arriving in the USA had revealed that a u boat base had been discovered on the Island the previous summer. In addition that 18 months previously the bodies of 170 Canadian troops had been washed ashore at Tory. This was in spite of the repeated assertion that no Canadian transport had been sunk. It is hard to attach significance to these reports. There is no mass burial on Tory which could not have been kept secret nor is there mention of the submarine base anywhere else. It would seem that this story is, therefore untrue. (145)

Lion

The 1000 ton transport *Lion* was wrecked at Baltimore on 20-5-1782. She was bound from Charleston to Liverpool. It is nor clear from the Lloyds account if Baltimore, West Cork was the location or Baltimore, Maryland.

Rockingham

When the *Rockingham* was wrecked in December 1765 in Rennies Bay the troopship was carrying the 32nd regiment bound for the America. One hundred and fifty men perished

Sovereign

The *Sovereign* was wrecked at Stradbally on 16-3-1837. Among those aboard were 80 men of the Royal Artillery. They were en route from their depot at Woolwich to the Barbados. All the men were saved.

Irlam

On 10-5-1812 the *Irlam* struck Tuskar Rock. She was from Barbados for Liverpool with cargo and 107 people aboard including 73 members of the 16th foot. Five people were lost at the time of the wreck and the rest were assisted by workers building the lighthouse. A passing ship took off most of the passengers leaving the crew and some of the soldiers who were rescued two days later by a boat from Wexford. Some details of the loss of the Irlam are nor clear and suggest greater loss of life but therc may have been some confusion.

Baring

The *Baring*, a former East India ship was wrecked on 10-10-1814 at Berehaven. She carried the 40th and York Chausseurs and their baggage. Of the 320 aboard 20 were lost and 300 saved

Rival

On 24-11-1832 wreckage was washed ashore at Galway. It was concluded that the *Rival* had foundered off shore while carrying troops from Glasgow for Portugal. It is not clear how many were aboard. This wreck may be the subject of a ballad. (42)

Britannia

A great mystery surrounds the loss of a troopship supposed to be the *Britannia* which was wrecked on Inisboffin. She carried the Orange Rangers from Canada bound for the USA 27-1-1780 about 60 lost and the survivors suffered terribly before they reached Galway. The name of the troopship is not recorded anywhere but a placename indicates the *Britannia* was her name.

ARMADA

After the initial flurry of activity on the Trinidad Valencera, Girona and Santa Maria de la Rosa there has been little work done or Armada wrecks in Ireland until the Streedagh expedition by an English group. (131)

The recoveries have been stunning and are the subject of awe wherever they were shown. Many documents and contemporary pamphlets exist on the Spanish armada of 1588 (24) but little new has come to light in recent times. The studies and grandiose proposals around the 400th anniversary in 1988 seems to have exhausted the appetite for research and excavation. There has been no encouragement to investigate any of the sites which are known nor has anything been published by Irish Government officials on the Armada. Some Armada items exist in scattered collections around Ireland but no effort has been made to exhibit these together in any context. The magnificent Ulster museum exhibition visited Greenwich in 1988 but there was insufficient official interest to attract it to Dublin.

An Armada exhibition was held at Drury Lane, London in October 1888. Among the items on show were four "Armada" chests, a Spanish matchlock taken from a Spaniard on the coast of Ireland, a spear head from one of the

Figurehead of a Spanish Galleon wrecked at Streedagh in 1588. It was in the possession of Simon Cullen, Sligo, in the 1890s but the present location is unknown.

Armada ships wrecked on the coast of Donegal and a spoon with a floral design cast ashore at Dunluce Castle about 1798. It is unclear where any of these items survive. Further Armada items are supposed to exist. These include a cannon removed to Northern Ireland from Carricktoorish lake, gold coins found on Gola and a chalice found on Cruit Island.

Table from an Armada vessel at Bunratty Castle.
Photo: Author

Six Armada wrecks have been located and material recovered from them in recent years. The Trinidad Valencera was discovered during a casual trainee dive and there followed a systematic removal of the material from the site. The Irish National Museum had insufficient interest in acquiring the material so it was sent to the Ulster Museum. There, it was in good hands and soon joined the treasures of the Girona which had been discovered near the Giant's Causway. (151) Some other items have been found at both sites since the initial discoveries. A concentrated search discovered the Santa Maria de La Rosa in Blasket Sound.

The English group worked on the Streedagh sites in 1985 and discovered ship timbers, cannon wheels and cannon. The vessels are La Lavia, La Juliana and Santa Maria de La Vision. There is excellent documentation covering the losses and fate of the crew. The work halted when a dispute arose over the ownership of the wrecks. The English group claimed to be salvors in possession under the current law of salvage. The Office of Public Works arranged to have legislation enacted which changed the law. Prolonged litigation ensued but not before several items had been raised and placed in OPW storage. The Streedagh site is unique in that three ships from the same squadron are there, they contain a set of artillery of the period as well as much more timbers than survive at the other three sites. The guns from La Juliana site have been traced by Spanish

Documents to her original armament and to extra guns allocated from the garrison at Palermo. Unfortunately The La Juliana site is most exposed to wave action and shifting sands. Some concreted material has been washed ashore and mixed with the rocks at the base of the sand dunes. Most of the timbers must have been washed ashore in previous years. It is not clear how much sand abrasion has occurred to the artefacts but this problem has been reported to have occurred on bronze objects. In the past material was recovered from two more wrecks by diving and another two by dredging. The location of six wrecks is known accurately and locations are hinted at for three more. This leaves an interesting body of work to be completed as these wrecks are explored. In all 26 Armada wrecks occurred on the Irish coast so 17 remain to be discovered. The exposed sites are a major obstacle to a classical archaeological investigation. Proper in situ indication of the wrecks by means of buoyage and roped trails would make them magnets for tourist diving just like any land site attracts visitors and the publicity would, itself be a protection. As the situation stands well informed individuals can visit the sites in secret and their activities are clandestine. The neglect of this heritage reflects the oft quoted view of a prominent archaeologist in the late 1960s that the Armada was not deserving of attention because it was not part of Irish history.

The Armada Chests

A number of Armada chests are held in various collections in both Britain and Ireland. These are assumed to have been washed ashore from shipwrecked Armada vessels even though they are made of iron. Many may have come from the Armada. There is another explanation that these were used as collection boxes to gather money towards the welfare of sailors. Christ Church in Dublin contains such a chest as does the Franciscan church in Kilkenny. The Chatham chest is a large oblong box with an elaborate locking mechanism. Eight bolts inside the lid secure its closure. Although such coffers are referred to as armada chests they were the strong boxes of the 16th and 17th centuries. The particular Chatham chest was constructed in 1625 to hold the "chest at Chatham" This fund or chest was established by the treasurer of the Navy Sir John Hawkins in 1590 to provide pensions for sailors in poor circumstances after the defeat of the Armada. Seamen were levied six pence a month to fund the pensions. The five locks had individual keys each kept by five officers to ensure security of the funds from embezzlement. There are a greater number of these chests preserved in Ireland than could have been from wrecked Spanish ships. However some are without doubt authentic Spanish items of the period. Treasure chests in the South Kensington museum have the same ornamentation and construction from 14th, 15th, and 16th centuries.

Armada chest at Christchurch, Dublin.
Photo: Cormac Lowth

They were not peculiar to Spain. In Ireland these chests were in use at the time of the O'Donnells and probably came from trading between Donegal and the continent. The lid of such a chest was dug up at O'Cleary's castle at Kilbarron, Ballyshannon. A chest found in Mayo could be authentic because it was supposed to have been taken from the sea at Blacksod and bears corrosion appropriate to sea water. Cuellar's narrative mentions the Irish breaking open money chests from Spanish arcas at Streedagh. These were iron chests with flat lids to hold money. (133). The State Papers of 1588 have several references to money chests on Spanish ships. Plate and ducats were rifled out of their chests. In the examination of Spanish Prisoners from Nuestra Senora del Rosario " a chest of the King's was taken wherein was 52,000 ducats, of which chest Don Pedro de Valdez had one key and the king's treasurer, the Duke had the other. The State Papers describing the capture of the carrack, San Salvador, describe a chest of great weight in the fore-peak of the ship. According to George Hill, historian of the McDonnells of Dunluce Castle the *Girona* carried two such chests which were kept at the castle. The Earl of Antrim has two iron chests of uncertain date. (162) There are, therefore, two sides to the Armada chest story, one of authentic chests, the other describing the collection chests relating to the sailors pensions. Then there also were the treasure chests of great families of the period unconnected with the Armada.

Armada artefacts in Ireland

Location Held	Items	1588 Armada Ship	Location found
Ulster Museum Collection	see Ireland's Armada Legacy (142)	Trinidad Valencera	Kinnigoe Bay
Ulster Museum Collection	Treasures of the Armada (162)	Girona	Lacada Point
Ulster Museum Collection	Matute plate	Santa Maria de La Rosa	Blasket Sound
National Museum	Lead Ingots, pewter	Unknown wreck	Poulathomas
National Museum	Cannon	Three wrecks	Streedagh
National Museum	Statue		Grange Co Sligo
Inisowen (private)	Cannon	Trinidad Valencera	Kinnigoe Bay
Franciscan Church Kilkenny	Armada Chest	unknown	Seen on request
from Kilkenny	Ingots of lead	unknown originally thought to be Roman	now in National Museum
Christ Church, Dublin	Armada Chest	unknown	
Clare Co Museum	Table		Quilty
Rossnoulagh Donegal Historical Society Museum, ex United Services Club, London	Anchor	Unknown	Recovered in 1853 by workers at local coastguard station
Tower Museum, Derry	Cannon	Trinidad Valencera	Recovered by City of Derry SAC
Ballyshannon Gillen Family	Cannon	Unknown	Dredged
C of I Carndonagh	Bell	Trinidad Valencera?	
Bamburgh Castle, Northumberland	Cannon	Unknown	Maybe ex Dundrum Castle
Mulranny	Cupboard door, timbers made into a table, one roundshot, Figurehead in possession of Simon Cullen in 1888		Eugene Gillan
Ballina	Figurehead of a Spanish soldier		Beleek Castle collection
Culdaff House Inisowen	Armada Chest		Eugene Gillan
Browne Hall Ballintra	Armada Chest		Eugene Gillan
On Seabed near Inisboffin	Anchor	Unknown	
Ballyferriter Museum	Shot and balls	Santa Maria de La Rosa	now in National Museum
Maritime Museum Dun Laoghaire	Cannon	ex Streedagh	now in National Museum
Bunratty castle	Table	Armada wreck	on Display
Dromoland castle	table		in Clare Co. museum ????
North of Ireland	Cannon		Ex Kiltoorish lake
Dundrum Castle Dublin	Bronze swivel	ex Blasket Sound	disappeared about 1921
In Private hands	anchors	ex Blasket sound	
Beleek Castle, Ballina	Many items	ex Armada wrecks	Privately held owner Marshall Duran
Maritime Museum Greenwich	Astralabe c 1580	Unknown	found at Valentia Island

MUSEUMS

The following museums and heritage centres in Ireland contain shipwreck and maritime artefacts. Some of these have come from wrecks. It is not possible to list all the items of interest.

National Museum Of Ireland, Collins Barracks, Dublin 7.

Maritime Trust, Grand Canal Dock Ringsend, Dublin 3

Dublin Civic museum, South William St, Dublin 2.

National Maritime Museum, Haigh Terrace Dun Laoghaire.

Arklow Maritime Museum, Former Vocational school, Arklow, Co Wicklow

Maritime Room, Wexford county museum, Enniscorthy

Cork Heritage Trust, Douglas, Cork.

Wexford Maritime Museum, MV Guillemot, Kilmore Quay. Co Wexford

Greencastle Maritime Museum, Greencastle Co Donegal.

Derry Maritime Museum, Guildhall, Derry.

Ulster Museum, Botanic Avenue Belfast.

Ceim Hill museum, Ballydehob Co Cork

Lathar Oidreachta, Cape Clear Island, Co Cork

Lusitania display at Cobh Heritage centre

Cobh museum

Tayleur display at Newbridge house Donabate

Ballyferriter heritage centre

Bushe's Bar at Baltimore

Kehoe's Bar, Kilmore quay, Co Wexford.

John Tim Collection at Castletownbere

Bantry town museum, French wreck pintail and cannonballs

Bantry Armada Centre Bantry House, Bantry Co Cork

Maritime museum Quaker Hall Tramore

Mexico memorabilia, Kilrane school Rosslare Co Wexford.

Church at Castletownsend *Lusitania* oars and lifejacket.

MUSEUMS

Several Museums and individuals possess diving helmets of the old hard hat type. Some might date to the last century and may have been used on many of the wrecks mentioned in the text. Many have been attributed to the turn of the century but close examination of the serial numbers has revealed that they are more modern.

Serial number	Type	Location	Period
11114	Siebe Gorman	Waterways Visitor Centre Dublin	c1930
15655	Siebe Gorman	Maritime Museum, Dun Laoghaire	1944
17481	Siebe Gorman	Limerick City Museum	1949
	3 Helmets	Paddy Power Museum Tramore	
	2 helmets	Dublin Port	
5047	Draeger	Kehoes Bar Kilmore Quay	

FIGUREHEADS

One part of a wooden shipwreck least likely to be smashed was the figurehead. There are many accounts of wreck which mention that a figurehead was washed ashore. Many were placed in gardens as ornaments and rotted away. It seems that very few have survived and some are listed below. One of the most remarkable was the Man O War which used reside on a plinth outside the pub in the district of that name near Balbriggan, Co Dublin. There was great mystery and confusion about the origin and representation of the figure. Some sources even alleged that the figure was stone. Serious research by Jim Walsh has elucidated much of the history but the classical scholarship of Cormac Lowth identified the figurehead as a representation of Hercules clad in the skin of the Nemean lion which he slew as his first labour. There was a ship named Hercules lost on the Irish coast in 22-3-1799 but the exact location is unclear. (137) (138). One clue to a marine origin for a wood carving is the damage by the shipworm otherwise known as Teredo (Teredo navalis) worm or gribble, a kind of woodlouse. This can be distinguished from woodworm by the longitudinal holes along the grain. Damage by the shipworm will indicate that the figurehead came from a wreck in deeper water which was washed ashore or one that had been immersed in an intertidal zone for a period. The worm is more prolific and larger in warmer waters. Figureheads were usually made of composite pieces of timber. Softwoods, usually pine was favoured for ease of carving. This facilitated working the wood in several directions regardless of the grain of the timber. (149)

The subjects of figureheads are varied. Deep sea vessels tended to have human figures. Both male and female figureheads were common at the beginning of the nineteenth century but by the end of the century females predominated. Coats of arms, warriors, statesmen and representations of the shipowner or his family predominated. The more profitable the trade the more likely was the ship to have a figurehead, thus the humble colliers were unlikely to be adorned. Ship registers for the ports after 1786 give a brief description of the figurehead. Warships tended to have huge, elaborate figureheads to symbolise power and majesty. Such examples survive on the *Vasa* (1628) but by 1760 the carvings on the warships were more modest and in 1796 the Royal Navy ceased fitting figureheads to new ships. There are fine collections on board the *Cutty Sark* and in the Maritime Museum at Greenwich, on the Victory at Portsmouth and in the Valhalla museum on the Scilly Isles.

FIGUREHEADS

Description	Ship	Location	Origin	Information source
Male head resembling Shakespeare	Thames	O'Shea's pub, Blackwater Co Wexford	washed ashore at Ballyconigar	
Lady in a green dress	Pomona	Wexford county Museum Enniscorthy	Wrecked on Blackwater Bank	28-4-1859
Bowsprit female figure	Mary Grace	Wexford county Museum Enniscorthy	Wrecked on Saltees	
Lady in a red dress with a rose	Unknown	Wexford county Museum Enniscorthy	Wexford shipwreck	
Lady in an orange and green with a dog	Unknown	Wexford county Museum Enniscorthy	Wexford shipwreck	
Figure of a man	Test	Wexford County Museum Enniscorthy	Wrecked at Morris castle	15-1-1861
Female figure	Unknown	Wexford County Museum Enniscorthy	Wexford shipwreck	
Albatross	Unknown	Clontarf Yacht Club	Found at store at Baldoyle coastguard station	
Queen Victoria	Queen Victoria	National Maritime Museum	Wrecked at Bailey, Howth	14-2-1853
Figure like an Indian	Unknown	National Maritime Museum		
Figure of Hercules	Unknown	Formerly at Man O War near Balbriggan	Possibly from wreck at Mornington	Now with Jim Walsh, Librarian Balbriggan
Female figure	Gipsy Maid		wrecked on Copelands 1-1-1911	Photo in shipwrecks of Ulster coast
	unknown	In a garden at Ballywalter		Jim Blaney
Diana	Wild Deer	formerly at garage in Ballyhalbert	wrecked 11-1-1883	bought by a man in Comber
Lion with an axe	Leo	formerly at Quentin Bay		Believed in New York Yacht club
Female figure	Village Bell	on wall of Old Ship pub Arklow		Taken away for repair

Description	Ship	Location	Origin	Information source
Red haired female figure	Unknown	on wall of Old Ship pub Arklow		removed after a short time
Female figure	Tarrgona	Arklow shipping office		
Unknown	Unknown	antique shop on road to Limerick		removed when shop was sold
Male figure with sickle and sheaf of oats	Harvest King	taken from ship when abandoned		Arklow Maritime Museum
Collection of figureheads	Unknown	In rectory garden at Ardagh Co Limerick	there c 1930s but current location unknown	Dr Smylie curator maritime museum
Lion holding a shield	Armada wreck at Streedagh Sligo in 1897	in possession of Simon Cullen JP,	current location unknown	reference 133
Black dog	Sirius	In Hull Museum UK	wrecked at Cork	
Male Figure	Alfred D Snow	On Guillemot lightship Museum Kilmore Quay	wrecked 4-1-1888 at Broomhill	
Female figure	Clara	On Guillemot lightship Museum Kilmore Quay	A Kilmore schooner dismantled c 1930	

LEGENDS OF THE LUSITANIA

The sinking of the *Lusitania* by a torpedo from U20 off the Old Head of Kinsale on Friday 7 May 1915 was the single greatest shipwreck tragedy in Irish waters. Some 1200 men, women and children died. A warning to intending passengers had been placed beside the sailing notice in the New York newspapers. A great storm of indignation was whipped up by British propagandists when the realisation sank in that the *Lusitania* had been managed in a negligent manner by the Admiralty. In later years some other legends arose around the somewhat conflicting circumstances of the loss of this prestigious liner. The truth lies somewhere between inept bungling and a murderous conspiracy.

The funeral of a Lusitania victim at Queenstown.

Photo: National Maritime Museum Collection

Diamonds

There are several stories of treasure aboard the *Lusitania*. They involve diamonds, gold bullion, personal goods of wealthy passengers and paintings. The story of the diamonds is true because a mailbag containing packets of diamonds was found floating near the wreck site. The Evening Herald of 13-12-1917 carried the information that the Cork correspondent of the Daily Chronicle reported the story that a poor Irish fisherman found a packet of diamonds which were washed out of the *Lusitania*. The gems were consigned to a London firm and were insured for $13,000 with the Union Insurance Company. The company paid the claim in full, and believed that they had heard the last of the matter, but a welcome surprise was in store. They received a letter about October 1917 stating that the diamonds had been recovered and that the owners had much pleasure in refunding the $13,000. It seems that the Irishman had found the packet of gems among a quantity of fish he had hauled up in his net and had thus made the catch of his life. Without telling anyone of his find he sent the diamonds to London as an ordinary postal packet, where enquiries were made and their ownership traced. The honesty of the fisherman was rewarded by a gift of some hundreds of pounds. This story tends to confirm the description of the mailbags being hauled on deck as otherwise they would not have floated free. If they had been in the area of the torpedo hit they would have been damaged. Postal records show that 32 packets of industrial gems were shipped and arrived intact with the consignee. (135)

Bullion

The truth about gold bullion aboard the *Lusitania* is somewhat different. Bullion was exported to the USA from Britain in enormous quantities during World War I. Such a consignment was lost and saved when the Laurentic was sunk by a mine off the Donegal coast. The bullion shipments are detailed in Nigel Pickford's book (88). There is no logical reason why a shipment would be made in the opposite direction as a simple banking transaction could reallocate gold already in Britain. The British Government, through the Bank of England, were transferring their reserves to the United States to support the pound sterling and to pay cash for armaments and munitions purchased in the then neutral America. If substantial gold was suspected to have been aboard the professional salvage companies would have attempted to recover it in the heyday of salvage between the wars and in the 1950s.

Personal wealth

There were many wealthy passengers aboard the *Lusitania*. There is no doubt that they would have had valuables among their possessions aboard the ship. If they did not retain the jewellery, money or documents in their cabin it would have been deposited in the purser's safe. There were two quite small Chubb safes available to the purser. Some say that there was a large 16 ton caged structure built into the ship but John Light indicated that this was not in the drawings. Divers from the Oceaneering expedition say that the "purser's safe " was gone when they searched the appropriate location in 1982. Furthermore they believed that the Italian company Sorima of Genoa had retrieved the safe when they visited the wreck in the 1930s. There is no doubt that Sorima worked in the South Coast area in the 1930s. They even worked on the nearby wreck the Spectator. However they did not send down divers other than in an observation chamber. Their method was to use a surface operated grab guided by a man in the observation chamber. There is no evidence of extensive explosive and grab demolition of the *Lusitania* and therefore it seems improbable that this story is true. The salvors *Risdon*Beazley got the safe out of the *Spectator* and this could be the origin of the story of the *Lusitania* safe. The Spectator was sunk very close to the *Lusitania*.

Paintings

One of the passengers was Sir Hugh Lane who was an art dealer and collector. His collection was shared between the galleries in Dublin and London after his death. There was a major dispute regarding a codicil to his will which left paintings to the Dublin Municipal Gallery. Lane sailed outward on board the Philadelphia with a Holbein insured well and kept in pursers safe. He returned from America with a crate insured for £2000. This crate was listed in the manifest. Due to the low insured value it is unlikely that this contained important paintings. A story circulated about tubes being seen on the wreck but there would be many lengths of tubing from the engine room and there appears to be no verification that any paintings could have survived. There was great excitement generated by this story. There was information that insurers had recommended that paintings should be packed in tubes sealed with lead for protection from water damage. There was no mention, however, on whether the tubes would float free nor whether they would resist 11 Bar hydrostatic pressure without admitting water. Another unnamed passenger was supposed to have a Mannet painting among his personal baggage. A Mr Archibald inquired of Cunard on 18-5-1915 if The Holy Family by Reubens carried by Mr Willimson was aboard. The paintings story became so bizarre that an Egyptian gallery asked in 1996 if a painting they held was a fake. press

A case of oil paintings was listed on outward cargo sheet held in papers of Franklin D Rosevelt. These were supposed to be two Reubens and a Monnet/ Mannet from Lord Duveen. Simpson gives no source for his suggestion that 27 masterpieces worth $4M were among the Lane consignment. The only documented paintings were a case of oil paintings insured for $2312.

The sonar echo behind the wreck

A distinct sonar echo lies behind the wreck and this is believed to be where the second explosion blew the bottom out of the ship. This would explain why the *Lusitania* sank so quickly. Investigation of this area could reveal the exact location of the second explosion and the heavy munitions are suspected to have been deposited here. Other heavy cargo would include the cartridges from Remington, the shrapnel shells, copper ingots and brass rods. The location has not been investigated thoroughly and it might be just a bed of Rock.

Missing radio messages

Transcripts of radio messages to the *Lusitania* were removed from the Admiralty message log as late as 1950 and there has been much speculation as to what instructions were given to the *Lusitania* about changing course for Queenstown. The original destination was Liverpool. If she was to have continued for Liverpool, standing orders from the Admiralty were that ships should stay well out to sea from headlands which were favourite submarine hunting grounds. The five *Lusitania* signals are the only ones missing for the whole of the war.

One of the missing messages seems to be from Valentia radio originating from Admiral Coke in Queenstown addressed to MFA (merchant fleet auxiliary), advising it to proceed to Queenstown and its escort Scadaun to search and locate a German submarine operating in the area. The Admiralty have always maintained that this message was meant for MFA tug *Hellespont*. However the *Lusitania's* call sign was MFA and the operators aboard assumed the message was for them. Captain Turner altered course for Queenstown exposing the *Lusitania* to the torpedoes of U20. (114) Patrick Beesley author of Room 40 was of the opinion that the missing signals were still in existence and if they showed the Admiralty is a favourable light then they would have been released.

The supposition is that the missing messages are a request from Captain Turner to go around the North of Ireland and the Admiralty refusal to allow this. There had been mines laid near Tory by the Berlin but they had been cleared. The damaged battleship *Jupiter* was escorted by that route. Indeed so safe was the route that instructions were given that there was no need to zig zag. (135),

Purpose of turning for land

It has been explained that Captain Turner approached the Old Head of Kinsale in order to obtain an accurate fix of his position. This is hardly the reason for the turn towards land because an approach to Queenstown was definitely intended as confirmed by third officer Bestic in a 1962 interview. He said that the mail bags were being hauled on deck and it would have been too early to complete this task if Liverpool was the next port of call. Sometimes mail was unloaded at Queenstown and transferred to Kingstown (Dun Laoghaire) for transfer to Holyhead by mailboats such as the *Leinster*. Apparently some valuable cargo was sometimes sent by that route to avoid submarines in St George's Channel.

The second submarine

There were several sightings of submarines which cannot have been Schweiger's *U20*. Patrol vessel no 47, a motor yacht, the *Seagull*, owned by the Shakelton family was lent to the Navy in September 1914. Though only 42 foot and 15 tons it was based in Baltimore as a patrol vessel. A letter dated 11-5-1915 describes an encounter between the yacht and a submarine. Cope, who may have commanded the yacht, wrote to his father a GWR station master in Wolverhampton describing the encounter. " we played a very active role in the last murder. (I enclose a cutting from the Cork Examiner which leaves one with a vague impression) We had been chasing an elusive submarine for several days without getting a glimpse of the bounder, in spite of being hot on his track. On Friday morning about 9.55 a.m. we saw a surfaced submarine. On sighting us about two or three miles off they made for us at top speed. They were greeted with a shot or two from my rifle which must have had the effect of making them smile, so futile was it. From then on matters became exciting. They had the legs of us by about eight or nine knots (nearly twice our speed) but our handy little boat was able to hold her own.2 They succeeded in keeping the German vessel in sight for twenty minutes before the submarine submerged. The *Seagull* got into Baltimore at 11.15 and the signal about the sighting was broadcast by 12.00. The *Seagull* was built by Percy See at Fareham in Hampshire in 1911 and still sails on the river Shannon. This sighting off Cape Clear is quite a mystery since it would be 30 miles from the Old Head of Kinsale and therefore three hours journey from the *Lusitania* sinking at 2 p.m. The mystery is that the *U 20* was coming from the East while this sighting was to the West. The signal to the MFA *Helespont* to proceed to Queenstown leaving the escort Scadaun to search for a submarine also points to a sighting other than *U 20* being taken seriously.

Coast watchers on a headland overlooking the sea reported a surfaced submarine at 1.40 and made a report to Queenstown. But a submarine in close to land cannot have attacked the *Lusitania* because she was attacked from seaward. These observers were official coast watchers and so their report must be considered reliable.

Passengers aboard the *Lusitania* reported sighting a submarine on the Port side at 2.00 before the *Lusitania* made the turn toward land. They interpreted this as the captain taking evasive action. This is significant because chart information shows that the *Lusitania* was directly on course for Queenstown BEFORE the evasive change of course. The alteration in course was not therefore the turn for Queenstown as some writers have indicated. It was this evasive manoeuvre thought to avoid a mystery submarine that exposed the *Lusitania* to the *U20*. Captain Schweiger in *U20* attacked from the Starboard almost immediately afterward. Significantly the Admiralty removed questions 14 and 15 form the list of queries to be put to witnesses at Lord Mersey's inquiry. These referred to submarine sightings and confirm that there was some evidence for mystery sightings.

Lookouts on the *Lusitania* say they saw two torpedoes but Captain Schweiger of *U 20* fired only one. This is explained by the track of the torpedo being slightly away from the track of bubbles as observed from a height. Bubbles take several seconds to rise from the torpedo depth and therefore "strike" the ship well aft of the torpedo.

Apart from *U 20* and *U30* to the North of Ireland en route to Germany, the next nearest German submarine activity was the sinking of a large number of trawlers between Aberdeen and Hartlepool. Even British submarines which became active in later years in the vicinity of Fastnet were considered. The nearest two recorded are training craft logged as tied up at Pembroke and Devonport. Their logs survive at the Public Records Office at Kew. Fleet dispositions are not necessarily free from misleading information as the battleship HMS Audacious is listed though she had been sunk. Q ships were never listed. Altogether some seven sighting Point to the existence of a mystery second submarine which cannot be explained. Conspiracy theorists believe that an unnamed British submarine was on location to ensure that the *Lusitania* was sunk.

German submarine activity

Though many observations have been made about the extent of submarine activity at the time and the warnings which should have been issued it is worth while just listing what activity occurred in the days before and after the *Lusitania* was sunk. *U20* cruised over towards Tuskar sinking the *Earl of Latham*, the *Centurion* & *Candidate* *U30* was around Eagle Island and sank *Fulgent* she was at Blaskets on 30 May at the end of her cruise. The presence of *U 30* contradicts the observation that *U 20* monographs say no subs within 600 miles.

Date	Vessel	Location	Fate
29-4-1915	Cherbury	27 m WNW Eagle Island	sunk
30-4-1915	Fulgent	20 miles WNW Blaskets	sunk
1-5-1917	Edale	45m NW by W Scilly	sunk
3-5-1915	Minterne	50 miles SW Wolf Rock	sunk
4 May	Cayo Romano	off Fastnet	torpedo missed
	Earl of Lathom	8 miles from Old Head	sunk
6 May	Candidate	13 miles from Coningbeg	sunk
6 May	Centurion	15 miles from Barrel LV	sunk
7 May	Etonian	off Queenstown	sub chased
7 May	Narragansett	off S Ireland	torpedo missed
7 May	City of Exeter	off Queenstown	chased
7 May	*Lusitania*	Old Head of Kinsale	torpedoed and sank
21-5	Glenholm	16 miles from Fastnet	sunk
30-5-1915	Megantic	S of Ireland	chased by sub

The second explosion

A second torpedo becomes a possibility only if a second submarine attacked the *Lusitania* simultaneously. Robert Ballard says that plates were bent outward from an internal explosion while a torpedo strike would cause them to bend inwards. He concluded that coal dust in the empty bunker was disturbed by the first and ignited to cause the second larger explosion. This theory is flawed because crew in vicinity of the coal bunker survived but crew near the forward hold unloading the mail were all killed. This observation suggests that the explosion was in the forward area which contained some cargo. The shell cases aboard were not filled with explosive however there were boxes of "margarine" in the deck. These were consigned to Woolwich Arsenal and had come from Du Pont chemical company. It is almost certain that this was a consignment of gun cotton. There were previous shipments of guncotton from Du Pont: 870 tons on the Arabic, 400 tons on the *Georgic*, and 3,200 boxes of guncotton on the *Ordiana*. Surprisingly this is quite stable unless allowed deteriorate but it could have exploded sympathetically with the torpedo. Paddy O'Sullivan indicates that there was a batch of 46 tons of aluminium powder manifested among the cargo. This is highly explosive and is used as an accelerant for other explosives. He believes that the aluminium itself exploded, ignited by the first torpedo explosion. There were cartridges aboard but their explosive potential was negligible.

A Sacrifice??

In 1914 Churchill was described as having passed the remark that a scheme to contrive an event to bring America into the First World War would be convenient. King George V, according to Colin Simpson, in a conversation with an American emissary, Colonel House asked "what will America do if the Germans sink the *Lusitania*" This suggests that there was an expectation of an incident involving the *Lusitania*. There was a message from Hope to Winston Churchill in 1941 suggesting a British submarine should attack a US navy escort to provoke a German - American incident. This would be incredible had not the same suspicion become attached to the *Lusitania* loss by the suggestion of a second mystery submarine. Even when the *Lusitania* was sunk the Americans delayed a further two years before they declared war on Germany. It took the additional threat of the Zimmerman telegram to convince them that there was a domestic danger from Germany. The cruiser *HMS Juno* was recalled to Queenstown on the morning of the 7th because of the submarine activity in the area. There was a significant concern about older cruisers because a squadron of three cruisers had been lost in the North Sea. The cruisers

HMS Aboukir, Hogue and *Cressey* were sunk by a single submarine on 22-9-1914 with disastrous loss of life. Their patrol was dangerous - so much so that their nickname was "the live bait squadron". The Admiralty was embarrassed that their tactics were so faulty. A cruiser was not of much use against a submarine in any case. The recall of the *Juno* must be seen in this light. During previous scares escorts had been rushed from Milford Haven to accompany cargoes of horses and mules, the *Ausonia* and *Transylvania* had been diverted into Queenstown on 30-1-1915 to avoid U21. Admiral Coke at Queenstown could only order ships under his command to safety, for example the cruiser *HMS Juno*. He also was instructed not to issue specific orders to a merchant ship but to limit his communications merely to indicate areas of danger. The Admiralty would have to have taken measures to divert the *Lusitania* directly. For some reason they did not do this. Churchill was not at the Admiralty himself, he was in France meeting Sir John French near Calais. The Admiralty did cancel the departure of the battleship *HMS Orion* from Devonport and delayed the return of the battleship *HMS Colossus* from the Atlantic to avoid the submarines known to be about. The Admiralty Room 40 had specific information about submarines because they had broken the German code, they also had seven powerful radio stations to locate the submarines by direction finding when they made their daily report. They knew more than the Germans suspected about submarine deployments.

It would have been normal practice during danger periods to divert shipping from the South coast by sending them around the North coast of Ireland. No such signal was sent to *Lusitania*. It is possible that the presence of *U 30* on the West coast made this action pointless. *U30* could have lingered off Tory before her return to Germany. The rescue of the passengers was accomplished by the 21 ton *Wanderer*, an Isle of Man trawler fishing in the vicinity. The only other vessels involved in the rescue were the tugs *Flying Fish* and *Stormcock* as well as the *Dan O'Connell* another fishing trawler. There were stories that the Kinsale fishing fleet was not permitted to sail to the rescue. There were four motor torpedo boats at Queenstown but they were restricted to minesweeping duties by an order dated 1910. While the *Lusitania* sank in only 18 minutes, the response from Kinsale was not very prompt or efficient. Bodies were recovered by the tug *Polzee*, the steamer *Heron*, and two trawlers.

Cover Up

In the early 1950s the Royal Navy reserve carried out exercises which involved dropping hedgehog anti submarine bombs on the wreck. The hedgehog fired forward and to the side of the patrol ship giving a wide spread of missiles falling on the supposed submarine position.These were wartime surplus and the explosives were being dumped as much as being used for training. An incredible number were fired off during the sessions and some remain unexploded on the sea floor today. Some sources suggest that this was an effort to pulverise the wreck and prevent any revelation of her secrets. It is also believed that the missing signals were removed at a late stage, maybe as late as the 1950s because the signal record was not interfered with in 1917. The sequence numbers of the signals are intact, clearly showing where the five missing signals should be filed. If any diving occurred, then it was during this early 1950s period. It would be credible to connect these events with Churchill's last term as Prime Minister between October 1951 and April 1955. Documentation was removed from files in the early 1920s and Churchill was believed to be directly involved. (135)

Guns aboard?

If there were naval guns aboard the *Lusitania* this would have made her a warship. As it stands she was listed in Jane's Fighting Ships as an auxiliary cruiser. The whole question is one of mere propaganda because with or without guns merchant ships were encouraged to turn and ram submarines. In any case it is beyond doubt that the *Lusitania* carried munitions and war material. The Germans had advertised in American newspapers that passengers were taking passage on a threatened ship.

The *Lusitania* was designed to be converted into an armed merchant cruiser on the outbreak of war. For this purpose she had rings and supports built under her deck planking to carry the weight and recoil of naval guns. In all the *Lusitania* was fitted for 12 six inch guns. This would have given her an armament stronger that regular naval cruisers but of course her armour would have been deficient. On the outbreak of war she went into Liverpool and was stripped of much of her fittings and some work was done on magazines and ammunition hoists. Some believe that guns were aboard but kept in the hold ready for fitting quickly. There was the suggestion that John Light observed two guns on the stern but later divers have not confirmed this. One piece of evidence suggests that the *Lusitania* guns were not mounted and ready for action. This is the absence of any ammunition around the site. While it could remain deep within a magazine or have been removed it remains a fact that any warship or wartime wreck site has scattered ammunition from the ready use lockers. Light suggested that there were two concealed guns at the stern but no later expedition has confirmed this. The stern was badly damaged by the spigot mortar bombs. Light also reported unexplained damage to the rails in the vicinity of the area where the gun mountings were situated. The implication was that the guns were indeed fitted but removed by divers prior to 1962. It is equally possible that the damage to the rails was done by anti submarine spigot mortars or depth charges.

Pre 1960 work on the Lusitania

When John Light visited the wreck in 1962 he reported that there was a square hole cut accurately probably by a thermal lance or very precise explosive work. The only documented visit to the wreck had been a single non working dive by Jim Jarrat in the Triton suit in 1937. There is no clear evidence that SORIMA, Risdon Beazley or the Royal Navy had visited the wreck though all were there according to various stories.

The allegation that the *HMS Reclaim* worked on the wreck cannot be substantiated. The logs of the *Reclaim* are in the Public Record office at Kew and contain no mention of diving on the *Lusitania*. A local diver Paddy Allen says that he never remembered the *Reclaim* working on the *Lusitania* and that he would have taken an interest.

Commander Shalford who joined *HMS Reclaim* about 1955 did not believe that the Navy had dived the *Lusitania* from the *Reclaim*.

Risdon Beazley certainly knew where the wreck lay. They were said to have used the site as a mark for calibrating their echo sounder. However when John Butler of Dunmore East and formerly of Castletownbere was 15 year old, Ted Aplin was pointed out to him as the diver who had dived on the *Lusitania*. He said *Lusitania* was upright and had 200 tons copper aboard. When Risdon Beazley were in the vicinity they were working from the *Help*. In order to observe that she was upright they must have dropped their observation chamber at least once.

Later John Butler joined Beazley's ship, the *Lifeline*, at Castletownbere and on the second time into Cork while the ship was coming up over the *Lusitania* the trace showed on the echo sounder. The story of the injured diver being landed at Kinsale could be an amalgamation of several diver injuries none related to the *Lusitania*. Ted Aplin who worked with RisdonBeazley had an injured left hand due a wound from an industrial bolt but he was an observation chamber diver not an open circuit diver. Another diver Barry probably worked on the Help which used to scout wrecks before the salvage ship Lifeline came to the area. John Butler of Dunmore worked with Wilfred Bunker Bollard, Lofty Yeates and Don Jones with Beazleys but they never dived the *Lusitania* while with the Reclaim nor did they reveal any diving on the *Lusitania* during their Royal Navy service. Bollard while aboard *HMS Reclaim* was involved in the record depth dives in 1949 while with the Royal Navy. Frankie Higgins also with Rieson Beazley had a wartime decompression accident again unrelated to the *Lusitania* but this could be woven into an injured diver story. Risdon Beazley's Help would have found and surveyed the *Lusitania* but the Lifeline was the working ship and would have conducted the dives on the *Lusitania* about 1951-2 before the Twyford came into operation. Risdon Beazley divers did know about the Lane paintings in the 1950s as they has researched valuables in the cargo of many vessels. Their researchers even spoke to dockers who had loaded the cargo.

Propaganda

Comparison of the photographs of lifeboats moored at the pier with one lifeboat photo shows that the name Cunard is painted in huge letters for propaganda photographs. The "Cunard" boat is not even a ship's lifeboat. Some of the photographs of bodies of children were also faked at the time. After the initial indiscreet questions in the House of Commons the enquiry was managed much more carefully by Lord Mersey.

Tall tales - The helmet

During the *Lusitania* exploration by John Light in the years 1959-1965, Kinsale was infested with storytellers who each claimed to have definite information regarding various aspects of the *Lusitania* sinking. These yarns were spun mainly in return for free drink in the pubs of Kinsale. The stories gained credence in the air of suspicion, intrigue and secrecy that surrounded the sinking of the *Lusitania*.

One such tale related that during the 1920s the IRA obtained a diving helmet and a diver with the intention of descending to the wreck to obtain explosives either for use during the war of independence or the Civil war. A Siebe Gorman helmet was on display in Tony Fitzsimons' pub allegedly with this provenance. It is more likely that this was one of two sets of diving gear provided for work on the Shannon and then Tony Fitzsimons bought the gear from Rinanna. The gear is thought to have been bought by people in Cornwall through Phil Dennis.

Tall tales -The Lost Diver

Another story told of a diver exiting a British submarine to carry out secret exploration of the wreck in the late 1940s. According to this tale the diver, an officer, got into difficulties and died. While this was the era of the midget submarines from which a diver could exit using the conning tower as an airlock there is no record confirming this story. The injured diver tale takes several forms but as mentioned above there was an injured diver among the Risdon Beazley crew and the story just might have its origins in this fact.

LUSITANIA BIBLIOGRAPHY

Lusitania Colin Simpson, Avid Publications, Garth Boulevard, Wirral L635LS (151 6452047) ISBN 0 952102064

Horrors and atrocities of the great war, including the tragic destruction of the *Lusitania*, Logan Marshall, 1915.

The tragedy of the *Lusitania*, Capt. Frederick D Ellis, 1915

The *Lusitania*'s last voyage, Charles Lauriat. 1915

German submarine warfare a study of its methods and spirit Including the crime of the *Lusitania*, Wesley frost. 1918.

RMS Lusitanaia, record of passengers and crew for office use only, Cunard SS Co Liverpool 1-3-1916 In Possession of Bob Ward Cobh. Passengers and burial locations

Lusitania unravelling the mysteries, Patrick O'Sullivan, Collins, Cork, 1998, ISBN 1 898256 51 9

Lusitania, Colin Simpson 2nd edition, Longmans, 1972.

Seven Days to disaster, Des Hickey and Gus Smith, G.P.Purnham, New York 1981

Hoehling, A.A. & Mary Hoehling, The last voyage of the *Lusitania*, Longmans, London, 1975.

Sauder, Eric, Marschall, Ken, RMS *Lusitania*: Triumph of the Edwardian Age. Trans Atlantic Designs, Redono beach, 1991.

Bailey, T. A. & Ryan, P.B. The *Lusitania* disaster, Free press, New York 1975

Lusitania, the Cunard Turbine driven Quadruple screw Atlantic liner, Mark D. Warren, published Patrick Stevens, Wellingborough, 1986.

REFERENCES

1. Limerick Reporter, contemporary account.
2. Iris Freeland, daughter of Thomas Ensor, personal communication. 1998
3. Naval Chronicles Vol. 17, 1807, p397
4. Irish Whales and Whaling, James Fairley, Blackstaff Press, Belfast, 1981 ISBN 0 85640 232 X
5. General Advertiser, contemporary account
6. Clare Champion contemporary account
7. Maritime Arklow, Frank Forde, Glendale 1988, ISBN 090 7606 51 2
8. Bright Lights, White Water, Bill Long, New Island Books, Dublin, 1993, ISBN 1 874597 40 5
9. For the safety of all, Commissioners of Irish Lights.

10 Conchur O Siochain, Seanchas Chleire, p155

11 Dictionary of disasters at sea during the age of steam, Charles Hocking, Lloyds of London, 1960

12 Waterford News, contemporary account.

13 Newsplan, J.O'Toole, catalogue of Irish newspapers held at libraries, ISBN 0907328 30X

14 Report of Irish Lights on wreck of Emily on Briggs reef, Groomsport, British Parliamentary Papers 1893-94 (52)

15 Conquest of the sea, Henry Siebe, Chatto & Windus, London 1873.

16 Irish Independent contemporary account.

17 Freeman's Journal contemporary account

18 By Swerve of shore Michael Fewer ISBN 07171 2718 4.

19 Donegal shipwrecks, Ian Wilson, Impact Coleraine 1998 ISBN 0 948 15456 X

20 *Lusitania* Unravelling the mysteries, Patrick O'Sullivan, Collins, Cork 1998 ISBN 1 898256 51 9

21 Death in the Irish sea, The sinking of the RMS Leinster, Roy Stokes, Collins, Cork 1998 ISBN 1898256 52 7

22 The Wrecking of the Tayleur, Emily Madden, a thesis for the Saor Ollscoil Na hEireann, 1991.

23 The shipwreck of the Tayleur, Manuscript, Veronica Oldham, 38 Russian Drive Liverpool L13 7BT.

24 Certain advertisements out of Ireland, concerning the losses and distresses happened to the Spanish navie, upon the West coasts of Ireland, in their voyage intended from the Northern isles beyond Scotland, towards Spain. Imprinted at London by I Vautroller for Richard Field, 1588.

25 The Tayleur Fund Medals, The Life Saving Awards Research Society Journal, 22, September 1994, pp4-49.

26 Danger Zone, the story of Queenstown Command, E Keeble Chatterton, Rich & Cowan, London 1934.

27 Saunders newsletter, contemporary account.

28 Cork Examiner contemporary account.

29 Dublin Historical record, Daws bridge by L Gogan, No 1, March-May 1952,pp12-17

30 Dublin Chronicle, 5-1-1788

31 Proposals for the improvement of the port of Dublin, a Report published for the Director General of the Navy Ireland 40th year of King George (III) (1801).

32 Evening Herald, Dublin, contemporary account.

33 Shipwrecks of the Irish Coast volume 1, Edward J. Bourke, ISBN 09523027 -0-5.

34 Shipwrecks of the Irish Coast volume 2, Edward J. Bourke, ISBN 09523027 -1-3.

35 Lifeboat, published by RNLI, Poole, Dorset, March 1961.

36 Irish Archives, Journal of the Society of Irish archives Volume 2, no 1 Summer 1992. Maritime History sources issue.

37 Dublin Port Archives, Port Centre, East Wall Rd, Dublin 3.

38 Letters from the West of Ireland, Alexander Innes Shand, Wm Blackwood, London, 1884.

39 Six miles from Bangor, the story of Donaghadee and the Copeland Islands, W.G. Pollock, Appletree Press, 1982, ISBN 0 86281 105 8.

40 Irish Times, contemporary account.

41 Out of the shadow, 1998, Liam Nolan, ISBN 1902011058

42 Freeman's Journal, contemporary account.

43 U boat operations of WW2 Volumes 1 &2, Kenneth Wynn, Chatham ISBN 186176 02x8 186176 0698.

44 The Storm Passed By, Trevor Allen, Irish academic Press, Dublin, 1996, ISBN 0 7165 2616 6

45 Riches from Wrecks, Fergus Hinds, Browne & Ferguson, Glasgow, 1995, ISBN 0 85174 623 3

46 Censorship papers in the Chief Secretary's papers at National Archives, Bishop St Dublin 2.

47 Dublin Port Archives, Port Centre, Alexandra Rd., East Wall, Dublin, 3.

48 Royal Proclamations 1485-1714, Betty Galley MS 1793 (196) cargo stolen

49 Accounts of moneys received for salvage for vessels wrecked on the Irish coast, House of Commons papers 1850, 546

50 Record of moneys received at wreck auctions, House of Commons papers,1850, 563

51 Loss of steamers Sirius, Tribune, Finn McCoul House of Commons papers,1851, 696

52 Vessels lost on the coast of Ireland 1848-1852, House of Commons papers,1852-3 385

53 Return of wrecks or ship casualties on the coast of Ireland, House of Commons papers,1864-66 1867, 231

54 Wrecks within five miles of Galley Head, House of Commons papers,1865-70 1871, 114

55 Report of the select committee on wooden shipwrecks 1839, (333) IX 223

56 Committee of inquiry into shipwreck of British vessels 1843 (549) IX, 1 and 1843 (581) IX 669.

57 Inquiry into increased number of shipwrecks 1836 (567) XVII 373.

58 Historical Manuscripts Commission Ormond, NS 2 p174

59 Historical Manuscripts Commission Ormond NS 2 p259. Mariners mirror 57, (4) Nov 1971

REFERENCES

60 Belfast Newsletter, contemporary account

61 The Man in the Helmet, Desmond Younge, 1963 Cassell, London.

62 Record Repositories in Great Britain, Ian Mortimer, PRO 1997 ISBN 1 873 162545

63 *Lusitania*, Merseyside special edition, 1999, Colin Simpson, Avid Publications, Garth Boulevard, Wirral L635LS (151 6452047) ISBN 0 952102064

64 Lloyds list 1827-1860 Microfilm at Merseyside maritime museum/Guildhall Library, London.

65 Wexford Herald, contemporary account.

66 Mizen Journal, No 7, 1999, Mizen Archaeological and Historical Society.

67 Cork Constitution 27-10, 10-11, 20-11, 11-12-1838.

68 Southern Reporter 25-7-1839.

69 Newry Telegraph, contemporary account.

70 The Grand Canal of Ireland Ruth Delany, David & Charles,1973, ISBN 07153 5972 X.

71 Dublin Port Archives, Dublin Port Centre, Alexandra Rd., East Wall, Dublin 3.

72 Freeman's Journal 16-3-1854.

73 Irish Times, Contemporary Account.

74 Trinity House alms people, Microfilm by LDS Family History centres, Society of Genealogists, London 1787-1854 in 102 volumes on microfilm.

75 Clare Freeman, Contemporary Account.

76 History of the parish of Caherdaniel, Padraig O'Loinsigh.

77 History of port of Cork steam navigation, William J Barry.

78 Port of Cork steamships, Barry, in J Cork Historical Society 1895.

79 Irish Shipwrecks, Images of Ireland, Edward J Bourke, Tempus Publishing, Stroud, Glos., 2000, ISBN 0 7524 1764 9

80 British Parliamentary papers, 1857, XIV p268 reports Committees on Harbours of Refuge.

81 Malahide Past and Present, Noel Flanagan.

82 Iron Clipper, Tayleur - the White Star Line's first Titanic, HF Starkey, Avid Publications, Wirral 1999 ISBN 1 902964 00 4

83 History Lore & Legend, Eamonn Breathnach, Published in Waterford c 1990

84 The Great Charter of the Liberties of Waterford 1626, Timothy Cunningham, 1881, grants Admiralty rights to the Corporation of Waterford but retains wrecks and the property of pirates to the High Admiral of England and Ireland.

85 Tramore of Long ago, Andy Taylor, Limited edition published locally

86 Waterford & Thereabouts, Bernie Colclough 1993, Published locally

87 Shipwrecks off Scotland, Ian G Whittaker, ISBN 095 3197700 CN Publishing, Edinburgh EH17 8EA.

88 Lost Treasure ships of the 20th century, Nigel Pickford, ISBN 1862 050791, Pavilion books London 1999

89 Epics of salvage, David Masters, Cassell, London 1953.

90 Index to the Freeman's Journal 1763-1771 prepared by prisoners at Mountjoy Jail c 1970, in National Library of Ireland.

91 A calendar of material relating to Ireland from the High Court of Admiralty 1536-1641, John C Appleby, Irish Manuscripts commission, 1992, ISBN 1 874280 03 7.

92 Waterford News, contemporary account.

93 Waterford Mirror, contemporary account.

95 The Forty Foot, Frank Power & Peter Pearson ISBN 09527198 1 9.

96 National Archives CHIEF SECRETARY'S OFFICE PAPERS 1854 13230, 13451, 13559 Wreck of the Robert Kelly.

97 A Gallant Barque, the story of the Port Yarrock, Sheila Mulcahy, Kerryman, 1999, ISBN 0946 277257.

98 Last Message 13.58, Death of the Princess Victoria, Bill Pollock, Greystone, 1990, ISBN 1870157 087.

99 Sea Breezes, Vol. 56, No 439, July 1982, In a first world war rescue tug, Captain T.H. Bull.

100 Military Archives, Cathal Brugha Barracks, Rathmines, Dublin. 6.

101 Guides to the Microfilmed records of the German Navy, 1939-1945, National Archives, Washington, Library of Congress Catalogue, 58-9982. (now available only as microfilm copy).

102 Guides to the Microfilmed records of the German Navy, 1914-1918, National Archives, Washington, Library of Congress Catalogue, 58-9982. (now available only as microfilm copy).

103 History of Dungarvan, 1922, Edward Keohan.

104 On a wave and a prayer, history of the Youghal lifeboat station, Brendan O'Driscoll.

105 Above and beyond the call of duty, John Power Kilmore Quay Printed CR Print Enniscorthy.

106 From Dauntless to Annie History of Wicklow lifeboat station, Ciaran Doyle 1990.

107 Home from the sea, Story of Courtmacsharry Lifeboat, 1825-95 Michael Hurley, 1995.

108 From the Boyne to the Mournes, History of Co Louth Lifeboats, Patsey McKenna, 1993.

109 Fethard Lifeboat story, John Doyle.

110 Palmers of Queenstown, Ships in Focus, Record Nos 6,7 2000, ISBN 0 9521179 9 1.

111 Express, Beaverbrook Newspapers 1960.

112 Immersed, Spring 1999.

113 Turmoil, Ewart Brookes, Jarrolds publishers London 1953.

114 Watchers of the Waves, A history of Maritime Coast Radio Stations, Brian Faulkner, Radio Bygones Publication, 1996, ISBN 1898805 09 1.

115 Minute books of the Commissioners of Customs and Excise, National Archives, Bishop St, Dublin 8. MFA 2-22, MFA 2 -23 Feb 1767-1830.

116 Minute books of the Commissioners of Customs and Excise, Public Records Office, Kew, 1730-1830.

117 The Customs & Excise Service in Fingal 1684-1765 Maighread Ni Mhurchada Irish Academic Press 1999 ISBN 0 7165267 2 7.

118 The Grand Canal, Inchicore, & Kilmainham, OPW 1994, ISBN 0 7076 0463 X.

119 A View of Society & Manners, John Gamble, Belfast 1812.

120 Val McCarthy, Dunmanway, personal communication.

121 Dublin Journal, contemporary account.

122 Cork Examiner, contemporary account.

123 Drogheda Journal contemporary account.

124 Freeman's Journal, contemporary account.

125 Tales of the Wexford coast, Richard Roche, Duffrey Press, Enniscorthy, 1993.

126 Irish History from 1700, A guide to sources in the Public Records office, Alice Prochaska, British Records No 6, 1986, ISBN 0900222 077.

127 Record books of Jaspar Walsh, receiver of wrecks at Wexford, 3 volumes, in private hands in Wexford.

128 Irish Revenue Police Records, Cust 111, National Archives, Bishop St., Dublin, 8.

129 A Cyclopaedia of Useful Arts, Charles Tomlinson, 1851, James Virtue, London.

130 Revenue papers, Administration papers and Calendar, 1778-1837, National Archives, Bishop St Dublin.

131 La Lavia, La Juliana & Santna Maria de Vison: Three Spanish Armada transports lost off Streedagh, Co Sligo, an interim report, Stephen Birch & D.M. McElvogue, International Journal of Nautical Archaeology, 28, (3) August 1999.

132 Walkers Hibernian Magazine, November 1807, p642-645.

133 The Spanish Armada, Captain Cuellar's Adventures in Connaught and Ulster 1588, Hugh Allingham, Ulster Journal of Archaeology, 1 (3) April 1895. Reprinted by Sligo County council 1988.

134 Donal Woodward, Shipowners of the Wirral, Mariners Mirror, 63, (3) Aug 1977 p 242.

135 Critique of Colin Simpson's *Lusitania* by John Light, Unpublished Manuscript.

136 Sea Killers in Disguise, Tony Bridgland, Leo Cooper, 1999.

137 Jim Walsh in Balbriggan Historical Society Journal.

138 Cormac Lowth unpublished notes.

139 Daily or Sunday Express, Beaverbrook Newspapers Ltd, 1960

140 The Safeguard of the Sea, a naval history of Great Britain, Vol. 1 660-1649, N.A.M. Rodger, Harper Collins, 1999.

141 Article in Rambler series in the Kerryman 1932.

142 Laurence Flanagan, Ireland's Armada Legacy, 1988, ISBN 0 7171 1593 3.

143 International Registry of Sunken Ships, database held at shipwreck@cableregina.com.

144 The Changing face of a coastal port, Bridgewater Mariners Mirror 81, (1) Feb 2000.

145 U Boat Alley, Roy Stokes, 2001 Manuscript in progress.

146 Index to the Belfast Newsletter, National Library of Ireland.

147 Marconi Mirror Jan Feb 1980.

148 Maritime Journal August 1994.

149 Ships figureheads, Shire album 109, MK Stammers ISBN 0 85263 650 4.

150 Blackrock Society proceedings 1996,, p8 Shipwreck near Blackrock House.
151 Treasures of the Armada, Robert Stenuit, David & Charles, 1972, 0 7153 5601 1.
152 Short sea stories, Robin Knox Johnston.
153 Wealth from the sea, Allan C Crothall, Starr Line, 1993, ISBN 0 9522747 0 1.
154 Treasure Hunters of the deep, New Scientist, 29-6-1996.
155 Dublin Journal, contemporary account.
156 Deep water, Moya Crawford 1999, Thomas Reed publications, ISBN0 901281 83 2
157 SS Hundson, Jim Blaney, Journal of Upper Ards Historical Society, 1979.
158 The RFA Industry, unpublished item by Roger Bullen.
159 Admiralty Wreck Register, Hydrographic Office, Taunton.
160 Freeman's Journal 8-4-1765.
161 Belfast Newsletter 8-4-1765.
162 Treasures of the Armada, Robert Stenuit, 1974, Cardinal, 0 351 18326.
163 Shipwreck Index of the British Isles, Richard Larn & Briget Larn, Lloyds of London.
164 An account of glass beads and cylinders found on the Strand at Dunworley Bay, William Chadwick Nelligan, private printing 1858.
165 We Own the Laurentic, Ray Cossum, Impact, Coleraine, 2000.
166 Lloyds list, newspaper published twice weekly by Lloyds of London.
167 Armada Guns, Professor Michael Lewis, 1961.
168 Clare Champion 8-3-1994.
169 Irish Independent, contemporary account.
170 Aidan Sharkey, Personal communication.
171 Mariner's Mirror, Vol 86, 3, August 2000.
172 Faulkners Dublin Jounal, 19-1-1804
173 Aid expedition 1987, Dublin University Sub Aqua Club.
174 Irish Georgian Society, Bulletin, vol xxvii, 1984, Lyons Co Kildare by June Eiffe.
175 Hell of Connaught - the Cromwellian colonisation of Ireland, Peter Berresford Ellis.
176 Long ago by Shannonside, Edmund lenihan, Mercier Publications, Cork, 1992.
177 Lloyds list from 1741 except 1745,1746,1754, 1756, 1759, 1771-1778 facsimile reprint, Greg international Publishers, 1969. Lloyds list published by Lloyds, London twice weekly newspaper which developed into a daily publication. The date in the text is the date of report unless a date of wrecking is available.

CORRECTIONS TO PREVIOUS VOLUMES

Volume two

p 184 re Bemis the ship mentioned is *Lusitania*

p145 Charles Astie ashore misprint

Teignmouth is in Devon not Tynemouth in Northumberland

p64 Wrecks described as 8-1-1783 are 8-1-1725 as referenced

p199 Submarine off Dublin position 55.43 07.51 should read off Antrim in account of UB 124

p 207 ref 130 German submarine losses from all causes during world war one, David J Perkins, Seaboot Publications, RR1 217 Hillside Drive, Boutilliers Point BOJ 1GO, Nova Scotia Canada.

Royal navy submarine losses 1914-1971, J. David Perkins. Seaboot Publications, Nova Scotia, ISBN 09699002-

Volume one

p 76 Photo has been confirmed as Hilda wrecked at Duncannon in 1898

p 159 reference to Cork Examiner, Quebra, 25-8-1986 is error the actual date has not been located

p117 *Lusitania* sank 7-5-1915 not 1-5-1915

p39 Confido owner was Mr Dann not Dunne

p41 Mersey 5-10-1892 three were lost not two as stated

p 21 The Gainsboro date was 28-11-1838 not 6-1-1839

BIM LIST OF SHIPWRECK LOCATIONS

The following list is known as the Bord Iscaigh Mhara (Irish Fisheries Board) list and was probably compiled by the Fisheries Board to record obstructions on the sea bed. That view is illustrated by the oil well listed. The main part of the data can be traced to the Admiralty wreck register. These positions have been found to be those reported by sinking ships and are not all accurate. This is because the ship may have drifted or sank at an angle.

No	Name	Type	Date	Latitude	Longitude	Notes
1	Magnolia	Trawler		5100 00	9 00 00	
2	Unknown			51 00 38.0	6 07 27.0	330 feet
3	Unknown			51 01 00	8 30 00	
4	Rita Rudi	Belgian Trawler		51 01 15.0	8 30 00	300ft
5	Missanabie	Br liner	1918	?? 02.00	7 30.00	12469t
6	Express	Br SV	1915	51.03.240	6.11.000	115t
7	Labud	Yuogslavian	1940	51.03.560	8.35.10	5336 t
8	Unknown			51 04 30	7.23.000	
9	Enafta	Br tanker	1918	51 05 00	7.56 00	
10	Unknown			51 05 00	8 55 00	
11	unknown			51 05 52.0	6 25 11.0	
12	Aurora Borealis	Br Trawler	1976	51 06 00	7 18 00	
13	Unknown			51 06 00	8 37 00	
14	Unknown			51 06 50	6 30 05	
15	Unknown			51 07 00	7 09 00	
16	Unknown			51 07 26	8 35 45	
17	Unknown			51 07 35	6 34 25	
18	Unknown			51 07 45	6 20 15	
19	Unknown			51 08 02.0	8 45 51.0	
20	Unknown			51 08 49.0	8 39 35.0	
21	Ellesmere	Br Merchant	1915	51 09 00	6 34 30.0	
22	Etonian		1918	51 09 00	8 00 00	
23	Scottish Monarch		1915	51 09 30	7 59 00	
24	Anguilla		1915	51 09 50	6 33 00	
25	Galv ar Mor	French Tr	1982	51 10.00	6 07 00	
26	Scantic	Dn Mv	1984	51 10 00	7 15 00	
27	Recovery 2	Pontoon	1972	51 10 00	7 25 00	
28	Unknown			51 10 78	8 35 00	
29	Stratharron	Br merchant	1915	51 10 50.0	6.15.30.0	
30	South Point		1915	51 11 00.0	6 16.30.0	
31	Unknown	Oil well Head		51 11 26.5	8 23 39.0	
32	Ellesmere or Anguilla			51 12 30.0	6 36 00.0	
33	Unknown			51 12 45	6 00 31	
34	Unknown			51 12 54	8 30 52.0	
35	Juliet			51 13 00	8 40 00	
36	Tresillian			51 14 00	7 30 00	
37	Miltown			51 14 01.5	6 00 20	
38	Crown of India			51 14 35	6 53 45	

BIM LIST OF SHIPWRECK LOCATIONS

No	Name	Type	Date	Latitude	Longitude	Notes
39	San Andros			51 15 00	7 50 00	
40	Gilles Et Michel	Fr Trawler	1977	51 16 00	6 10 00	
41	U 400			51 16 00	8 05 00	
42	Arklow Bay		1973	51 17 08.0	6 11 18.0	
43	Unknown			51 17 12.0	6 50 48.0	
44	Unknown			51 17 30	6 27 00	
45	Unknown			51 18 00	6 43 00	
46	Unknown			51 18 30	8 42 18	
47	Iwate	steam trawler	1946	51 18 30	9 00 00	
48	Kilgarran Castle		1940	51 21 00	8 35 00	
49	Lilian H	Br SV	1917	51 21 40	8 27 20	
50	Ben Lomond		1918	51 22 00	7 41 06	2814t
51	Vancouver City		1939	51 23 00	7 03 00	4955 t
52	Caliph	Br trawler	1941	51 24 24	8 31 57	226 t
53	*Lusitania*			51 24 49	8 37 43	
	El Zorro			51 26 70	8 31 55	
54	Unknown			51 27 00	7 55 00	
55	Cliftonian			51 27 24	8 56 10	
56	Akassa			51 27 45	8 46 00	
57	Spectator			51 27 55	8 41 10	
58	Unknown			51 28 00	8 58 00	
59	Earl of Latham			51 28 30	8 34 24	
60	Pegu			51 28 30	8 47 00	
61	Unknown			51 29 00	7 51 42	
62	Dumfriesshire			51 29 13.5	6 06 33.5	
63	Gafsa			51 24 24	8 19 24	
64	Alyssum	HMS sloop		51 30 00	8 48 00	
65	Ghazee			51 30 00	8 58 20	
66	Ludgate			51 30 00	8 59 00	
67	Mignonette	HMS sloop		51 30 30	8 55 30	
68	Kayside correction Tayside		1921	51 31 30	8 49 00	Error on Admiralty list
69	Unknown			51 32 00	6 54 18	
70	Norwegian			51 32 20	8 55 47	
71	Gafsa see 63			51 31 22	8 57 28	
72	Bell Rose			51 32 30	8 39 30	
73	Colemore	Br merchant	1917	51 32 59	6 30 58	
74	Ghisloire Renes	Fr trawler	1978	51 33 00	8 10 00	
75	East Wales		1917	51 35 00	8 16 00	
76	City of Chicago		1892	51 36 40	8 32 45	
77	Meadowfield			51 36 48	7 09 30	
78	Charleston			51 36 53	6 27 52	
79	Unknown			51 36 56	6 08 07	
80	U 58	Submarine		51 37 00	8 12 00	
81	Artist	Collier		51 37 20	7 12 40	
82	Unknown			51 38 04	6 51 55	

BIM LIST OF SHIPWRECK LOCATIONS

No	Name	Type	Date	Latitude	Longitude	Notes
83	Unknown			51 38 07	8 40 09	
84	Raylight	Br MV	1978	51 38 15	6 35 30	260 t
85	Unknown			51 38 23	6 01 35	
86	Unknown			51 38 30	7 53 30	
87	Unknown			51 33 30	8 05 00	
88	Kinoccary			51 38 30	8 34 45	
89	Unknown			51 38 40	7 55 05	
90	Unknown			51 39 17	6 34 19	
91	Unknown			51 39 58	5 43 55	
92	Carrabin			51 40 00	5 08 00	
93	Belville	Sw SV		51 40 57	6 42 49	992 ton
94	Aud			51 42 39	8 14 23	
95	Idrami			51 42 40	6 45 21	
96	Richard De Laranaga			51 42 48	7 42 12	
97	Killarney	Paddle steamer	1846	51 42 57.0	8 72 30.0	
98	Pinewood	Steamer	1915	51 43 00.0	7 12 00.0	
106	UC 42			51 44 00	8 12 00	
107	Unknown			51 44 15.0	8 10 00	
108	Souvenir			51 45 00	7 26 00	
109	Unknown			51 45 24	6 33 56	
110	Canova			51 45 30	7 28 00	
111	Gold coast			51 45 30	7 35 15	
112	Unknown			51 45 42	6 07 33	
113	Edith			51 45 50	7 39 45	
114	Exeter	Br trawler	1941	51 45 52	8 04 48	
115	Westwick			51 46 04	8 17 40	
116	Elizabeth Jane			51 46 30	8 12 45	
117	HMS Vervain	Br Corvette	1945	51 47 30.0	7 09 00.0	
118	Unknown			51 47 30	7 42 00	
119	Unknown			51 47 30	8 11 48	
120	Manchester Engineer		1916	51 47 48.0	8 08 24.0	
121	Centurion			51 47 44	6 29 20	
122	Irish Plain correction Plane		1916 ?	51 47 48	8 08 24	
123	Unknown			51 47 49	6 38 57	
124	William Martin			51 47 54	7 46 12	
125	Inniscarra			51 48 00	7 30 00	
126	U 1208			51 48 12	7 02 30	
127	Joseph Mitchell			51 48 40	8 02 10	
128	Hebburn			51 48 41	7 24 20	
129	Lucena			51 48 50	7 51 10	
130	Brika			51 48 58	6 78 03	
131	Unknown			51 49 00	7 22 00	
132	Karina			51 49 23	7 02 53	
133	Bredah HMS	Br 3rd Rate	1690	51 49 34	8 15 45.5	
134	Candidate		1915	51 49 51	6 33 15	

BIM LIST OF SHIPWRECK LOCATIONS

No	Name	Type	Date	Latitude	Longitude	Notes
135	Unknown			51 49 51	8 19 37	
136	Unknown			51 49 57	8 19 13	
137	Unknown			51 50 02	6 25 10	
138	Unknown			51 50 30	7 59 30	
139	Unknown			51 51 00	77 11 00	
140	Greta		1917	51 51 45.0	7 22 45	
141	Whoal Geever	Trawler	1981	51 52 00.0	6 47 48.0	
142	Zeta			51 52 00	7 34 00	
143	Folia			51 52 30 actual 51 52 85	7 48 00 actual 7 41 33	
144	Unknown			51 52 43.0	6 46 48.0	
145	UC 33	German sub		51 53 00	6 13 56	
146	Unknown			51 53 00	6 43 59.0	
147	Unknown			51 53 24	6 4307.0	
148	Unknown			51 53 30.0	6 31 10	
149	Garmoyle			51 53 30	7 14 30	
150	Lough Fisher			51 54 00	7 19 30	
151	Ardmore			51 54 45	7 00 11.0	
152	Barrister			51 54 50.0	7 43 30.0	
153	HMS Lavender	Sloop		51 55 00.0	7 19 00.0	
154	Crispin			51 55 22.0	6 55 02.0	
155	Copeland	British SS		51 55 25	6 15 33	
156	Lincolnshire	British SS		51 56 13	7 01 00	
157	Thoral	Danish Barque	1918	51 56 34.0	6 14 ???	
158	Rhodesia	British SS	1917	51 57 15	6 45 06	
159	Exelsior	Irish ketch	1917	51 57 15	7 40 30	
160	Cooroy	British SV	1917	51 57 36	6 55 50	
161	Sandsend	Br Merchant	1917	51 58 00	7 26 00	
162	Bandon	Br Merchant	1917	51 58 00	7 38 00	
163	Anne Sophie	French Tr	1984	51 58 00	7 40 00	
164	Unknown			51 58 03	6 33 18	
165	Hildefjord	Norwegian Tanker	1941	51 59 26	6 10 01	
166	Unknown			51 59 48	6 38 55	
167	Carlo	British SS	1917	52 00 00	6 46 01	
168	Unknown			52 00 07	7 00 16	
169	Etal Manor	Br collier		52 00 12	6 53 56	
170	Unknown			52 00 22	6 37 39	
171	U 106		1918	52 00 38	6 27 13	
172	Anthony	Liner	1917	52 00 30	7 10 10	
173	Trafford		1915	52 00 54	6 57 15	
174	Grainville	Br merchant	1981	52 02 04	6 12 13	1770 t
175	Unknown			52 02 30	6 53 24	
176	Unknown			52 02 46	6 18 56	262 ft
177	Unknown			52 02 59	6 26 40	290 ft
178	Castle Bay	Br Trawler	1971	52 03 30	6 56 00	
179	Lode Star	Ir Trawler	1971	52 03 30	6 56 00	

No	Name	Type	Date	Latitude	Longitude	Notes
180	Unknown			52 04 30.6	6 14 29.5	
181	Ary	steamer	1947	52 05 00	6 55 00	
182	Alfred D Snow		1888	52 05 00	7 01 00	1987 t
183	San Conrado	Br Tanker	1941	52 05 17.8	6 11 59.5	7986 t
184	Viferedo	SS	1863	52 05 55.0	6 34 48.0	
185	Wheat Flower		1918	52 06 46.0	6 04 13.0	
186	Lennox		1916	52 07 00.0	6 36 00.0	
187	Ythan	schooner		52 07 10.0	7 23 05.0	
188	Providence	Br Merchant	1917	52 07 12	6 23 48	
189	Margaret	British SS	1919	52 07 19	6 55 55	
190	Isolda	Ir Lights Vsl	1940	52 07 30	6 23 00	
191	Shapinsay	Trawler	1967	52 07 30	5 55 00	
192	Kerick	Fr Trawler	1969	52 07 36	7 06 24	
193	Sustain	Trawler	1975	52 07 45	7 01 30	
194	Croghan	Irish MV	1973	52 07 47	6 56 13	
195	Tourmalet	FrenchTrawler	1972	52 08 00	6 35 30	
196	Hazael 3			52 08 01.5	6 54 28.0	
197	Seahorse	Br Transport	1816	52 08 06	7 10 15	
198	Unknown			52 08 46	6 16 36	
199	Unknown			52 08 48.0	6 16 43.0	
200	Pilar de Larenga	British ss	1917	52 08 54.5	6 02 39.5	4316 t
201	Halronell	Irish MV	1961	52 09 00	7 06 00	
202	Margaret Ann	trawler	1958	52 09 00	7 06 00	
203	Michael	Cypriot MV	1975	52 09 03	7 07 03	423 ton
204	Langsdale	British SV	1879	52 09 24	6.24 50	
205	Unknown			52 09 38.0	6 34 50.0	
206	Atxeri Medi	Spanish SS	1918	52 04 44.9	6 03 25.6	2484t
207	Rask	Norwegian SS	1941	52 10 06.7	6 11 11.3	
208	Unknown			52 10 18	6 33 15	
209	Ceres		1866	52 10 30	6 21 36	3512t
210	Ydun	Norwegian SS	1915	52 11 30.4	6 08 49.4	1266 t
211	Tripoli		1872	52 11 36	6 17 46	
212	EI AOM	Aer Lingus Viscount	1968	52 11 54.0	6 09 28.0	
213	N Dame de Sacre Coeur	British Trawler	1978	52 12 00	6 06 00	
214	Unknown U Boat	German		52 12 15	6 12 26	
215	Stetz	tug		52 12 15	6 12 30	
216	Manchester Market	British SS	1903	52 12 20	6 12 33.0	
217	Avance	ketch	1923	5212 30	6 13 30	
218	Unknown	obstruction		52 12 38	6 12 28	
219	Unknown			52 13 50	6 11 05	
220	Earl			52 14 21	6 17 48	
221	Unknown			52 14 33	6 18 29	
222	Unknown			52 14 43.0	7 03 05.5	
223	Unknown	obstruction		52 14 47	6 14 31	

BIM LIST OF SHIPWRECK LOCATIONS

No	Name	Type	Date	Latitude	Longitude	Notes
224	Unknown			52 14 53	7 03 41	
225	Unknown			52 15 03.5	7 03 49.0	
226	Margaret Edna	trawler		52 15 12	6 19 24	
227	Unknown			52 15 33	7 05 55	
228	Unknown			52 15 40	7 06 02	
229	Unknown			52 16 13	6 03 58	
230	Jimmy	Br Barge		52 17 30	6 23 00	
	Cumberland	142 ft		55 31 36	7 15 15	
	Unknown			55 30 38	7 19 37	
	Unknown			55 29 54	7 15 57	
	Argo Delos			55 23 36	7 03 24	
	Castle Eden			55 19 30	7 03 30	
	Laurentic			55 18 13	7 35 27	
	U 1003			55 25 00	6 53 00	
	Unknown			55 14 10	6 43 15	
	Santa Maria			55 14 00	6 09 20	
	Unknown			55 13 20	6 14 15	
	U Boat	scuttled		55 28 50	7 20 40	
	U 110			55 23 00	7 39 00	
	Saldahana	Frigate		55 17 00	7 35 00	
	Drake			55 17 08	6 12 30	
	Unknown			55 01 30	7 17 13	
	Micky Willy			55 22 22	7 10 13	
	Linda Blanche			53.34	3.51	sunk by U21
	Spanish	trawler		51.33.913	9.51.398	
	Exodus			51.23.83	10.15.98	
	Malmanger					Owned by Aodh O'Donnell
	Miami					Owned by Aodh O'Donnell
	Minnehaha					Colin Barnes Paddy Barnes
	Councillor					Owned by Paddy O'Sullivan
	HMS Vanguard					Owned by Eugene Houlihan
	City of Lancaster			53 30 790	5.57.080	Dive an hour off Dublin slack i.e. summer GMT
	Leinster			053.18 88 N	005 47 51 W	Owned by Des Brannigan
	Guide Me Two			50 16 58 N	06 02 94 W	
	Lennox	Saltees		52 06 789N	06 36 757W	
	U 104			51 59N	06 26 W	
	Bolivar	Kish Bank		53 16.55	05 55.54	

This list assembles data from Shipwrecks of the Irish Coast volumes 1,2,3 with wrecks mentioned in Shipwrecks of the Ulster coast and local lists to form a more complete list.

Date	Ship Name	Captain	Voyage	Cargo	Location	Comment
924	Viking fleet				Dundrum Bay	
1591	Spanish Ship			treasure	Ardglass	
1700	Fame		from Africa	rum & ivory	Groom's Point	
1714	Unknown				North Rock	18 lost
10-1715	Eagle's Wing				Strangford Bar	76 Lost
22-9-1741	Cloverland	Robinson	New England to Liverpool		Strangford	
22-9-1741	Mary	Harisson	from Lancaster		Strangford	
22-9-1741	Lowther	Barrow	of Bristol		Strangford	two more wrecks
5-2-1747	Sarah		Liverpool to West Indies		Dundrum Bay	
9-2-1747	Swarthe	Cooke	Liverpool to Tortola		Dundrum Bay	
30-12-1748	Wolf			warship	Kearney Point	
23-2-1749	sloop		Liverpool to Belfast		Ballywalter	
22-12-1749	Ranger	Swan	Derry to the Straits		Dundrum Bay	
5-3-1750	Molly		from Maryland	Tobacco	Donaghadee	
5-3-1750	Durham			flax seed		
20-11-1750	Hambden	Monroe	from Nantwick		Newry	
3-2-1756	Britannia		Liverpool to Guinea		North Rock	37 lost
18-2-1757	Success		Liverpool to West Indies		Dundrum Bay	
20-11-1759	Fanny		Workington to Dublin		Gartar Rock	
19-5-1761	Good Hope	Montgomery	Glasgow to Dublin		Dundrum Bay	3 more ships wrecked
28-4-1761	Polacca		New York to Newry		Newry	
10-11-1761	Lily	Montgomery	Glasgow to Dublin		Dundrum bay	
10-11-1761	Cleveland	Jackson			Killough	
13-11-1761	Squirrel	Godfrey	Cardigan to London		Killough	
4-1762	Young Miriam	of Rotterdam			Strangford	
20-4-1762	Young Adrian	Suckling	from Bordeaux	wine		
24-12-1762	Grandberg	M'asland	Bristol to Liverpool	gun carriages	Strangford	
31-12-1762	Active	Hope	Liverpool to Guadaloupe		Ringboy	
31-12-1762	James	Harisson	Guadaloupe to Liverpool		Cloughey Bay	
8-3-1763	Betty		Liverpool to Virginia		Cranfield Point	
6-12-1763	Phoenix	Fulton			Donaghadee	
12-3-1765	Unknown		Whitehaven to Dublin		Ardglass	
12-3-1765	Sloop	Milford		coal	Donaghadee	
10-3-1767	Hannah		Port Glasgow to Holland		Cloughey	
28-5-1767	Nightingale	Rice	Dundalk to Belfast	oats	North Rock	

DOWN CHRONOLOGICAL LIST

Date	Ship Name	Captain	Voyage	Cargo	Location	Comment
June 1767	Emanuel			deals	Dundrum Bay	
19-12-1767	Betsey	Hadskins	Liverpool to Waterford		Ballyquentin Point	
23-1-1768	Three vessels				Ards coast	
5-11-1772	Mary	Henry	Belfast to West Indies		Kearney Point	
24-2-1773	Jennet	Colclough	Virginia to Dublin		Portaferry	
19-1-1774	Brothers			coal	Strangford	
7-2-1775	Dublin	Johnson	Whitehaven to Dublin		Ballywalter	
7-2-1775	Isaac	Jefferson			Ballywalter	
9-2-1776	Unknown		Campbelltown to Dublin	Herrings	North Rock	
28-2-1777	Peggy	Conk	Liverpool to Newry		Crosbie Point	
2-5-1777	Draper	Boyd		provisions	Killough	
31-1-1780	Peggy	Linsay	to Belfast	tea, linen, hemp	North Rock	
24-2-1780	Amazon			Privateer	Donagahdee	
24-2-1780	sloop		Dublin to Belfast		Donagahdee	
24-2-1780	Three Sisters	Archdeacon	Bristol to Belfast		Donagahdee	
2-3-1782	St John Baptista		Oporto to Dublin	wine & fruit	Strangford	
8-3-1782	Industry	Parry	Bristol to Derry		Downpatrick	
31-7-1783	Wachlaren				Strangford	
22-9-1783	Peggy				Cloughey	
25-3-1783	Peggy	White	Clyde to West Indies		Downpatrick	
18-11-1783	Fruitful Vine		Cork to Le Havre	beef pork candles	Benbridge ledge	
1783	Hector		Leghorn to Dublin		N of Newcastle	
1-1784	Peggy	Carson	Glasgow to New York	wine	Cloughey Bay	
7-2-1784	Unknown			tobacco	Newry	
27-4-1784	William	Bell	to Liverpool		Portaferry	
4-1784	Unknown			meal & salt	South Rock	two vessels lost
13-12-1784	Unknown		from Scotland	coal	Bangor	
1784	Nancy		Liverpool to Drogheda		Dundrum Bay	
1785	Recovery		Glasgow to Carlingford		Dundrum Bay	
1786	Margaret		Bristol to Belfast		Dundrum Bay	
27-1-1786	Hume		Cork to Bristol		Portaferry	
1787	Britannia		Newport to Wicklow		Dundrum Bay	
1788	Kent		Glasgow to Jamaica		Dundrum Bay	
1788	sloop		Dublin to Belfast		Dundrum Bay	
26-2-1788	William & Mary	Butler	to Derry		Strangford	
2-1-1788	brig		Liverpool to Hull		South Rock	
1789	James		Greenock to Cork			
17-10-1790	Santissima Trinidad	Cuchullo	Bilbao to Belfast	wine	Ballyquentin	
25-1-1791	Henderson	Hannah	Leghorn to Belfast		Carlingford	
12-1791	Charlestown	McKillar	Greenock to Charlestown		South Rock	
12-10-1792	Lord Bangor		Whitehaven to Belfast	coal	South Rock	two more vessels lost
2-1794	Letter of Marque				South Rock	
2-11-1794	Jean		Liverpool to Tralee	salt	Ballyquentin Point	
11-1794	unknown		Liverpool to Madeira		Tara	
2-12-1794	Experiment	of Maryport			North Rock	
2-12-1794	Union	Bennett	London to Liverpool		Portaferry	

Date	Ship Name	Captain	Voyage	Cargo	Location	Comment
2-12-1794	Large Vessel				Ballyhalbert	
12-1796	Hope				Killough	
1796	Nymph		St Ives to St Johns		Dundrum Bay	
1797	Amite		French	frigate	Ardglass	
12-1797	New Loyalty	Ellison	Liverpool to Belfast		Dundrum bay	
1797	Mermaid		Liverpool to Africa		Newcastle	
1794	Surprise		Liverpool to Guinea		Annalong	
1799	Barmouth		Liverpool to Newry		Newcastle	
1800	May		Whitehaven to Dublin		S of Dundrum	
27-1-1801	Eve	Gilmore	Dublin to Newry		Carlingford	
1802	smack		Liverpool to Drogheda		Dundrum Bar	
1803	brig		West Indies to London		Tyrella	
27-1-1803	Unknown		Liverpool		Copeland Islands	
23-2-1803	Union	Peggs			Ballywalter	
24-2-1803	Shamrock	McIlroy	Liverpool to Belfast	cotton & flour		
26-4-1803	Orr		Irvine to Dublin		Strangford	
5-6-1804	Castor	O'Hara	Jamaica to Liverpool		Dundrum bay	
10-1-1804	Pincent	Wells	Lisbon to Liverpool		Newry	
25-9-1804	Diamond	Nesbitt	Dublin to Limerick		Strangford	
6-11-1804	Auspicious		to Dundalk		Cranfield point	
15-1-1805	Minerva		Delaware to Liverpool	turpentine, tar, timber	North Rock	
1-1805	Three Sisters	Donnan	Dublin to Portaferry		South Rock 130 years old	Built in 1670 and
3-3-1807	Ann	Cochrane	Liverpool to Glasgow		Dundrum Bay	
21-8-1807	Satisfaction	Middleton	Liverpool to Picton		Dundrum Bay	
10-11-1807	Fame		Rothsay to Galway		Killough	
8-10-1808	Unity	Davidson	Workington from Belfast		Bangor	
7-2-1809	John	Taylor	St Ubes to Gothenburg		Down coast	
1809	Lucy		Savannah to Liverpool		Dundrum Bar	
1810	John		North Sheilds to St John's		Newcastle	
1810	Letter of Marque		Liverpool to South America		Dundrum	
1810	Hornby		Liverpool to Newry		Newcastle	
23-1-1810	Magnet	Thompson	Newry to Liverpool		Strangford	
6-2-1810	Elizabeth	Neil	Jamaica to Belfast		Dundrum Bay	
24-3-1810	Molly	Parkinson			Kirkstown spit	
25-3-1810	Juno		Barnstaple to Derry		Ardglass	
25-3-1810	Britannia	Shannon	Kinsale to Liverpool		Dundrum Bay	
2-11-1810	Drondtheim	Block			Donaghadee	
31-1-1811	Lady Dunbar		Whitehaven to Belfast		Donaghadee	
31-1-1811	Warrington	Read	Workington to Dublin		Ballywalter	
1-2-1811	Emelia	Dunstone	Philadelphia to London	cotton, indigo	Dundrum bay	
8-2-1811	Jubilee	Carnegie	Greenock to Surinam		Killough	
5-10-1811	Thomas	McKennon	Liverpool to Tobermory		Dundrum bay	
17-2-1812	William	Watt	Clyde to Buenos Aires		Mileste Bay	
25-2-1812	Britannia	Dauvers	Strangford to Liverpool		Duddon Bay	

DOWN CHRONOLOGICAL LIST

Date	Ship Name	Captain	Voyage	Cargo	Location	Comment
22-3-1812	Jane	Busby			Ardglass	
19-1-1813	Lagan		Belfast to London		Donaghadee	
5-3-1813	Gatcombe	Henderson	Whitehaven to Dublin	coal	Ardglass	
20-9-1813	Loyalty	Stewart	from Workington		Portaferry	
21-10-1813	Caesar	McLarty	Greenock to Jamaica		Portaferry	
1813	Neptune		Milford to Liverpool		Tyrella	
1814	Duke of Richmond		Liverpool to drogheda		Clanmaghery	
10-1-1814	John & Sarah		Greenock to Strangford		Dundrum bay	
10-1-1814	William & Sally	Shaw	Harringdon to Belfast		Bangor	
11-1-1814	Leda	Watts	Belfast to Swansea		Kilkeel	
3-12-1814	Janet & Peggy	Morgan	Liverpool to Newry		off Carlingford	
3-12-1814	Phoenix	Fearan	Liverpool to Newry		off Carlingford	
30-12-1814	Betsey	Campbell	Greenock to Newry		Copeland Islands	
1814	Industry		Dublin to Strangford		Newcastle	
1815	Roberts		Irvine to Dublin		Newcastle	
1815	Auspicious		Liverpool to Newry		Newcastle	
1815	Recovery		Liverpool to Newry		Newcastle	
9-11-1816	Vine				Ballywalter	
9-11-1816	Helena	Kerr	Greenock to Limerick		Briggs reef	
21-11-1816	Paroquet		Liverpool to West Indies		S of Strangford	
21-11-1816	Queen Charlotte	Wells	Whithaven to Dublin	coal	Ballywalter	
24-12-1816	Ann & Mary	McWilliam			Ballywalter	
13-12-1817	Brothers	Myler	Wexford to Glasgow		Strangford	
13-12-1817	John	Hayes	Wexford to Glasgow		Strangford	
14-6-1818	Providence	Lyons	Chester to Dublin		Ballywalter	
4-8-1818	Ann	Turner	Glasgow to Cork		Ballyhalbert	
9-10-1818	Ruby	Wylie	Liverpool to Newry		Dundrum bay	
11-1818	Gallant				Strangford bar	
1818	Brothers		Dublin to Glasgow		S of Strangford	
1818	Minerva		Liverpool to Newry		Dundrum	
1819	Hamlet				Ballywalter	
15-1-1819	Louisa		Liverpool to Killough		Dundrum Bay	
15-1-1819	Messmate		Liverpool to Killough		Dundrum Bay	
15-1-1819	Marygold	Hodgson		coal	Ballywalter	
28-1-1819	Eliza & Mary	James	Killough to Newry		Carlingford	
22-3-1819	Peggy & Helen	Bloom	Sligo to Liverpool		Copeland Islands	
8-6-1819	Brothers	Marshall	Carlingford to Greenock		off Copeland Islands	
24-9-1819	Rebecca	Livingstone	Clyde to Charleston		Donaghadee	
24-1-1820	Collins	Ashridge	St Johns to Liverpool		Dundrum bay	
10-1820	Hardwick			revenue cutter	Dundrum Bay	
21-11-1820	Bordeaux Packet	McFee	Liverpool to Derry		Copeland islands	
26-11-1820	Isabella	Barkley	Newry to Preston		Newry	
6-1-1821	Anna McLean		Greenock to Waterford	sugar, rum	Newry	
6-1-1821	Friendship	Evans	Whitehaven to Dublin		Carlingford bar	
29-1-1821	Perseverance		Liverpool to Buenos Aires		South Rock	
20-10-1821	Emperor Alexander	of Sunderland			South Rock	
22-10-1821	Glenore		Dublin to Belfast		Mew Island	

Date	Ship Name	Captain	Voyage	Cargo	Location	Comment
19-11-1821	Jean	of Ayr	Liverpool to Bahia		South Rock	
26-11-1821	Hope		to Newry		Ballyhenry	
26-11-1821	Brothers	Anderson	Archangel to Dublin		Mica Island	
26-12-1821	Erin		Newry to Glasgow		Carlingford	
1821	Prosperity		Westport to Liverpool			
12-2-1822	Aurora		Liverpool to Dundalk		Dundrum bay	
13-10-1822	London	Hazell	Quebec to Liverpool		Bangor	
13-10-1822	Rose		Strangford to Liverpool		Drumore	
6-11-1822	Ann	Bowman	Quebec to Liverpool		Donaghadee	
2-1823	Ann				Strangford bar	
24-9-1823	Agnes	McFee	from Saltcoates		Strangford	
22-12-1823	Flora	Baghley			Ballywalter	
12-1823	William Hobbs				South Rock	
18-1-1824	Barbara & Janette				Newry Bar	All lost
18-2-1824	Barbara & Janette		Irvine to Dundalk		Newry	
28-12-1824	Phoenix		Greenock to Liverpool		Donaghadee	
28-12-1824	Maxwell		Waterford to Liverpool		Ballyferris	
1825	Superior		Greenock to America		Tyrella	
26-1-1825	Nancy				off Carlingford	
25-3-1825	John Little	Muirland	Liverpool to Nova Scotia		Dundrum bay	
1-12-1825	Usk		Liverpool to Adra		Dundrum Bay	
9-2-1826	Unknown		from Dublin		Dundrum bay	Large flat
23-2-1826	Three Brothers	Workington	Belfast	coal	Strangford bar	rescuers lost but refloated
7-2-1826	Maid of Selma	Bell	Dundrum to Belfast		Mew Island	
5-3-1826	Sophia	McRee	Whitehaven to Belfast		Mew Island	
6-3-1826	Richard Pope		Liverpool to Sierra Leone		Newcastle	
17-4-1826	Verheldersum	Visser	Rotterdam to Newry		Newry	
10-5-1826	Minerva	McKay	Belfast to Cork		Portaferry	
1827	Blue Eyed Maid		Liverpool to Dundrum		Newcastle	
1829	Sir James Kenp		St John's to Liverpool		Tyrella	
1829	brig					
1829	Henry				Mew island	
9-3-1830	Sally	Rodham	Maryport to Dublin		Dundrum Bay	
4-4-1830	Friendship		Cushendall to Dublin		Ballyberries Rock	
16-11-1830	Ann	Littlejohn	Newport to Aberdeen		Dundrum Bay	
14-3-1831	New John			coal	Killough	
16-11-1831	Fanny	Sangster	Wick to Dublin		Ballyferris	
1831	Delaford		Liverpool to Lisbon		Tyrella	
7-1-1832	New Diligence	Wale	Newport		Dundrum Bay	refloated
12-1-1832	John	Scotland	Liverpool to St Thomas		South Rock	
1832	Warrenpoint	Westmoreland	Portrush to Liverpool		Killough	
1833	Heroine		Swansea to Liverpool		Tyrella	
1834	unknown		Liverpool to America		Tyrella	
1835	Charlotte		of Drogheda		Dundrum bay	
1835	Helen		Riga to Newry		Strangford bar	
1835	Dale	Maryport			Killough	all lost
16-12-1836	Minipia				St John's point	all lost

DOWN CHRONOLOGICAL LIST

Date	Ship Name	Captain	Voyage	Cargo	Location	Comment
1837	Coeur de Lion		Liverpool to America		Tyrella	
1837	George		Swansea to Liverpool			
1837	Bellona		Liverpool to Mobile			
20-1-1838	Margaret	O'Neill			Newry	
17-2-1838	John Stamp		Bombay to Liverpool		Kilkeel	
17-2-1838	Kennedy		of Balbriggan		Ardglass	
20-2-1838	Eagle				Ballywalter	
21-2-1838	Hope		Campbeltown	Barley	Ardglass	
21-2-1838	Thomas				Ardglass	
1838	Mary Stewart				Balagan point	
1838	Elizabeth					
7-11-1838	Farnham	Wylie			Cranfield Point	
29-11-1838	unknown				Tyrella	
1838	Constitution		Liverpool to America		Newcastle	
1838	John Stamp		Bombay to Liverpool		Rossglass	
1838	Friendship		Bangor to Belfast		Lee stone	
1838	brig		Liverpool to Derry		Tyrella	
1838	Rapid		from Bangor		Tyrella	
1838	British Heroine		Liverpool to Mobile		Tyrella	
7-1-1839	Bonnie Lass				Ardglass	
7-1-1839	Rusden Castle		from Isle of Man		Ardglass	
7-1-1839	William & Mary	Race			Strangford	
7-1-1839	Margaret	Patton	from Irvine		Strangford	
8-1-1839	Ellen		from Belfast		Portaferry	
8-1-1839	Waterloo		from Carlingford		Portaferry	
14-2-1839	Lady Downshire				off Copelands	
14-2-1839	Shannon	Little	Maryport to London		Ballywalter	
17-2-1839	Antrim	McCracken		cotton	Cloughey	
10-3-1839	United Friends		Barmouth to Strangford		Killard Point	
1839	smack				Newcastle	
1839	schooner		Belfast to Strangford		Tyrella	
1840	Eagle		Liverpool to Newcastle on Tyne		Tyrella	
25-1-1840	Trevor		Marseilles to Belfast		Dundrum bay	
11-11-1840	Susannah	Rule	Maryport to Strangford	coal	Garter rock	
19-11-1840	Susannah	McKenzie			Bangor	
14-2-1840	Clarence	Hughes	from Runcorn		Newry	
22-3-1840	Mary Gordon	Canning			Donagahdee	
1840	Kincardineshire		Liverpool to Aberdeen		Tyrella	
1840	Trevor		Marseilles to Belfast		Tyrella	
3-1-1841	Aurora	Welch	from Wexford		off Strangford	
28-2-1842	Adonai	Roche	Ardrossan to Plymouth		Portavogie	
1842	Tagus		New Brunswick	timber	Carlingford	
26-1-1842	Brutus		Clyde to St Thomas		Ballywalter	
26-1-1842	Lerwick				Ballyferris	
1843	Peace & Plenty		Drogheda to Campbeltown		Dundrum	
21-2-1844	Northumbrian Maid				Strangford	

DOWN CHRONOLOGICAL LIST

Date	Ship Name	Captain	Voyage	Cargo	Location	Comment
12-11-1844	Europe	Brodie	to Narva			
15-1-1845	Belisle	Huddart	Maryport to Dublin		Kearney Point	
3-3-1845	Orissa		Liverpool to Bombay	general cargo	Carlingford	repaired
1845	Frolic		Liverpool to Dort		Newcastle	
1845	Red Diamond		to Newry			
6-3-1846	Caledonian				Strangford	
6-3-1846	William		of Donaghadee		Ballyhenry	
22-9-1846	Great Britain		Liverpool to New York		Dundrum Bay	refloated the next year
18-1-1849	Mantura	of Ardrossan			North Rock	
18-4-1849	Marquis of Normanby			hemp	South Rock	
9-2-1850	Nimble				Ballyhenry bay	
31-3-1850	Preston	Mateer	Dundalk to Llanelly	ballast	The Ridge, south rock	
31-3-1850	Peggy		Liverpool to Glasgow	salt	Cloughey bay	
19-12-1849	Garland		Belfast to Venice		Killough	burned
10-1850	Favourite				Newry bar	
1851	Ebeneezer	Fletcher			off Carlingford Lough	
31-1-1852	Glencapple	Rodick	Ibrael to Newry		Cranfield	refloated
16-6-1852	Providence				Strangford Bar	
7-11-1852	Louisa C	Soich	Ibrael to Newry		Cranfield	
15-1-1853	Queensbury				Strangford Bar	
21-1-1854	Catherine Corrigan	Davison	Cardiff to Cork		Dundrum bay	
21-1-1854	Lively	Whittle		coal	Dundrum bay	
2-7-1854	Nova Providenza	Genoa			Ringfad	
28-10-1854	Jupiter		to Vera Cruz	coal	Tyrella	
28-10-1854	Sarah Ann		to Cuba	coal, railway chairs	Sheepland harbour	
15-11-1854	Johns				Killard point	
9-12-1854	Duke of York				South Rock	6 lost
5-4-1856	Nautilus				Dundrum Bay	
22-10-1856	Harriet Matilda		Larne to Killyleagh	lime	Carrstown Point	
22-10-1856	Robert E Ward		Troon to Castle Espie	coal	Plady Lug	
4-1-1857	Lion				Angus Rock	
4-1858	Sylvia				Dundrum Bay	nine lost
4-1858	Triton		Liverpool to Barcelona	rails	Ballymartin	
4-1858	Welsh sloop				Carlingford	
9-12-1859	Saxon King				Struck the Ridge at Strangford	refloated but sank at Corsewall Point
12-3-1860	Providence		from Java		Strangford Bar	
5-2-1861	Manchester		Whitehaven to Dublin	coal	St Patrick's rocks	
14-8-1861	Coriolanus	Kinnear	Liverpool to Quebec		Cannon Rock	House built with a dish of sovereigns found aboard
5-1-1867	Gardella	Italian	Ardrossan to Genoa	pig iron	Pladdy lug	
12-10-1870	Favourite		Ardrossan to Dublin	coal	Ballyhoran	
2-3-1872	Conflict	of Belfast			Ballyquentin Point	

DOWN CHRONOLOGICAL LIST

Date	Ship Name	Captain	Voyage	Cargo	Location	Comment
2-1872	Newry		Cardiff to Newry	coal	Warrenpoint	
21-1-1873	Margaret Ann				Killowen point	foundered
5-1-1873	Marseilles		Moulmein to Glasgow	teak	Cannon rock	6 lost
29-11-1874	Lancashire Lass	Holliday	Drogheda to Workington		Ringfad	
1-2-1877	Amoy	Dundee	Pernambuco to Greenock	Sugar	Ridge at Strangford	
20-2-1877	Mary Ann				rocks north of Strangford	
14-9-1877	Irishman	Morisson	Dublin to Glasgow		Burial Island	
24-12-1877	Friends		Girvan to Killeigh	coal	South Rock	
4-6-1878	Jason		Dundalk	iron	Carlingford	
2-10-1878	Maria Lowther				Bloody Bridge	
7-1-1897	William & Mary	Workington			The Ridge at Strangford	
17-3-1881	Sally & Anne				Annalong	
16-11-1880	Speedwell				Angus rock	
27-1-1881	Eleanor				Leestone point, Carlingford	
27-2-1881	John Kendall		Greenock to Barbadoes	coal	The Ridge at Strangford	
3-3-1881	Albion				Annalong	
26-6-1881	Amanda	Sandefjord	Garston To Kronstat	coal	North Rock	
13-12-1881	Craigownie		Bilbao to Troon	Iron ore		
11-1-1883	Wild Deer	Kerr	Glasgow to Otago	Emigrants	Canon Rock	
6-2-1883	Beagle	McIlgorm	Maryport to Derry	coal	Ballyhoran	
22-9-1883	Emily		Bilbao to Glasgow	Iron ore	Belfast Lough	
9-10-1883	Strathdon		Abergele to Clyde	Limestone		
25-1-1885	R.Liverpool.Alston		Bilbao to Glasgow	Iron ore	Killard point	
19-9-1885	Zebra		Carnavon to Broughley	Slate	Ballyquentin	
22-10-1885	Bertha		Carrickfergus to Ramsgate	granite	Annalong	
23-2-1886	Lelia	Padstow			Garter Rock	
8-2-1886	Eureka			Iron ore	South Rock	Refloated
9-6-1886	Urania		Liverpool to Vyborg	Salt	North rock	
6-11-1886	Eclipse	Frances			off Donaghadee	
29-12-1886	Wembdon		Huelva to Troon	Copper ore	Cannon Rock	
3-1-1888	Kate	Hansen	Mersey to Christiania	coal	South Rock	
13-10-1891	Grid	Farsund	Liverpool to Buenos Aires	coal	Cannon rock	
1892	Margaret Ann				Carlingford bar	
26-10-1892	Annie		Port Dinorwic to Dundee	Slates	Killard point	
7-7-1895	Emily				Briggs reef	Wreck caused loss of Ranger
7-7-1895	Ranger			tug	Briggs reef	
7-7-1895	Davaar				Briggs reef	refloated
2-10-1895	Helen		Ardrossaan to Christiania	coal		
25-9-1897	Sulby Glen		Whitehaven to Quoile Quay		Killard point	Coal gas explosion
9-4-1898	Beaconsfield		Rangoon to Greenock	teak	north Rock	
7-12-1899	John R Noble		Irvine to Newry	coal	Ballyquentin Point	
10-11-1901	Meridian				Donagahdee	towed off

Date	Ship Name	Captain	Voyage	Cargo	Location	Comment
12-11-1901	Whiteabbey				Belfast Lough	
12-11-1901	Nil Desperando		Kircubbin to Killyleagh	sand	Killyleagh bay	
15-12-1906	Anglia			cable steamer	Ballyquentin point	
1906	Febo		Almeira to Clyde	iron ore	Cannon Rock	
1906	Hazeldene			iron ore	Cannon Rock	
14-1-1905	Beechgrove	Woodall	Ardrossan to Penarth	coal	Dunmore	
7-2-1907	Ascalon	Sivertson	Mersey to Ollofjord		Murphy's point	
26-12-1907	Vamos	Larsen	Oporto to Garston	ballast	south of Murphy's point	
1-3-1907	Rippling Wave		Par to Glasgow		South Rock	
16-10-1908	Glassford		Neath to Belfast	coal	South Rock	
13-11-1908	Croisset		New Caledonia	nickel ore	South Rock	
1909	Martha Anne		Annalong to Liverpool	granite	Helyhunter rocks	
5-11-1913	Reading		Seville to Glasgow	iron ore	South Rock	
9-2-1914	Loch Long	Polly			Strangford bar	
18-3-1915	Upas		Ayr to Warrenpoint	coal	Burial Island	
3-11-1916	Retriever	O'Neill	Garston to Newry	coal	Carlingford Lough	Collided with Connemara
3-11-1916	Connemara					94 lost
11-1916	Fulvia				Newcastle	
11-1916	Frieda	Donner	Mobile to Greenock	pine	South Rock	
18-12-1916	Benshaw		Bilbao to Ayr	iron ore	South Rock	
24-12-1917	Daybreak				off South Rock	
5-4-1918	Saint Barchan				4 m off St Johns Point	
18-10-1918	Hunsden	Beedie			3 m E of Ballyhoran	
18-10-1918	Industry				SE Strangford light buoy	
9-10-1918	Neatsfield				off Skulmartin	
18-11-1920	Scarpa				North Rock	refloated
18-7-1928	Lucy				Ringfad point	
21-11-1936	Pine	McKee			Narrow water	struck by Olive
4-4-1937	Alder		to Newry		Narrow water	raised and scrapped
15-10-1940	Bellavale		Dundalk to Ayr		Rossglass	
28-1-1941	Alhena		Liverpool to Egypt	war stores	South Rock	
23-9-1941	Bereby		Liverpool to port Harcourt	war stores	Ringfad point	
30-4--1946	Georgetown Victory		Fremantle to Glasgow	1,200 sailors	Killard Point	
c1946	Alisdair			yacht	Strangford	burned
30-11-1954	World Concord			oil	Tara Point	
6-3-1962	Frida Blokzul				Kearney Point	
21-1-1973	Tide	Tooke			Guns Island	caught fire
21-1-1977	Jeanette			fishing	Kilkeel	
5-4-1977	Anna Catherina				Kearney Point	refloated
13-1-2000	Solway Harvester				between Down and IOM	sank

WATERFORD CHRONOLOGICAL LIST

Tony Caulfield of Tramore listed Waterford wrecks in chronological order for a 1993 book by Bernie Coughlan (86). His sources were the Jacob material and the Waterford Mirror. Additions to this list from Lloyds records added some 200 extra wrecks. This serves yet again to illustrate the huge number of wrecks mentioned in Lloyds list and not in newspapers and vice versa. The puzzle is that in the relevant period there is little duplication between the Lloyds agent, Jacob's list and the newspaper data as well as the Lloyds list data.

Date	Vessel	Master	Voyage	Cargo	Wreck location	Comment
1566	Post			warship	Tramore	
1697	Hastings			32 gun warship	off Waterford	
6-3-1749	Cole		Lisbon		Waterford river	
18-2-1757	Joseph & Jane	Wardell	Philadelphia to Dublin		near Waterford	
1753	Anne & Margaret				off Waterford	
before 1758	East Indiaman	French			off Credan Head	
20-12-1757	Unknown	DuCarnen	Cork to Bristol		near Dungarvan	
20-12-1757	Ann & Isabel		to Dublin		near Waterford	
14-1-1763	Betsey	Ball	of Teignmouth		off Dungarvan	60 drowned
14-1-1763	Ann	Spencer	Virginia to Bristol		off Dungarvan	
7-1-1764	Providential Friends		Liverpool		Tramore	
22-12-1764	unnamed	Hogan	London to Waterford		Waterford river	
30-11-1765	Unnnamed		Cadiz to Cork	wine	Islandkeane	
28-3-1776	Hawke	William McCarthy	Bristol to Barcelona	wheat	Dungarvan bar	
28-3-1767	Unnamed		Dungarvan		Waterford harbour mouth	
27-12-1768	Unnamed				Bonmahon	Hull ashore
21-1-1769	Duchess of Leinster	McCarthy	Waterford to Liverpool		Opposite Hook	
14-3-1769	Two Friends	Henry	London to Waterford	sugar, hops, tobacco	Tramore	
14-3-1769	Serviceable	Terry			Kings Bay	
12-8-1769	Friendship			Staves	Tramore	
10-11-1770	Bonny Jane	Dominic Waters	Malaga to Dublin	Wine & raisins	Passage	
11-10-1770	St Henrick	Selinen			Waterford	
15-10-1770	Henry		Sielem to Stockholm		Waterford river	
5-11-1772	Hero	Smith	Rotterdam			
5-10-1772	St Simone Sacramento	Antonio Simone	St Ubes to Waterford		Tramore	
4-5-1773	Lyon		Newfoundland to Waterford		Drumroe bank	
4-5-1773	Venus		Newfoundland to Waterford		Drumroe bank	
4-5-1773	Eagle		Newfoundland to Waterford		Drumroe bank	
19-1-1774	Young Cornelius	Reilly	Cork to Grenades		Ardmore	
10-12-1774	Hereford	Harisson	South Carolina			
10-12-1774	Hampshire	Channel	from Southampton		Waterford	
20-1-1775	Mermaid	Pulleins	Bristol to Waterford		Dungarvan	

WATERFORD CHRONOLOGICAL LIST

Date	Vessel	Master	Voyage	Cargo	Wreck location	Comment
29-1-1776	sloop			ballast	Graingers, Dungarvan	crew lost
6-2-1776	Juffpionn Maria	Hendrik Berkel	Bordeaux -Rotterdam	wine, vinegar, chestnuts	Coxtown	4 crew survived boy lost plundering
24-2-1776	Unknown				Islandkeane	
12-4-1776	Two Brothers	Peter Nielsen Morek	Dram - Ross		Tramore Bay	Danish ship
27-2-1776	Dutchess De Clerk	Drevillard	Bordeaux to Guadaloupe	flour, brandy bales & gunpowder	Near Waterford	
12-4-1776	Pike	Linthorn	Liverpool to Waterford & Newfoundland		Waterford river	
18-4-1779	Montague		Bristol to Waterford		14 miles from Waterford	
31-1-1777	St Mary	Ellworthy	St Ubes to Waterford		Dungarvan	
12-4-1777	Four Sisters	Meldall	Arundel -Waterford	baulks and deals	Tramore Bay	crew and
Cargo						saved
28-12-1781	Solidade	Santos	Lisbon to Waterford			
4-8-1782	Swan				off Waterford	
16-4-1782	Patty	Scriven	Cork to Newfoundland		Tramore	
4-3-1783	Rose	Sheal	Newry to London	Linen	Minehead	
25-9-1783	Draper	Robinson	Bordeaux to Belfast		Waterford	
25-9-1783	Unknown	Dutch			West of Waterford	
9-9-1783	Unknown	Foreign			Tramore	
20-12-1785	Adventure	Wiley	North Carolina		Near Waterford	
6-1-1786	Thomas & Mary		Ross to Bristol		Minehead	
6-1-1786	Peggy		Waterford to Bristol		Minehead	
13-1-1786	Hibernia	Doyle	Waterford to London		Tramore	four other ships were lost
24-1-1786	Pomona	Granger	Belfast to Malaga		2 m East of Waterford Light	
30-1-1789	Douglas		Waterford to Greenock		Waterford	
20-11-1789	Lowther	Rothery	Whitehaven to Ireland		Waterford	
7-4-1790	Lewis		London to Newfoundland		Waterford	burnt
28-1-1791	Mary	Dwyer	Waterford to London		Tramore	
20-3-1792	Lovel	Mudge	Waterford to Lisbon	wheat	Waterford	
30-3-1792	Fille Unique	Hamel	Martinique to Harvre		near Waterford	
May 1792	Fanny				Woodstown	
May 1792	Barbados Packet		bound for Newfoundland		Giles Quay	
12-6-1792	Barbadoes Packet	Orchard	Waterford to Newfoundland		Waterford	
Aug 1792	Fan	Matthew Parle			Tramore Bay	
30-12-1794	Mary	Gladcot	London to Waterford		Waterford	
12-10-1799	Countess of Leicester	Richards	from Waterford	packet boat	Waterford	
19-2-1799	Dennis	Griffith			Dungarvan	

WATERFORD CHRONOLOGICAL LIST

Date	Vessel	Master	Voyage	Cargo	Wreck location	Comment
19-2-1799	London Packet	Glass	London for Newry		Tramore	
1-3-1799	Three Brothers	Sullivan	Cork to Liverpool		Tramore	
19-10-1799	Neptune	Cavenaugh	Chester to Wexford		Waterford	
4-2-1800	Victoria	Wood	St Kitts to Liverpool		Waterford	
2-2-1802	Harmony	Baird	from Philadelphia	flax	Tramore	
10-6-1803	Happy	England	Wilmington to Liverpool		Waterford	
20-12-1803	Britannia		Ipswich to Liverpool		Waterford	
27-12-1803	Peggy	Rogers	Newport to Camarthen		Waterford	
26-1-1804	Charlotte & Ann	Kirby	Liverpool to Galway	Salt	Tramore Bay	
4-5-1804	unknown brig		from Liverpool			
30-1-1804	Fanny		Jackson to liverpool	flour corn bacon butter	In Waterford river	
7-1-1804	Dilligence	Gorman	Cork to Waterford	Staves	Leaked and beached on Tramore strand	all saved
3-5-1804	Brig		Liverpool	ballast	Falskirt Rock, Portally	7 saved
15-5-1804	Little Charles	Martin	Liverpool to St Michaels			off Waterford
3-10-1804	Queen Charlotte	Gorman	Cork	wine, spirits, sugar, iron	Ballystraw Bay Duncannon	crew saved
Oct. 1804	Liberty	Lovels	Swansea to Waterford	Coal	Passage	
9-11-1804	Elizabeth & Margaret		Waterford to Swansea		Dungarvan	
11-3-1805	Sampson	Prize captured by frigate Melpomene	Havana	rum, brandy, sugar coffee	Annestown	
6-11-1804	Charlotte & Anne	McKirdy	Liverpool to Galway		Tramore	
6-4-1805	ferry		Ballyhack to passage			horses caused boat upset
1-2-1806	William	Sinclair	Liverpool to Cork	West Indiaman for convoy to Trinidad	Dunmore Strand	
2-11-1806	Cheshire		Newport - Cork	coal	Tramore Bay	
19-11-1807	Betsey	Chapman	Boston to Cork		Dungarvan	
19-11-1807	Endeavour		Dublin to Whitehaven		Waterford	
16-8-1808	Matty		of Kinsale		Woodstown strand	
17-1-1809	Trinity	James White	Bristol - Tobago	earthenware goods	Brazen Head near Brownstown Head	master buried at Stradbally
27-1-1809	Appledore	of Barnstaple			Tramore	
27-1-1809	Caledonia	John Stewart	Alicante - Belfast	500 Bales Bartilla	Tramore Bay	
8-2-1809	Warren	Davis	to Whitehaven		Dungarvan	
1809	Dispatch		Whitehaven	coal	Credan Head	crew lost
Feb. 1809	Warren	Davis	Whitehaven -Waterford	coal	Clonea Strand	
26-10-1809	La Sainte Anne		of Livourne	wine	Rhineshark Harbur	deserted and salvaged by fishermen
7-11-1809	Jane	Adams	Plymouth-London	Provisions	Buttermilk castle	crew Saved
6-12-1809	Eliza	Tromp	St Johns NB	fish	Islandkeane	Master and two lost

Date	Vessel	Master	Voyage	Cargo	Wreck location	Comment
6-12-1809	Sloop		Tralee	kelp	Tramore	
20-9-1810	Chasse Maree Les Deux Soeurs	Prize of HMS Cadmus	Nantes		brought in to Rhineshark	
16-11- 1810	Princess Royal	David Richards	Milford	ballast	Islandkeane	
Nov. 1810	James	Robert McLea	Liverpool- Limerick		Duncannon	
5-2-1811	Fox	Le Gresbey	From Jersey		Tramore	
17-2-1811	Grinder	Robert Werre	Lisbon -Dublin	Spanish wool	Tramore	
17-2-1811	Commerce	John Wilcox	Waterford- London	Bacon	Tramore	
19-2-1811	Leopard	Clarke	Waterford - Oporto		Duncannon	Lost anchors cables, rudder
27-3-1811	Fleece		Waterford - London	Oats	Cheekpoint	
24-9-1811	Phesant		Whitehaven - Cork	Coal	Islandkeane	
1811	Fox				Tramore	
1-12-1811	Albion	Robert Thomas	London - Waterford	Merchants goods	Tramore	Vessel got off
15-12-1811	Jason	Henry	Newfoundland to Waterford		Waterford	
30-1-1812	Lancaster	Wm McMullan	Lancaster - Dominicia		Broomhill	Crew saved
27-6-1812	Friends	cooke	Liverpool to Waterford		Waterford river	
23-9-1812	Yeoman's Glory		Teignmouth - Liverpool		Kings Channell Waterford	Sank
7-12- 1813	Neptune	Copestone	Bristol- Cork		Ballinacourty	4 passengers lost
20-2-1813	Conceico	Soares	Waterford to Lisbon		Waterford	
24-3-1814	Venus		Cork- Bristol		Credan Bay	refloated
14-6-1814	William I		Liverpool - Amsterdam	rock salt & earthenware	outside Hook Head	
23-11-1814	Shamrock		Cardiff - Kinsale			
Dec. 1814	Nelson	French	Liverpool	Coal and dye	Duncannon	
Dec. 1814	Active		Chepstow to Workington	timber	Dunmore	Captain, mate and another drowned
3-1-1815	William	Hall	St John NFL - Waterford	Fish & Oil	Tramore	Vessel got off
29-11-1815	Bellona		Newport to Waterford	Coal	Broomhill	
4-1-1816	Norwood		Plymouth to Poole	pipe clay	Rhineshark	
29-1-1816	Mary Cummings		Ayr to Cork		Waterford Harbour	Crew saved
30-1-1816	Sea Horse	Gibbs	Ramsgate to Cork	Troop transport	Tramore Bay	363 drowned
31-1-1816	Appolonia	Parry	London -Cork	Clothes tea sugar	Tramore	7 saved
31-1-1816	Caroline		Vienna to Waterford	fruit	Waterford Harbour	
19-9-1816	Mary		Ayr to Cork		Waterford	
29-9-1816	St Patrick		Cork to Dublin	Flour	Rhineshark	refloated
28-12-1816	Agnes		Greenock to Meditteranean	sugar	Rhineshark	reefloated
1816	Fanny			salt	Tramore	5 lost
17-2-1817	Oscar Pleasant	Meyers Gibson	Baltimore to Liverpool Whitehaven to Cork	flour	Rhineshark Tramore	Cargo saved
1817	Fox			fruit	Tramore	9 lost
23-8-1817	Industry		Wales to Dungarvan		Mine Head	

WATERFORD CHRONOLOGICAL LIST

Date	Vessel	Master	Voyage	Cargo	Wreck location	Comment
24-8-1817	San Johannes			Gravel	Bonmahon	refloated
8-12-1817	Patrick & Briget	Veal	Cork to Dublin		Dungarvan	
1-1-1818	Briget & Mary				Metal Man Tramore	
1818	Shamrock			ballast	Tramore	all saved
1818	Matthew	Quinlan	Dungarvan-Waterford		off Dungarvan	crew saved
1818	Enna		Newfoundland	fish	Tramore Bay	five lost
1818	Rose			Potatoes	Tramore Bay	saved
1818	Sir John Cameron		Quebec to Liverpool	Timber, flaxseed, salmon	Fornought Bay Waterford harbour	saved
1819	Hope	Steel	St Johns	timber	Duncannon	
1-2-1819	Billet				Newtown Head	
1819	Active		Dungarvan	Barley	Tramore Bay	
17-12-1819	James & Henry	Ridley	Marianham to Liverpool	cotton	Rhineshark	Saved
20-2-1820	William & Mary	Veale	Ross to Youghal		ballyhack	
15-8-1820	Jane Mary				Dunmore East	
8-12-1820	Lord Collingwood	Henry Fudge	Cork to Portsmouth	Oats	Whiting Bay Ardmore	crew lost
1820	Eliza			flax	Tramore Bay	saved
1820	Dart				Tramore Bay	Five lost
21-11-1820	Heart of Oak		Baltimore to Liverpool		off Waterford	
Dec 1820	Schooner	Pierce Kirwin			Ballinacourty	Crew lost
1820	John & Mary	James Fitzgerald				
Dec 1820	Friends	of Maryport			Dungarvan Bay	crew lost
16-12-1820	Thetis	Peregrine			Dungarvan	
Dec 1821	Endeavor	Hector McCann	Newport to Cork	Coal	Dungarvan Bay	crew lost
Dec 1821	Thomas	Thomas Fox	St Johns to Liverpool	Fish oil, rum	Booley Bay Waterford harbour	
Dec 1821	Susan	Huxtable	Ilfracombe		15 leagues off Hook tower	Foundered
Mar 1822	Martha	Arthur Daly	Waterford to Liverpool	Grain	Broomhill	Master, pilot and nine lost
Apr 1822	Asia	Otis	America to Liverpool	Flaxseed & Rum	Rhineshark	All saved
Apr 1822	Celestial				Metal man Tramore	Wrecked
1-1-1823	Harriet	Collins	St Johns NB - Liverpool	timber	Woodstown	stranded
4-1-1823	Flora	McColl	Quebec- Liverpool	timber	Broomhill	crew saved
29-1-1823	Hope	Clark			off Ardmore Head	crew lost
30-1-1823	Swift		St Michaels to Bristol	Oranges	Near Dungarvan	crew saved
1823	Harmony		Aberdeen	Timber	Tramore Bay	crew saved
30-11-1823	Susquahana	McManus	Liverpool to New York		Waterford river	
12-6-1824	Thomas & Judith	Oliver Nelson	Newport	Coal & Iron	Kings Channel	
1824	Bridget			Ballast	Tramore Bay	Three lost
1825	Mary		Youghal	furniture	Tramore Bay	crew saved
1825	Ellen		Glendon	Potatoes	Tramore	Four Lost
1825	Spanish lugger			Fruit & wine	Tramore Bay	crew saved
1825	Kitty		Cork	Flour	Tramore Bay	crew saved

Date	Vessel	Master	Voyage	Cargo	Wreck location	Comment
6-12-1825	Dove		Bristol to Marseille	iron	Dungarvan	crew saved but two locals lost in salvage
27-12-1825	Bolton		from Maryport		Tramore Bay	
27-12-1825	Flora	Jarmond	from Brixham		Tramore Bay	
1-11-1825	Brilliant	Skinner	Castlehaven to Cork		Passage	
19-12-1825	Flora	Peter Jarman	Brixham	ballast	Lady's Cove Tramore	Eight lost
19-12-1825	Bolton		Maryport	ballast	Between Newtown Head and Islandkeane	crew Lost
19-12-1825	brig				Stradbally	all lost except master & mate
27-12-1825	Royal Oak	of Plymouth	Youghal to Dungarvan		Dungarvan	
27-12-1825	Endeavour	Davis	Pwelly to Cork		Dungarvan	
27-12-1825	Esther	William	California to Liverpool		Ballyroney	
1826	Victory	Maurice Jones	Cork to Portsmouth	Provisions & Whiskey	Bonmahon	crew saved
5-1-1826	Perseverance	William Clewston	Newport to Glasgow	Iron	Red Head Dunmore East	crew saved
1827	John T				Annestown	
13-2-1828	Mermaid		Newport to Cork		Whiting Bay Ardmore	5 saved by coastguards
1828	Helen				Dungarvan	
1828	Clyde		of Alowa		Tramore	
1828	Enterprise	Richard Williams	Newport to Limerick	coal	Foundered off Credan Head	Crew lost
Dec 1828	William & Mary		Bideford	ballast	Tramore Bay	crew saved
Sep 1829	Josias		Newport to Kinsale	coal	Tramore Strand	crew saved
1829	James		Ross	Ballast	Tramore Strand	crew saved
20-11-1830	Providence	John James	Newport to Cork	Iron coal tin	Lady's cove Tramore	crew saved
21-11-1830	Favourite	Edward Trevett	Swansea	Culm	Templetown	crew saved
3-5-1830	Christian			Timber		
1830	Maud		sunderland	wine	Tramore Bay	crew saved
1830	brigantine		North Shields	coal	Tramore Bay	crew saved
1830	Diana		Newport	coal	Tramore Bay	crew saved
1830	Hound		Swansea			crew saved
1830	Mary Susanah		Youghal to Ross	ballast		crew saved
2-12- 1830	Unity	Andrew Power	Cardiff to Ross	coal	Dunmore	one saved
6-12-1830	Picton	William Grinnel	Oporto to Liverpool	Oranges	Credan Bay	crew saved
23-10-1831	Lusitania		Liverpool to Oporto		Ardmore	
30-9-1831	Eliza	Williams	Cork to London		off Waterford	
7-10-1832	Elizabeth & Anne	Lewis			Waterford	
24-11-1835	Les Deux Soeurs	Jean Pierre Manet	Niece to Rouen	tallow, oil, dye	Tramore Bay	Crew Saved
22-11-1835	Hebron	Frederick Higginson	New Brunswick to Dublin	coal and deals	Kilmurrin	crew saved
28-11-1835	Le Patriote			cognac	Portally	
21-11-1835	Collins	Alexander Smart	Quebec to Liverpool	Timber	Flat Rocks, Tramore	three lost
1836	Briton	Thomas	Llanelly to Ross	coal	Rathmoylan	one lost
1836	Grecian		Mobile	cotton	Tramore Bay	crew saved

WATERFORD CHRONOLOGICAL LIST

Date	Vessel	Master	Voyage	Cargo	Wreck location	Comment
1837	Jane	William Wakeham	Newport to Waterford	coal	Dungarvan bar	
16-3-1837	Sovereign	Turner	Woolwich to Dublin & Barbadoes	Detachment of eighty Royal Artillery	Killeton near Stradbally	all saved
1837	Yacht		Cork		Tramore Bay	crew saved
1837	Sir Edward		Liverpool	coal	Tramore Bay	crew saved
1838	Active		Poole	corkwood	Tramore Bay	crew saved
1838	Swain		Cork to Newport	Ballast	Bonmahon	crew saved
1838	Ellen	Thomas Harris			Arthurstown	
1838	Swan		Ross	ballast	Tramore Bay	crew saved
23-10-1838	Brothers	David Evans	Newport for New Ross	Coal	Tramore Bay	
28-11-1838	Le Speculator	John Gilbert	St Malo	ballast	Tramore Bay	seven crew lost
1838	Breeze				Tramore Bay	three lost
Nov 1838	St Patrick	George Schute	Liverpool to Waterford	steamer	Churchtown	six lost 23 saved
28-11-1838	Isabella	Ryder	Pernambuco to Liverpool	Cotton	Drumroe Bank	crew saved
29-11-1838	Comala	Donald McNeil	Signapore to Liverpool	cloves, pepper, tea, tin	Ballinacourty	16 saved
1838	St John	Curran	of Dungarvan		Ballinacourty	six lost mate swam ashore
5-1-1838	Favourite		Cork to Waterford			
20-1-1838	Olive Branch	Adams			Dungarvan bar	
10-2-1837	Jane	Wakeham	Newport to Waterford			
19-12-1837	Edward		Cork to Waterford		Ballymacaw	
16-2-1838	Sir Francis		Liverpool to Demerera		Ardmore	
	Burton Linsay					
16-2-1838	Jubilee	Edwards	Mobile to liverpool			
24-10-1838	Brothers	Evans	Maryport to Ross		Tramore Bay	
1839	Cuba	Dunlery	Alexandria to Liverpool	cotton	Rhineshark bar	three lost
1839	Leopard		Cardiff	iron ore	Clonea	crew saved
Mar 1839	Letitia	Titus Rees	Cardigan to Bannow	culm	Tramore	Crew saved
1839	Phoenix	Galway	Loading from Knockmahon mines	Copper ore	Bonmahon	
1839	Prince Regent	Pierce	Newport to New York	Passengers and rod iron	Tramore strand	13 crew, 28 passengers saved
19-1-1839	Ellen Pope		Newport to Cork	Coal	Bonmahon	crew saved
1839	Jane		from Swansea		Tramore Bay	crew saved
17-1-1840	Swift				Tramore	
23-2-1840	Medora				Ardmore	
1-12-1840	Glencoe	J.Keith	Glasgow to Calcutta	Coal, Ale, bale goods	Ballymacaw	local drowned
Dec 1840	Liske		Malaga to Glasgow	fruit	Bonmahon	crew saved
7-8-1841	Mary	Nichols	St John to Dungarvan			
12-2-1841	Harmony		Wicklow to Bristol		off Dungarvan	collided with Cockburn

Date	Vessel	Master	Voyage	Cargo	Wreck location	Comment
3-1 1842	George		Lisbon to Glaggow		Clonea	
11-10-1842	Kirby		From Dudden		collided with brig Dundonald off Waterford	one saved
1842	William		from Wales		Tramore Bay	crew saved
1842	Abraham		from Mobile	cotton	Tramore Bay	
11-1-1844	Elizabeth	Travers	Newport to Kinsale		"Tramond Bay"	
1844	Kate		from Glendon	Potatoes	Tramore Bay	crew saved
1845	Dove		from Ross	bricks	Tramore Bay	crew saved
1845	Elizabeth		From Newport	Ballast	Tramore Bay	one lost
1846	Joseph		from Dungarvan	fish	Tramore Bay	crew saved
1847	Casket		from Cork	ballast	Tramore Bay	crew saved
1847	Mystery		from Portmadoc	Maize	Tramore Bay	one lost 13 saved
13-12-1848	Dartagnan		from Nantes	corn	Tramore Bay	crew saved
14-12-1848	Petit Alexre		from Nantes	corn	Tramore Bay	crew saved
15-12-1848	Lomville		from Nantes	corn	Tramore Bay	crew saved
17-12-1848	St Vincent		from Nantes	corn	Tramore Bay	crew saved
1852	Achilles		New Ross	ballast	Tramore strand	crew saved
29-12-1852	Anne	Graves	Odessa to Limerick			
Dec 1852	Selim Rephy	Anastatin	Beyront to Liverpool	corn	Bonmahon	8 Greeks and 5 Arabs saved
Dec 1853	Old Kirwan	Nugent	Bonmahon to Swansea	Copper ore	Ballinacourty	crew saved
18-12-1853	Salacia	William Morgan	Cork to Bristol	Oats	Ring beach	
Dec 1856	Eliza	Jones	Llanelly to Cork	coal	Tramore Bay	crew saved
25-1-1858	La Capricieuse		Llanelly to St Malo	coal	Rhineshark	one lost and also two locals
1858	Neptunius		from Norway	ice	Tramore Bay	crew saved
17-8-1860	Hope	Edward James	from Ross		Sunk in collision with SS Malvina in river Siur	crew and pilot saved
1861	Tycoon	J. Lewey	Galveston to Liverpool	cotton	anchored off Brownstown	crew and ship saved
16-2-1861	San Spiridon	Gazzule	Swansea to Barcelona	coal	Rhineshark	six lost 2 rescued by LB which capsised
20-2-1861	Voyadore Du Voga	Jose Piuts	Viaua to Cork	Indian corn & figs		crew saved
1861	Nancy	Ournus	Marseilles	rock salt	Burrow House Tramore Bay	crew saved
21-1-1862	Sarah Anne	John McCarthy	Cardiff to lWaterford	coal	Ballinacourty	Master and 4 lost
22-1-1862	Sophia	Barry	Cardiff to Waterford	coal	Credan Head	crew saved by pilot cutter
22-1-1862	Schooner		to Waterford		off Red Head Dunmore	all aboard lost
22-1-1862	Queen of Commerce	Calvert	Liverpool to Antwerp		Ballymacaw	23 rescued
22-1-1862	Active	James Lewis	from Liverpool	coal		5 lost

Date	Vessel	Master	Voyage	Cargo	Wreck location	Comment
22-1-1862	Tiger	Lowell	Liverpool to Boston	general Cargo	Templetown	2 crew lost 24 saved by pilot cutter, Gannet
24-2-1862	Indian Ocean	Russell	Liverpool to Sydney		Benvoy strand near Annestown	25 rescued
24-1-1862	Nairn	Ness	Cardiff to Havana	railway iron	Brownstown Head	boy lost 5 saved
24-1-1862	Ellen Morris		Falmouth to Waterford	Wheat	Crook	vessel refloated
27-1-1862	Angelica	Domina	New York to Newcastle	grain	Credan Bay bank	
19-10-1863	Marinatta		Lisbon to Cardiff	ballast	west of metal man	locals saved 9 LB saved one
1863	Westock		Dungarvan		stranded at Rhineshark bar	drunken crew rowed ashore and vessel refloated
17-11-1864	Sarah	Galger	Waterford to Cardiff	hay & turnips	Tramore Bay	crew saved
3-12-1866	Jane				Tramore Bay	crew saved
6-1-1867	Anemone	Tardif	Glasgow to Nantes	pig iron	Rhineshark	crew saved
23-3-1867	Wild Horse	William Parr	New York to Liverpool	Petrolium and turpentine	Tramore strand	crew saved
Aug 1867	Willie		from Cork		Falskirt Rock, Ballymacaw	
12-1-1868	Oasis	George Irwin	Demrera to Liverpool	linseed	Metal man, Tramore	crew saved
29-11-1868	Mea	D Tomonavich	Constantinople to Waterford	maize	Tramore	crew saved
30-11-1868	Betsey	Samuel Jennings	Cardiff to Crosshaven	coal	Ballymacaw	Master and 2 lost, mate saved
19-9-1869	Belle		Of Londonderry		Capsized in Siur	
Mar 1869	Proteus	Capt Grady	Cardiff to Waterford		caught by a squall off Hook	crew saved
Jan 1870	Betsey		of Falmouth		Smuggling Rock B allymacaw	
Apr 1870	Harvard				Cromwell's Rock	
30-5-1870	Bertholly		Portmadoc to Cork	slates	Dungarvan bar	crew saved
Oct 1870	Mincalm		of Swansea		Credan head	
11-2-1871	Stranger	William Berry	Glouster to Waterford	salt		crew saved
12-2-1871	Content	Matthews	Waterford to Penzance	bones	Annestown	crew saved
21-11-1871	Adelaide	Nicholas Saul	Cardiff to Waterford	coal	Tramore	crew waded ashore but captain died
Nov 1871	Ejeria	Starrett	Boston to Liverpool	flour	Ballymacaw	8 saved, five lost
22-11-1872	Re Di Spagna	G Nicholich		wheat	Bonmahon	master and 16 saved
22-11-1872	Kinsale	Anderson	Cork to Glasgow	butter, flour porter	Broomhill	All 26 lost

Date	Vessel	Master	Voyage	Cargo	Wreck location	Comment
6-1-1875	Gwennissa		Falmouth to Glasgow		Bonmahon	
4-1-1875	Fanny	W Conc	from Cardiff	coal	Tramore	crew saved
8-3-1876	Aurora Australis	Frederick Meyer	Java to Queenstown	sugar	Tramore	crew saved
7-12-1877	Susanna		Bideford	coal	Waterford Bridge	
1879	Pevieur		Tenby	trawler	Tramore	crew saved
13-12-1881	Polly Pinkham			calcine, bone	Annestown	five lost, two saved
14-2-1881	Scotland	Marien			Ballymacart, Mine Head	11saved
8-2-1881	Victory		of Cork		Broomhill	
3-3-1881	Day Spring			coal	Broomhill	master survived but five lost
July 1881	Stormy Petrel	Dwyer	Baltimore to Waterford	wheat & maize	Brownstown Head	towed off
7-4-1882	Ellen				Ardmore	
8-8-1882	Silkstone	Burns			Rammed whilst alongside at Waterford	two lost
1-9-1883	Slaney				Hook	
13-2-1884	Earl Beaconsfield				Abandoned off Hook	Towed into Waterford
Feb 1884	Stowell Brown		Cardiff to Rio de Janeiro		Bar shoal, Waterford	23 saved
11-6-1884	Welcome Home		Lossiemouth	trawler	Falskirt Rock	6 saved
8-2-1884	Victory				Waterford	collided with brig
21-2-1841	Camilla	John O'Brien	Newport to Cork	coal	Rhineshark	three passengers and seven crew lost
21-2-1885	Venus B		Liverpool to Rio	general Cargo	Ballymacaw	Crew lost
13-12-1882	Silkstone				Quay, River Siur	
21-1-1886	Friends			fishing yawl	Waterford	3 lost
15-9-1886	Kingfisher		Helvick	fishing	run down	2 crew lost
4-1-1888	Alfred D Snow		San Francisco to Liverpool	wheat	Broomhill	all 23 abord lost
Dec 1888	Etta	Arthurs	St Johns to Fleetwood	timber	Credan Bay	captain lost but 16 saved
25-8-1891	Albert	George Fletcher	Newport to Youghal	coal	Tramore Bay	crew saved
14-9-1891	Garland		from Cork	slates	Tramore Bay	crew saved
22-2-1892	Paul		France to Newport	pitwood	Dungarvan harbour	
Dec 1893	Sybil				Broomhill	nine saved
9-12-1893	Vivid		of North Shields	coal	Arthurstown	nine saved
12-1-1894	Monmouthshire	Radford	Cardiff to Santos	coal & machinery	Tramore Bay	crew saved
17-11-1894	Scott Harley	Spillane	Glasgow to Cork	coal	Tramore Bay	crew saved
1895	Nautilu		of Barnstaple		Bonmahon	3 saved
20-4-1895	Olga		to Waterford	coal	Broomhill	7 crew saved
29-7-1895	Louisa		of Bideford		Bonmahon	3 saved
24-12-1895	Moresby	C Comber	Cardiff to Pisagua	coal	Dungarvan	20 lost, 5 saved

WATERFORD CHRONOLOGICAL LIST

Date	Vessel	Master	Voyage	Cargo	Wreck location	Comment
24-12-1895	Mary Sinclair				Clonea strand	crew saved
8-10-1896	Jessie		to New Ross	coal	off Hook	all lost
30-12-1897	Kedda		of Bridgewater	coal	Duncannon	
jan 1898	Hilda		Swansea to New Ross	timber	Duncannon	
1898	Shamrock		Kinsale to Isle of Man	fishing	Ballinancourty	3 rescued
1898	Dunvegan		Cardiff to New Orleans	coal	Dungarvan	Crew saved
12-12-1899	Unicorn		Cardiff to Ballyhack	coal	Tramore Bay	crew saved
9-3-1900	Eliza O'Keefe	John Flynn			Dungarvan	Crew saved
April 1900	Hansa		St Johns to Waterford	timber	Swedes bank, Waterford	
5-10-1900	TBL		of Liverpool		Dunmore	
5-10-1901	Cintra		of Arklow	coal	run down by Elt de Leo in Barrow	4 saved
2-12-1902	Frane Jack		To Arklow	wheat	Drumroe bank	4 saved
31-12-1902	Anne		of South Shields	wheat	Tramore Bay	crew saved
2-11-1907	Peri		Newport to Cork	coal	Dungarvan	
March 1909	Nestor				off Dunabrattan	
5-4-1909	Twin Brothers	Patrick Welan	Newport to Dungarvan	coal	Dungarvan Harbour	crew saved
5-5-1911	Christiania Davis		Cork to Lynton	fertiliser	Tramore	refloated
18-3-1911	Teaser	Thomas Hughes	Swansea to Killorglan	coal	Curagh, Ardmore	crew of three lost
12-12-1912	Marechaille de Noailles	Dominique Huet	Glasgow to New Caledonia	coke, coal, limestone, railway material	Mine Head	crew of 24 saved
19-12-1913	Nellie Fleming	Donovan	Bristol to Youghal		Ardmore	
27-6-1914	Jama				Church Bay	three saved
8-10-1915	Morning Star	Christopher	Cardiff to Cork	coal	Dunabrittain pier	four lost one saved
27-3-1916	Manchester Engineer				Torpedoed off Tramore	
31-12-1916	Montezuma	of Falmouth			2 miles from the Smalls	foundered with all aboard
31-1-1917	Motor launch				Ballinacouty Lighthouse	
11-3-1917	Folia				Torpedoed 4m ESE Ram head	
16-3-1917	Pencaer				8 SE Mine Head	bomb from submarine
29-3-1917	Lincolnshire				Torpedoed 8 miles off Hook	
13-4-1917	Bandon		Liverpool to Cork		Torpedoed 2.5m SW Mine Head	28 lost 4 crew saved
20-4-1917	Loch Eye				Dunmore	mined
11-5-1917	Barrister				7 m S of Mine Head	torpedoed
12-7-1917	George Milbourn				Dunmore	mined
1-8-1917	Karina				17m SSW Hook	Torpedoed
4-8-1917	UC 44	Kurt Tebbenjohanns			Mined off Dunmore	28 lost, captain survived

Date	Vessel	Master	Voyage	Cargo	Wreck location	Comment
29-8-1917	Cooroy				10m SW Hook,	Torpedoed
19-9-1917	Etal Manor				Torpedoed 7m from Hook	Master and five lost, 16 saved
30-3-1918	Lough Fisher				12 m SSE Helvick	gunfire from submarine
7-12-1919	St Margaret	David Kerr	Troon to Waterford	coal	Hook Head	12 lost
1920	Village Bell		of Arklow		Passage East	
27-11-1921	Industrial		to Milford		Churchtown	
Oct 1924	Ythan	Lemy	Newport to Dunabrittin	coal	founderd off Bonmahon	four saved
24-10-1924	Waft		Cardiff to Waterford	coal	Wrecked at Kilfarrissey	crew saved
May 1925	Lismore		Cork to Liverpool	cattle	Sank off Mine head	only one survived
1926	Cirilo Amoros	Haerrera	Spain	rice, fruit, china clay	Stradbally	30 rescued
July 1912	Baltic				Woodstown Strand	
1929	Mount Claing		Cardiff to New Ross		Churchtown	
1930	Bernard		from Bridgewater	bricks		three rescued
by LB						
1931	Berkdale	Evans			Buttermilk point	aground
12-2-1936	Nellie Fleming		Wales to Youghal		at sea off Waterford	
1942	Gozo				The Burrows at Tramore	ashore
1946	Happy Harry		Dublin to Cork	salt	Ballyhack	refloated
Feb 1947	Ary	Kolt	Port Talbot to Cork	coal	off Carnsore	14 lost, one washed ashore in boat
Feb 1958	John Buchan		Killybegs	trawler	300 yards from Dunmore East	five lost
1964	Jan Brons		Dutch		Ardnamult	all saved
19-2-1966	Schisein			trawler	hook Head	
6-12-1969	Kerick	Claude Maree	from Lorient	trawler	Coolum, Ballymacaw	nine escaped
15-1-1975	Michael		Poland to Letterkenny	coal	Tramore strand	broken for scrap
15-1-1975	Nestindor			trawler	Arthurstown	refloated
28-1-1975	Ocean Searcher			trawler	Tramore Strand	skipper drowned
13-10-1975	French Yacht		St Malo	yacht	Tramore Strand	refloated
7-6-1979	Business Girl		from Holyhead	yacht	Tramore Strand	refloated
13-1-1984	Anne Sophie			trawler	Ballymacart	8 rescued
8-8-1989	Adrupani		Dublin	yacht	Tramore strand	refloated
13-1-1989	Gladonia	D Pringle	Avonmouth to New Ross	grain	Tramore strand	lightened and refloated
31-10-1991	Matrishia				Bonmahon	refloated
28-3-1995	Trawler			Trawler	Rathmoylan cove	
5-2-1996	Jenalisa			Trawler	off Dunmore East	

CHRONOLOGICAL WEXFORD LIST

This Wexford list is derived from several sources. Initially, a list of Wexford shipwrecks was kept by William Powell a local Lloyds agent. It was first published in 1846 in the Independent, Wexford. The list was republished in the Wexford Guardian on 19-7-1851 in an item supporting their campaign for a harbour of refuge at Rosslare. Then a list was assembled by Richard Roche and Tom Williams and published by Roche in Tales of the Wexford coast. Both have been augmented by addition of material from the 1700s & 1800s. Wicklow and foreign material was removed for clarity and missing dates added where known. It is clear from records that not all the shipping casualties in this list were total losses. Many of the vessels mentioned were recorded in the Wexford List printed in Volume one. Despite this huge list the cross checking of different sources continues to yield more shipwreck accounts and so it must be concluded that a substantial number remain to be added. The list from the Wexford newspaper presents somewhat of a mystery as the large number designated pre 1852 do not seem to come up in the data from Lloyds. This remains an enigma. Some of the information from the Roche - Williams list is from folklore and thus can be inaccurate though substantially true. The amount of information varies according to the source. Generally Lloyds List provided the captain's name, voyage and the date of report is about three days after the loss.

Date	Ship Name	Home port or Captain	Voyage	Cargo	Wreck Location	Comment
10-1-1549	Unnamed		Spain to Limerick	wine	Off Wexford	Ship plundered
12-1549	Turtledove		Spain to Antwerp	silver plate	Fethard	few lost
3-4-1643	Loves Increase	Moody	Duncannon to Dublin	supplies	Duncannon	all lost
23-7-1643	Hopewell		Dublin to Duncannon	troops	Saltees	
26-1-1645	Great Lewis		siege of Duncannon fort	warship	off Hook	300 lost
11-10-1649	Unnamed				Wexford	150 lost Hoares hist.
10-1649	Unnamed				Wexford	
6-12-1670	Unnamed				Off Wexford	
15-12-1694	HMS Talbot	Tollat	chasing privateers	warship	Glasgorman bank	
1717	Unnamed				Carne	
	Unnamed				off Wexford	
8-1-1725	30 ships				Greenore pt. to Wexford	report Dublin Journal
9-1743	Greyhound	Liverpool	Liverpool to Guinea	bale goods	Wexford	
29-11-1743	Prince Augusta				Wexford	
20-3-1749	Limington	Scut	London to Dublin		Wexford	
1753	Unnamed					
17-10-1757	St Nicholas			prize ship	Wexford	captured
25-7-1767	Speedwell	Murphy	Seville to Dublin		Wexford	
27-1-1761	King of Prussia	Faulkner	San Sebastian to Isle of Man		Fethard	

CHRONOLOGICAL WEXFORD LIST

Date	Ship Name	Home port or Captain	Voyage	Cargo	Wreck Location	Comment
20-10-1761	Adventure	Davis	Chester to Bristol		Wexford	
29-12-1761	King of Prussia	Duncan	Barbados to Belfast		Wexford	
1762	Prussia				Carnsore	
29-1-1762	Delight	Adam	Bordeaux to Dublin		Wexford	
29-1-1762	Three Friends	Maxwell	Senegal to Liverpool		Wexford	
1762	Fishing fleet				Off Wexford	70 lost
20-1-1764	Nancy	Hanson	Liverpool to Wexford			
13-4-1764	The McDowell	Wallage	Maryland to Glasgow	Tobacco	Tuskar	
1764	Unnamed				Co Wexford	Salvage forgiven by R.Paliser
22-1-1765	seven ships unnamed				Off Wexford	report of Capt. Curran
1765	Unnamed				Off Wexford	
1765	Unnamed				off Wexford	
18-2-1766	Welcome	Crosstead	Virginia to Whitehaven	Rum & Tobacco	Castle Talbot	
24-11-1766	Yawl				Wexford	
4-3-1766	Unnamed		Wexford to Cork	coal	Wexford bay	all lost
10-3-1766	Providence	Staples	Lynn to Liverpool		off Wexford	
24-2-1766	Welcome	Crosswhite	Virginia to Whitehaven	tobacco	Wexford	
30-11-1767	Recovery	Weatherhead		Baggage	Wexford	
8-3-1768	Diligence		Liverpool to Boston		near Wexford	
13-2-1768	Exchange			wine & Brandy	Near Wexford	
18-12-1768	Caravile				Blackwater bank	
25-7-1769	Nancy	of Liverpool		tar, cotton	Saltees	
29-8-1769	Favourite	Bastable	Bristol to Cork	Mahogany	Duncannon	
18-10-1771	Hibernia		Riga to Dublin		Wexford	
24-3-1771	Commerce		London to Dublin		Wexford	
20-12-1771	New Blessing	Walth			Wexford	
20-12-1771	Fortune	Byrne			Wexford	
20-12-1771	John	Bell	Oporto to Dublin		Wexford	
20-12-1771	Vine	Whittle	Liverpool to Oporto		Wexford	
12-11-1773	Mary & Sally	Dalling	Malaga to Dublin		Wexford	
9-9-1774	Dolphin	Kerr	Glasgow to Limerick		Wexford	
23-3-1771	Commerce		off Cardigan		Blackwater hill	
13-2-1781	Zee Fortune			tobacco	Wexford	
6-2-1781	New Judith		Newry to Cork			
6-2-1781	Henry & Maria			prize	Wexford	captured by Stormont
20-4-1781	Mary	Snowball	St Kitts to London		Wexford	
8-3-1782	Goede Vrienden		Ostend to Newry		Wexford	
29-1-1784	St Barbara	De Silva	Lisbon to Dublin	fruit & cork	Bank off Wexford	
1784	Unnamed		to Duncannon	turf	Blackwater bank	all lost
1784	Mayflower			coal	off Fort	3 lost
11-7-1784	Frances & Mary		off Wexford	coal	Ballytrent	expected to be refloated
9-3-1787	Ross	Capt. Mortimer		Revenue Cutter	Between Black rock and Little Saltee	Goods ashore from Carne to Ballyteigue

CHRONOLOGICAL WEXFORD LIST

Date	Ship Name	Home port or Captain	Voyage	Cargo	Wreck Location	Comment
25-9-1787	Unnamed			Timber	Duncannon	
12-1787	Recovery			Art treasures	Off Wexford	
2-2-1790	Jane	Power	Woodbridge to London			
31-3-1790	Minerva		London to Greenock	porter	near Wexford	
26-4-1791	Liberty		Cork to Greenock		Wexford	
20-1-1791	Little Neptune	Queripel	St Domingo to Dunkirk		Kilmore	
22-11-1793	Industry		Bristol to Dublin		near Wexford	
4-3-1794	Adventure	Diamond	from Chepstowe			
9-12-1794	Aurora	Richardson			Saltees	
2-12-1794	Eldest Daughter	Birch	Danzig to Bristol		near Wexford	
1796	Euphrasia				Near Wexford	
29-1-1799	Lavinia		Oporto to Belfast		Near Wexford	
19-2-1799	Little		Falmouth to London		Wexford	
7-3-1799	Peace & Plenty	Hunter	Dundee to Dublin		Near Wexford	
22-3-1799	Robert & Jean	Allison	St Michael's to Dublin		off Saltees	
6-4-1800	North Star	Binchsman			Wexford	
3-2-1801	Brilliant				Wexford	
14-8-1801	Friendship		Dublin to Cork		Wexford	
7-1-1803	Mona	Foulkes	Jamaica to Liverpool	silver dollars	Bonmahon	
27-12-1803	Peggy	Campbell	Greenock		Wexford	
30-12-1803	Hector	Davis	Milford		Wexford	
1-4-1803	Nymph	Blight	Lisbon to Cork		Saltees	
15-5-1803	Daphne	Forster	Liverpool to Quebec		Wexford	
23-12-1803	Tar	Crisp	Liverpool to London		Wexford	
1803	Unnamed				Between Kilmore and Hook	many
6-11-1804	Grezzie	McKinlay	Liverpool to Tralee		Tuskar	
9-11-1804	Joseph & Mary Ann	Cornith	Poole to Liverpool		Wexford	
14-11-1804	Swan	Bell	Liverpool to Milford		off Saltees	all lost
1804	Polly & Mary		Glasgow to Liverpool		Rosslare	
1805					Ballyteigue bay	many
15-2-1805	Elizabeth		Wexford to Dublin		Wexford	
15-2-1805	Vigilance	Harris	Wexford to Dublin		Wexford	
30-4-1805	Hope	Jennys	Liverpool to St Leuchars		Wexford banks	
24-10-1805	Betsey	Buffet	Dartmouth		Wexford	
5-11-1805	Thomas & Mary	Gibson	from Bristol		Wexford	
1806	Brilliant Star			wheat	Ballyteigue beach	many
4-3-1806	Margaret & Mary	Dale	Africa to Liverpool		Wexford	
11-2-1806	George & Ann	Stephens	Liverpool to Waterford		Bonmahon	
18-11-1806	Favourite	Allen	Liverpool to West Indies		Greenore	
16-3-1806	Jane	Parker	Workington to Cork		Wexford	
25-3-1806	Swallow		Limerick to Liverpool		Wexford	
31-7-1806	Hope	Cuffe	Oporto to Wexford		Wexford banks	
18-121807	Liberty		Wexford to Dublin		Wexford	
1-1-1807	Industry	Cooper	Glasgow to Waterford		Wexford	
6-9-1807	Industry	Gutherie	Newfoundland to Cork		Wexford	

Date	Ship Name	Home port or Captain	Voyage	Cargo	Wreck Location	Comment
9-10-1807	Concordia		Leghorn		Saltees	
23-10-1807	Abeona	Allen	Liverpool to Charleston		Wexford	
3-11-1807	John		Wexford		Wexford	
20-1-1808	Mary Anne		Kinsale to Dublin	Potatoes	Wexford	
20-1-1808	Catherine Greene		Kinsale to Dublin	Potatoes	Wexford	
1-4-1808	Ann	Williams	Conway to Neath	copper ore	Wexford	
19-5-1809	Minerva	Rookin	Youghal to Whitehaven		Great Saltee	
29-1-1809	Foxwell	Clapp	Dominica to London	Sugar, rum	Bannow bar	
10-1-1809	Francis	Burke	Whitehaven		Wexford	
16-11-1809	Peter	James	Dublin to Bristol		Wexford	
10-12-1809	Elizabeth		Cardigan to Liverpool		Wexford	
30-3-1809	Chance	Boyle	Dublin to Wexford		Wexford	
29-12-1809	Barbara & Mary		Liverpool to Derry			
21-11-1810	Fanny	Griffin	Dublin to Cork		Tara Hill	
25-3-1810	Sally	Morris			Wexford	
25-3-1810	Havant	Cooper	Arundel to Plymouth		Wexford	
8-4-1810	Hammond	Pinder	Whitehaven to Ireland	coal	Tuskar	
2-11-1810	James & William	Sinnot	Arklow to Dublin		Wexford	
16-11-1810	Friendship	Toole			Wexford	
16-11-1810	James		Liverpool to Limerick		Duncannon	
25-12-1811	Aimwell		Lisbon to Clyde		Wexford	
31-1-1811	Little George		Greenock to Trinidad		Wexford	
26-2-1811	Leopard	Clarke	Waterford to Oporto		Duncannon	
25-11-1811	Mary	Power	Drogheda to St Ubes		Kilmore	
1811						
25-9-1811	Rattler			cattle	In Channel	
20-3-1812	Wellwood		Brazil to Liverpool		Off Wexford	
6-4-1812	Welland	Liverpool			Holdens Bed	
10-5-1812	Irlam			General & troops	Near Saltees	
12-5-1812	Kitty				Tuskar	
7-12-1812	Emanuel	Graham	London to Dundalk		Carne	
27-1-1812	Peace	Edmonson	Swansea to Dublin		Wexford	
11-12-1812	Ann	Roach	Bristol to Dublin		Ballyneshar	
9-2-1813	Third Mary	McAllister	London to Cork	Butter	Wexford	
1813						
1-1813	Star			barley /butter	Ballyhealy	
5-2-1813	Mary	Dumbarton		butter & pork	Ballyhealy	
1-4-1813	Harmony	Williams	from Exeter	ballast	Rostoonstown	
1-4-1813	Sophia		for Liverpool			
10-1-1814	Frederick			china clay	Carne	
10-1-1814	Ruby			ballast	Carne	
12-1-1814	Soho			provisions	Ballyneskar	
17-1-1814	Sokal		Liverpool to Havana	crockery	Ballyneskar	20 saved
14-6-1814	Jane	Shaw	Havana to Glasgow	sugar & coffee	Carne	
26-11-1814	Thorne	Ludlow	Chester to London	Muskets	Sandeel bay	
12-12-1814	Dove	Phelan	Cork to London	pork	Hook	cargo saved
3-12-1814	Conception				Ballyneskar	

Date	Ship Name	Home port or Captain	Voyage	Cargo	Wreck Location	Comment
21-2-1815	Will				Carne	
23-10-1815	Peace	Tregarthen	Scilly to Waterford		Wexford	
27-10-1815	George Frederick		Saltcoates to Dublin	coal	Wexford	
20-1-1816	Alert		San Domingo to Portsmouth		Wexford	
15-1-1816	Anne	Connolly	Wexford to Liverpool		Ravenglass	
1816	Demara				Off Wexford	
23-12-1816	Elizabeth		London to Cork		Wexford	
3-3-1816	Indian Lass		Marienham to Liverpool	cotton wool	Carne	
10-4-1816	Fair Reaper		Dublin to Cork	general	Blackwater bank	
27-8-1817	George Ponsonby	Hill	Wexford to Milford		Greenore	
1818	William	Weymouth			Off Wexford	
9-1-1818	Frances	Waldron		grain	Saltees	
22-2-1818	George	Doyle	Liverpool to Waterford		Wexford	
18-4-1818	Caledonia	Hingstone	Liverpool to Prince Edward island	ballast	Ballyteigue	
18-7-1818	Sprightly	Keal	Liverpool to Kinsale		Wexford Bank	
3-4-1818	Shellegh	Keale			Wexford	
11-12-1818	Union	Davy	Belfast to London		Wexford	
20-2-1818	William			grain	carne	
4-4-1818	Shillelagh			general	Wexford bar	
5-12-1818	King George		Clonakilty to Liverpool	wheat	Saltees	
9-4-1818	Caledonia			ballast	Ballyteigue	
11-4-1818	Shitelack	Steele	London to Belfast	tea, wine, sugar	Wexford bar	
11-12-1818	Union	Davy	Bideford to Waterford		Wexford river	
12-12-1818	Unknown	collier			Wexford	
16-2-1819	Anne	Barmouth	London to Dublin	tea, sugar, wine, spice	St Patrick's Bridge	
13-6-1819	Earl of Leicester	Steele	Milford to Waterford		Hook	
17-1-1819	Alice	Leonard	Kinsale to Dublin		Duncannon	
16-12-1819	Demerera			coffee and gold	Keeraghs	
27-3-1820	Albion	Thompson	Charleston to Liverpool		Ballyteigue	
19-6-1820	Mary	McLachan	Gibraltar	general cargo	10 m SE Tuskar	
17-11-1820	Robert Stewart	Bibby	Wexford to Liverpool		Kockbeggar	
26-11-1820	Anne		Liverpool to Cork		Rosslare	
15-12-1820	Coquette	Taylor	Liverpool to Africa		Wexford	
12-6-1821	Peggy & Jenny		Galway to Waterford		Saltees	
1-11-1821	Britannia	Hancock	Oporto to Liverpool		Ballyteigue	
6-3-1821	Susannah	Graham	Palermo to Dublin		Carne	
20-4-1822	Esther	Colshead	Charlestown to Liverpool	Cotton & Rice	Hook	
24-10-1822	Hero	Hudson	New Orleans to Liverpool	Cotton	Forlorn point	
30-10-1822	Victory		Swansea to Dungarvan		Carne	
1-1-1822	Betsey & Mary	Kingston	Cork to Glasgow		South Bay	
11-10-1822	London Packet	Aspell	Newfoundland to Dublin		Cullenstown	
19-3-1822	Lady Warren	Hump	Oporto to Dublin	wine & fruit	Ballyteigue	
21-4-1822	Sandwich	Stubbles	Waterford to Milford		Hook	
14-2-1823	Susannah	Evans	Waterford to Chichester		Churchtown	

Date	Ship Name	Home port or Captain	Voyage	Cargo	Wreck Location	Comment
22-12-1824	Rebecca	Alexander	Glasgow to Jamaica		Blackwater bank	
26-1-1824	Dorethea	Clooney	Savannah to Liverpool		Bonmahon	
19-4-1824	Lively Kate				off Saltees	
14-6-1824	Elizabeth		Cork to Liverpool		off Tuskar	
5-7-1824	Margareth		Glasgow to Dunmore		Rush bank	
15-9-1824	Generous Planter		St Johns to Liverpool		Kilmore	
9-6-1824	unknown				Courtown	
1-11-1825	Union		Ayr to Waterford		Wexford bay	
1-12-1825	Sam				Tacumshane	
1-12-1825	Favourite				Tacumshane	
1-12-1825	Macedonia				Tacumshane	
1-12-1825	Ann				Tacumshane	
1825	Mary & Eliza				off Wexford	
6-11-1825	Mary	Chivers	Stakisco to Waterford		Moneyweights Bank	
20-9-1825	Fame	Rennie	Mirimichi to Wexford		North bay	
16-9-1825	Robert	Crowe	Bangor to Newcastle		Tuskar	
29-8-1826	Progress	Harper	Nipsignit To Dublin		Saltees	
19-11-1826	Flora	Parle	Liverpool to Wexford		Wexford	
29-8-1826	Progress	Harper			Wexford	
28-10-1827	Elizabeth				Ballymoney	
1827	Bolt	of Wexford			Wexford	
1827	Clio	of Exeter			off Wexford	
1828	Venus	of Glasgow			off Wexford	
1828	Fanny				Wexford Bar	
1828	Fairfield	of Liverpool			Wexford	
1829	Thomas Farrell	of Wexford			Rosslare	
24-4-1829	Two Brothers				Banks off Wexford	
22-10-1830	Ranger	Holt	Marseilles to Liverpool		Ballyteigue	
1830	Sarah Lynn				Greenore	
26-11-1831	St Patrick	W.E Forrest	Dublin to Waterford	Passengers	Doornogue Pt Hook	
2-12-1831	Aid	Stubb			Blackwater Bank	
2-12-1831	Horatio	Gotham	Liverpool to Newfoundland		Cahore	
12-1831	Vulcan			iron	Tacumshane	
12-1831	Friends				Carne	
16-12-1831	La Bonne Julia			oil & fish	Bannow	
5-2-1832	Crown			salt	Blackwater bank	
4-12-1832	Unknown			iron	-	
7-10-1832	Eliza & Ann		Waterford to Larne	wheat	Hook	crew lost
13-4-1832	Hawk	Capt. McEntire	Belfast		Blackwater bank	
22-11-1832	Malta		Mirimichi to Wexford		Wexford Bar	
29-6-1833	Flora		Liverpool to St John's	ballast	Long Bank	15 saved
9-10-1833	Zephyr		from London	general	Tuskar	all lost
12-1833	William Donald		Liverpool to Havanna	salt	Blackwater Bank	
8-12-1833	Michael Wickham		Wexford to Dublin	malt	Wexford bar	
19-12-1833	Faythe Fishing Fleet	Faythe		fishing	Curracloe	

CHRONOLOGICAL WEXFORD LIST

Date	Ship Name	Home port or Captain	Voyage	Cargo	Wreck Location	Comment
21-12-1833	Water Witch	Stacy	Bristol to Waterford	cotton	St Patrick's bridge	7 lost 36 saved
23-1-1834	Subernacaddie		Brazil to Liverpool	cotton, wool, hides	Crossfarnogue	
30-1-1834	Argyle		West Indies to Dublin	sugar &coffee	Blackwater Bank	
1-1834	Mary Ann		from Tenby	coal	Curracloe	3
14-6-1834	St Patrick		from Dungarvan		Rostoonstown	3
17-3-1835	Unknown		fort to Wexford	passengers	Wexford Harbour	12 lost
25-11-1835	Subnacadie	Murphy	from Quebec	timber	South Bay	
25-11-1835	Brig		from Spain	passengers	Slade	
1835	Sarah				near Wexford	
1835	Hawk				Wexford bar	
1835	Cordelia				Hook	
1835	Arthur Jones				off Wexford	
5-5-1835	Merchant			mahogany	Blackwater bank	
16-5-1835	Tagus		From Liverpool	salt	Tuskar	
9-1835	Frances			oil	Kilmore	
3-11-1835	Anna Maria		From Liverpool	coal & iron	Blackwater bank	
3-11-1835	Prince Ferdinand		Liverpool to Leghorn	boilers	Blackwater bank	
24-11-1835	Brunette		Cardiff - Liverpool	iron	Rostoonstown	6 lost
24-11-1835	Auley		from Jersey	apples	Kilmore	
25-11-1835	Cordelia	Capt. Bragg	Spain to Cardiff	ballast	Hook	one lost
26-11-1835	Arthur Jones		from London	fruit	Carnsore	3 lost
1836	unknown			logwood	Off Kilmore	
30-1-1836	Intrinsic		Rosslare fort to Wexford		Wexford Harbour	
19-1-1837	Sultana		to England	Cotton Wool	Long Bank	
15-1-1837	James Hadden	Beatty	Campeachy to Liverpool		Ballyteigue	
15-1-1837	Perseverance	Beatty	Liverpool to Wexford		Blackwater	
5-2-1837	Maria		Cape to Dublin	Wine & Silk	Bar o Lough	
6-2-1837	Mary		to Dublin	salt	Kilmore	
6-3-1837	Betsey		Catania to Glasgow		Ballyteigue	
6-2-1837	Mary & Betsey		to Dublin		Kilmore	
7-2-1837	Spanish Packet				Black Rock	
7-2-1837	Betsey Millar		from Sicily	Fruit & Sulphur	Bar O Lough	
7-2-1837	unknown			apples	Bar O Lough	
13-2-1837	William Whitty				Wexford harbour	
13-2-1837	Pearl				Wexford harbour	
10-2-1837	Spanish Packet	Wooton	Genoa to Liverpool		Black Rock	
13-2-1837	Mary				Wexford harbour	
13-2-1837	George				Wexford harbour	
13-2-1837	The Rose Bank				Wexford harbour	
1to4-1837	Mexico				Tuskar	
1to4 1837	Bristol				Tuskar	
1to4 1837	Jane				Tuskar	
15-2-1837	Glasgow		Liverpool to New York	Passengers & wheat	Barrels	
17-12-1837	Molly Moore				Tacumshane	
15-2-1837	Water Witch		Liverpool to Barbados	general	Blackwater bank	

Date	Ship Name	Home port or Captain	Voyage	Cargo	Wreck Location	Comment
18-1-1838	Water Witch			timber, Geneva & turpentine	Blackwater bank	
28-11-1838	Water Witch	Glasgow	to Leghorn	coal & bale goods	Carnsore	
29-11-1838	St Patrick		from Liverpool		Hook	4 drowned
21-2-1838	Arran		Wexford to Gloucester		Hook	
2-1838	Orissa		Glasgow to Bristol		Wexford coast	
2-1838	Kingston		Plymouth to Liverpool		Wexford coast	
24-2-1838	Paragon		Liverpool / Pernambuco	general	North Bay	
28-2-1838	Anne & Elisabeth				Carnsore	
11-6-1838	Aedicia	Johns	Fethard to Llanelly		Wexford Harbour	
29-11-1838	Belina		Strangford to Quebec		Ballyteigue	
28-11-1838	Thistle		St Andrews to Liverpool		Kilmore	
28-11-1838	Ariadne	Belfast			Tuskar	
31-1-1839	Thistle		coastal	ballast	South bay	
2-1839	Alert	Duggan	Cardiff to Waterford		1/2 mile from Hook	
25-11-1838	Ariadne		Quebec to Belfast	timber	Tuskar	
29-11-1838	Robert Noble		from Cork		Carnafarraige	
29-11-1838	Frances				Small Saltee	4 lost
29-11-1838	Lord Ebrington				Ballyteigue	
1-1839	Union		Chepstow to Wexford		Wexford bar	
1-2-1839	Phoenix	Galway		copper ore	Bonmahon	
21-2-1839	Alert		Cardiff to Wexford		Wexford	crew lost
11-3-1839	Elizabeth & Alidia		Amsterdam to Liverpool		Wexford harbour	
8-9-1839	Brenton	Haliburton	Halifax to Liverpool		Bannow	
9-1839	Felix Pensamiento		St Ubes to Sligo		Wexford harbour	
9-1839	unknown				Kilmore	
1840	Edniada				Wexford Bar	
13-11-1840	Mary				Banks off Wexford	
1-1840	Francis		Cork to Liverpool	grain	Little Saltee	
1-1840	Six Brothers		Cork to Newport		Off Wexford coast	
1-1840	Elisa & Abbey		Wellington /Liverpool	Turpentine	Ballyteigue	
8-2-1840	Urania	Malta			Saltees	
14-2-1840	Eagle		Yarmouth to Wexford		Wexford bar	
5-2-1840	Mercury		from Wexford		Moriscastle	
18-2-1840	Margurite		Bangor to New Ross	slates		
3-1840	Belina		Quebec to North	timber	Kilmore	
2-12-1840	Perthshire				Codling	
16-10-1841	Theseus	Renell	St John's		Tacumshane	
28-8-1841	Palace	London			N of Wexford	
22-1-1842	Honor		Messina / Liverpool	fruit	Tacumshane	
26-1-1842	Sarah		Bristol /Fethard	timber	Ballyhealy	
26-1-1842	Urania	Marengo	Malta to Liverpool		Saltees	
9-11-1842	New Expedition		Portmadoc to Wexford	slates	Blackwater Bank	
12-1842	Vermont		Savannah to Liverpool	Cotton Wool	Ballyteigue	
24-12-1842	Alfred			Brandy	Kilmore	
26-1-1843	Urania		Malta to Liverpool	wheat	Great Saltee	6 of 17 lost

CHRONOLOGICAL WEXFORD LIST

Date	Ship Name	Home port or Captain	Voyage	Cargo	Wreck Location	Comment
26-1-1843	Commerce				South bay	
25-12-1843	Salvatore		Liverpool to Naples	general	Blackwater Bank	3 0f 8 lost
13-1-1843	Santon 11		Calcutta to Liverpool	Sugar rice salt	Ballyteigue	4 lost
11-1843	Rover		Arklow to Swansea		-	
1-12-1843	Zeno		Liverpool to Jamaica	general	Blackwater bank	
2-12-1843	Unknown			wine	-	
5-12-1843	Minerva		Glasgow to Bombay		Blackwater bank	
28-12-1843	Royal Albert		Liverpool to Ichiboe		Blackwater Bank	towed to shore by fishermen
8-3-1844	Georgia		Liverpool to Palermo	general	Carnsore	
17-3-1844	Georgianna		Liverpool / Pernambuco	general	Blackwater bank	12 lost
18-3-1844	Caroline				Blackwater bank	13 lost
12-1-1844	James Mathieson		Liverpool / Hong Kong		Blackwater bank	
12-1844	Victory		Chepstow		Off Wexford coast	
1-1845	Jager		L /Calcutta		Off Wexford Coast	
2-1845	Burley		L /Africa		Carnsore	
21-2-1846	Jacob Pennell	Martin	Mobile to Liverpool		Tacumshane	
22-2-1846	Iride				Blackwater bank	
23-1-1847	Macao		New York to Cork		Blackwater bank	
26-1-1847	Niobe				Keeraghs	
27-1-1847	Tribune				Tacumshane	
13-12-1848	Emma			coal	Hook	
18-12-1848	Republic				Blackwater bank	
19-4-1849	Royal Albert		L/ Ichiboe		Blackwater bank	
1-4-1849	Prince Albert		Liverpool to Ichiboe	ballast	Blackwater bank	
28-1-1849	Trio				Splaugh rock	
22-10-1849	Repealer				Blackwater bank	
12-1-1850	Geisler Adolph		Koenigsberg / L		Ballygeary	
12-1-1850	Hottingeur		L to New York		Blackwater bank	
13-1-1850	Adile				Tacumshane	
30-1-1850	Fairfax		Sierra Leone to Liverpool		Ballyteigue	
1-2-1850	Horatio		Alexandria / Dublin		Kilmore	
19-2-1850	Adoline				Curracloe	
1-4-1850	John R Skiddy		from New York		Cahore	430 saved??
3-4-1850	Eliza Taylor				Ballygeary	
19-11-1850	Adeline		To America		Blackwater bank	
19-11-1850	Strabane				Curracloe	
1851	Ann		Plymouth To Waterford		north Bay	
16-1-1851	Grace		Alexandria To Preston		St Patrick's Bridge	
3-5-1851	Lief Zaritza		Lima to L		St Patrick's Bridge	
13-7-1851	Witch		Bristol to Cork		Tuskar	
4-10-1852	Therese	Venice			Tuskar	
pre 1852	Unknown				Splaugh Rock	
pre 1852	unknown				Carnsore	
pre 1852	Shamrock				Morris Castle	
pre 1852	Veloz				Ballyhealy	
pre 1852	Unknown				Ballyhire	

Date	Ship Name	Home port or Captain	Voyage	Cargo	Wreck Location	Comment
pre 1852	Unknown				Ballyhire	
pre 1852	Unknown				Ballyhire	
pre 1852	Unknown				Ballyvaloo	
pre 1852	Unknown				Long Bank	
pre 1852	L'Aventeen				Ballygeary	
pre 1852	Maria				Kilmore	
pre 1852	Fly				St Patrick's Bridge	
pre 1852	L'Active				Tacumshane	
pre 1852	Unknown			Coffee & Sugar	Tacumshane	
pre 1852	St James			cotton	Kilmore	
pre 1852	Morca			wheat	Kilmore	
pre 1852	Rambler			General	Tacumshane	
pre 1852	Amelia			Indian corn	Bannow	
pre 1852	Britannia			general	Ballyhealy	
pre 1852	Invincible			Indian corn	Cullenstown	
pre 1852	Seagull			wheat	Tacunshane	
pre 1852	Gazelle			timber	Baninoulart	
pre 1852	Ottoelle			flour	Ballintrent	
pre 1852	Ann			general	Ballyhealy	
pre 1852	Albiona			general	Blackwater bank	
pre 1852	Fiora			sugar	Blackwater bank	
pre 1852	Hawk		to Liverpool	grain	Blackwater bank	
pre 1852	Coqueta			sugar	Blackwater bank	
pre 1852	Twlight			potash	north Bay	
pre 1852	Hunter			general	North banks	
pre 1852	Peggy			general	North bay	
pre 1852	Rochester			passengers	Blackwater bank	
pre 1852	Unknown		to Wexford	timber	Wexford bar	
pre 1852	General Moore			coal	Wexford bar	
pre 1852	Wild Irish Girl			general	Blackwater bank	
pre 1852	Alcutta			general	Blackwater bank	
pre 1852	Swallow			grain	South bay	
pre 1852	Hector			ballast	Wexford bar	
pre 1852	Unknown			ballast	South bay	
pre 1852	Maria			coal	South bay	
pre 1852	Thomas Farrell			timber	South bay	
24-1-1837	Subernacaddie			Timber	South Bay	
pre 1852	unknown			grain	Wexford bar	
pre 1852	Fame			timber	North bay	
pre 1852	Fame			coal	Long Bank	
pre 1852	Brothers			grain	South bay	
pre 1852	Sea Flower			grain	Raven Pt.	
pre 1852	Edward			grain	Raven Pt.	
pre 1852	Chance			coal	Wexford bar	
pre 1852	unknown			grain	South bay	
pre 1852	Clonmel			general	Long Bank	
pre 1852	Shelmalier			timber	South bay	

CHRONOLOGICAL WEXFORD LIST

Date	Ship Name	Home port or Captain	Voyage	Cargo	Wreck Location	Comment
pre 1852	Star			coal	South bay	
pre 1852	Ellen			coal	Wexford bay	
pre 1852	unknown			general	Off Tuskar	
pre 1852	Sally			ballast	Tacunshane	
pre 1852	Ponsonby			cattle	South bay	
pre 1852	unknown			lumber	South bay	
pre 1852	Esther			grain	Wexford Bar	
pre 1852	unknown			-	Off Tuskar	
pre 1852	Sally			general	Carne	
pre 1852	brothers			salt	Tuskar	
pre 1852	Margery & Mary			general	Whilkeen Rock	
pre 1852	Wellwood			general	Long Rock	
pre 1852	Rebecca			general	Nr saltees	
pre 1852	unknown			wine	Splaugh Rock	
pre 1852	Victorine		to Liverpool	wine	Tacumshane	
pre 1852	Unknown			lumber	Splaugh Rock	
pre 1852	Newfriendship			grain	South bay	
pre 1852	Maid of the Mill			sulphur	Ballyteigue Beach	
pre 1852	Waldo			earthenware	Ballyhealy	
pre 1852	mary			flour & Malt	Tuskar	
pre 1852	unknown			timber	Bannow	
pre 1852	unknown			grain	Ballyteigue Beach	
pre 1852	Belisle			timber	Ballyteigue Beach	
pre 1852	unknown		to Liverpool	grain	Slatees	
pre 1852	Prince of Wales			Pipeclay	Kilmore	
pre 1852	Thomas Peel			Grain potash	Tacumshane	
pre 1852	unknown			potatoes	Saltees	
pre 1852	Lively Kate		Coastal	grain	Saltees	-
pre 1852	Hero			Cotton wool	Kilmore	
pre 1852	Royal George			grain	Saltees	
pre 1852	Progress			timber	Saltees	
pre 1852	Surrey			fruit	Ballyteigue	
pre 1852	Ecord			Ballast	Ballyteigue	
pre 1852	Britannia			fruit	Ballyteigue	
pre 1852	Unknown			Fruit	Ballyteigue	
pre 1852	James Hadden			Logwood	Ballyteigue	
pre 1852	Britannia			Coal	South Bay	
pre 1852	Unknown		to England	Wine & brandy	St Patrick's Bridge	
pre 1852	Aimwell			Fruit	Kilmore	
pre 1852	Unknown		to Belfast	Barilla	-	
pre 1852	Prince Royal			Madder root	Ballyteigue	
pre 1852	Sam			General	Rostoonstown	
pre 1852	Erin			iron	Splaugh Rock	
pre 1852	Favourite			iron	Rostoonstown	
pre 1852	Neptune			Wine cotton wool	Saltees	
pre 1852	Eliza			copper ore	North Bay	
pre 1852	Unknown			iron	?	

Date	Ship Name	Home port or Captain	Voyage	Cargo	Wreck Location	Comment
pre 1852	Tiger			Sugar	Black Rock	26 lost
pre 1852	Argo			Barilla	Ballyteigue	
pre 1852	Unknown			oil fish	Bannow	
pre 1852	Margaret			timber	Ballyteigue	
pre 1852	Unknown			cola	Saltees	
pre 1852	America		to Liverpool	Cotton Wool	Saltees	
pre 1852	Unknown			General	Wexford bar	
pre 1852	John p Esther			malt	South bay	10 lost
pre 1852	Marchioness Wellesley			General	Wexford Bar	
pre 1852	Unknown			Barilla	Carne	
pre 1852	John P Samuel			Potatoes	South bay	
pre 1852	Native			coal	Wexford Bar	
pre 1852	Tubbermurray			coal	Splaugh Rock	
pre 1852	Unknown		to Liverpool	beans	Tacumshane	8 lost
pre 1852	Jeager			General	Blackwater bank	
pre 1852	Juliana			Cotton Wool	Long Bank	
pre 1852	Indian Chief			General	Blackwater bank	
pre 1852	Betsey			Ballast	Blackwater bank	9 lost
pre 1852	Baron Ardrossan			Copper ore	Blackwater bank	4 lost
pre 1852	Huldah			Grain	Blackwater bank	
pre 1852	Arnan			General	Blackwater bank	
pre 1852	-			steam engines	Blackwater bank	
pre 1852	Margaret			Iron ore	Blackwater bank	
pre 1852	Margaret			coal	Blackwater bank	
pre 1852	Margaret			lumber	Blackwater bank	
pre 1852	Barrack			timber	Blackwater bank	
pre 1852	Neptune			grain	Blackwater bank	
pre 1852	Perseverance			grain	Blackwater bank	
pre 1852	Mercury			coal	Blackwater bank	
pre 1852	Blackbird			Grain 7 bale goods	Blackwater bank	
pre 1852	Sprightly			salt	Blackwater bank	
pre 1852	Laura			ballast	Blackwater bank	
pre 1852	-			salt	Blackwater bank	
pre 1852	Venus			general	Blackwater bank	
pre 1852	Shilmalier			timber	Long bank	
pre 1852	Vine			malt	Ballyhealy	
pre 1852	Hyacinth			coal & bale goods	Blackwater bank	
pre 1852	Slaney			timber	Wexford bar	
pre 1852	Elizabeth			general	Kerraghs	
pre 1852	Primrose Hill				Ballyhealy	
1852	Curliana			iron ore	South bay	
8-1-1852	Columbia		New Orleans to Liverpool	cotton & maize	Hook	
8-1-1852	Caroline		New Orleans to Liverpool	Indian corn	Hook	
11-1- 1852	Regalia		From Jersey	barley	Ballyhealy	

CHRONOLOGICAL WEXFORD LIST

Date	Ship Name	Home port or Captain	Voyage	Cargo	Wreck Location	Comment
27-2-1852	Szarpey		from Austria	flour	Bannow bay	
18-9-1852	Burthpoer		Liverpool to New York	Emigrants	Long bank	
4-10-1852	Theresa			Indian corn	Tuskar	
29-12-1852	-			Indian corn	St Patrick's bridge	
9-1853	Victory				off Wexford Coast	
22-10-1853	Tancred				Kilmore	
1854	Niagara			Emigrants	Ballyteigue	
1854	Maria				Hook	All the crew were named Carr
15-1-1854	Chattenochee		Liverpool to Savannah	salt	Carrig rocks	
18-1-1854	James Calder		New Orleans to Liverpool	cotton & Maize	Ballyteigue bay	
11-11-1854	Greenville	Young	Fleetwood to Dalhousie		Hook	
11-1854	James			coal	Tacumshane	
11-1-1855	Holyhock		St Johns to Dublin		Carne	
18-12-1855	Isabella				Saltees	
19-12-1855	Bon Accord		Penang to London		Saltees	
6-1-1856	Elvira		Liverpool to Havana	general	Splaugh Rock	
23-1-1856	Alciope		Liverpool to Malabar	general	Barrels	
6-2-1856	Spec		Cardiff to Cork	coal	Ballyteigue Bay	
12-2-1856	Proteus		Liverpool to Jamaica	general	Blackwater bank	
18-2-1856	Bess		Liverpool Wexford	grain	Wexford bar	
22-2-1856	Catherine		Queenstown to Cardiff	ballast	Barrels	
10-3-1856	George		Liverpool to Quebec	salt	Tuskar	
5-4-1856	Exchange				Blackwater bank	
28-8-1856	Rover		Ayr to Wexford	coal	Glascarraig	
27-9-1856	Expert		Llannelly to Wexford	coal	Wexford Bar	
27-9-1856	Helena		Cork to Cardiff	grain & passengers	Raven point	
7-10-1856	Chance		Newport to Wexford	coal	Whitehouse bank	
13-10-1856	Irrawaddy				Blackwater bank	
20-11-1856	Star of Hope		Bristol to Swansea	general	Tuskar	
2-12-1856	Elizabeth Martin		Liverpool to Singapore	general	Tuskar	
5-12-1856	J.L Warner		New Orleans to Liverpool	cotton	Tacumshane	
6-12-1856	Cassivelauness		Liverpool to Calcutta	salt	East of Tuskar	
9-12-1856	Blonde		Tarangay to Falmouth	linseed	off Fethard	
12-12-1856	Dione		Cardiff to Bordeaux	coal	Greenore	
17-12-1856	Johanna Kirwan		Waterford to Liverpool	coal	Slade	
16-2-1857	Chattanochee		Liverpool to Savannah	salt	Greenore	
28-3-1857	Elizabeth Huddleson		Newport to Waterford	coal	Kilmore	
28-3-1857	Emperor		Liverpool to Bahia	general	Blackwater bank	
17-4-1857	Conquest		Liverpool to Quebec	salt	Blackwater bank	
18-4-1857	Diamond		Cardiff to Waterford	coal	Ballygrangans	
22-10-1857	Vulcan		Waterford to Newport	ballast	Wexford	
3-11-1857	Purtndiada		Alfandigo to Liverpool	fruit	Kilmore	
21-1-1858	Elerslie		Liverpool to Barbados	emigrants	Hill of Sea	
6-4-1858	L'Amiable Elisa				Blackwater bank	

Date	Ship Name	Home port or Captain	Voyage	Cargo	Wreck Location	Comment
6-4-1858	Florentine Glenville				Curracloe	
1859	Eiderslic				Rosslare	
6-4-1858	Arctic				Kilgorman	
? 1859-1883	Tiger			iron	Waterford Harbour	2 lost
?	unknown American Barque		Leghorn to Dublin	marble	hook	tried to land pilot
7-1-1859	Stella		Sicily to Glasgow	sulphur		
11-3-1859	Fleetwood		Alexandria to Belfast	wheat		
13-3-1859	Nemisis					
2-4-1859	Perseverance		Cardiff to Waterford	coal	off Cullenstown	
2-4-1859	Forrester				off Lady's island	
3-4-1859	Loodianah		Mobile to Liverpool	cotton	off Lady's island	
2-4-1859	unknown			corn	Graet Saltee	
29-4-1859	Pomona		Liverpool to New York	Passengers	Blackwater Bank	360 lost
28-9-1859	Grace Darling			coal	Kilmore	
12-1859	Lady Rebow		from St Michael's	oranges	St Patrick's bridge	
1-1-1860	Arethusa			tobacco mahogany	Bannow	
11-1-1860	Jeune Marie			beans	Fethard	
18-1-1860	Unknown		Liverpool to Genoa	general	Dogger Bank	
19-1-1860	H Fidden		Liverpool to Cuba	coal	Ballygeary	
4-1860	Neptune				Ballyteigue bay	
4-1860	Vanguard				Blackwater bank	
27-11-1860	Lydia			general	Ballinamona river	
10-12-1860	Sommauth		Liverpool to Montevideo		Blackwater bank	
20-12-1860	Frela		Seeborg to Dublin	vetches	Dogger bank	
29-12-1860	Golden Star			cotton	Baginbun	
1861	-	Greek		training ship	Ballyteigue	
18-1-1861	Versailles		Liverpool to Shanghai		Rosslare	
2-1861	Test		Mauritius to Glasgow	sugar	Morriscastle	
7-2-1861	-					.seven wrecks that day
10-2-1861	Guyana		Glasgow to West Indies		Carnsore	
8-2-1861	Sarah Bell		Boston to Liverpool	logwood	off Fethard	all lost
2-1861	Grace Evans				Tuskar	
9-2-1861	Louisa				Blackwater Bank	
9-2-1861			Savannah to Wexford		Saltees	
10-3-1861	Sir Allan McNab				Courtown	
15-11-1861	Maid of Fife				Blackwater bank	
25-11-1861	Empress		Alexandria to Liverpool		Ballyvaldon	
10-12-1861	General striker		Peru to Liverpool	salt & hides	Tacumshane	
12-12-1861	Cumloden Castle.		Quebec to Ardrossan	timber	Ballymadder	
1-1862	Brandywine				Carnsore	
23-5-1863	La Vifrido		Bilboa to Liverpool	Fruit wine ivory	Brandies rocks	
16-1-1864	Caluna		Glasgow to Turkey	barley	Ballyhealy	
28-1-1864	G. H. Warren				Fundale rock	
2-1864	Royal Arthur			Ivory, copper silver	Hook	

CHRONOLOGICAL WEXFORD LIST

Date	Ship Name	Home port or Captain	Voyage	Cargo	Wreck Location	Comment
11-1864	Eurocydon				Tuskar	
1-1865	unknown				Dogger Bank	
29-1-1865	Panope		Liverpool		Hook	
30-1-1865	Stirlingshire		from West Indies	Sugar, rum	Tuskar	
19-3-1865	Teazer		from Goole	flour	Wexford	
4-1865	Peep O Day				Dogger bank	
5-1865	Speed				off Cahore	
1-12-1865	Tasmania				Blackwater bank	
9-12-1865	Barbadian				Blackwater bank	many lost
25-12-1865	Tennessarian				Blackwater bank	
2-2-1866	Carrie Davis				Carnsore	
10-11-1866	Ceres				Carnsore	50 lost
9-2-1867	Johnstone		Demerera to Liverpool	Rum, sugar	Ballyteigue	
2-3-1867	Orcadian				Tuskar	
23-3-1867	unknown				Keeraghs	
2-3-1867	Ness	Power	Dingle to Cork	butter	Crow Head	
9-5-1867	Ayrshire lass				Off Wexford coast	
21-5-1867	Nonpariel				Off Tuskar	
6-5-1867	Blanche Moore		Liverpool to Calcutta		Long Bank	
1-6-1867	Assaye				Blackwater LS	
17-8-1867	Robert Husdon				Dogger Bank	
11-1-1868	Ullswater		from Liverpool		Ballymoney	
3-1868	Loreto				Long Bank	
11-3-1868	La Touche				Ballyteigue	
3-1868	Civil service				Off Rosslare	
30-4-1868	Clementine			bone ash	Tacumshane	
14-8-1868	Annie Jane				Courtown	
7-9-1868	R.H.Tucker				Blackwater Bank	
9-1868	Vivid				Poulduff	
20-3-1869	Porteus		Cardiff to Waterford	coal	Bannow Bay	
7-7-1869	Josephine		to Liverpool	sugar	off Kilmore	
1869	Helinio				Arklow bank	
1869	William Linsay				Off SE Coast	Bell in Hotel Rosslare
1869	Mary Bangor				Rosslare	
1869/70	Meridian				Carnsore	
1870	Dove				Arklow Bank	
1870	Sea Rest				Carnsore	
1870	John Calvin				Fundale perch	
16-1-1870	Ripple		Israel to Wexford	grain	Tuskar	
12-10-1870	Aberfeldy			copper ore	Tacumshane	
16-10-1870	Sydney				-	
21-12-1870	Bubona				Tuskar	
22-12-1870	Mary			ballast	St Patrick's Bridge	
1870	Astria		Of Whitehaven		hook	
22-4-1871	Royal Arthur	Hingston	San Francisco	wheat, silver & copper	Hook	crew saved
3-1871	Rose				Fundale Perch	

Date	Ship Name	Home port or Captain	Voyage	Cargo	Wreck Location	Comment
17-12-1871	Thermitas				Blackwater Bank	
1872	Fanny Palmer				Arklow bank	
26-3-1872	Jane & Sarah		to Dublin	fertiliser	Carnsore	
17-5-1872	Tripoli				Tuskar	
5-9-1972	unknown				Tuskar	
11-1872	Emma Kay				Blackwater bank	
29-11-1872	Kinsale		Clyde to France	Passengers	Broomhill	27 lost
5-12-1872	Belamyu		Newcastle to Windsor		South rock	
13-12-1872	Euphemia		Quebec to Scotland		Tuskar	
1873	Calcutta				Kilmore	
13-1-1873	Idaho		Liverpool to New Orleans		Courtown	
13-1-1873	Polyxna				Baginbun	
13-5-1873	Little Dorit				Dogger Bank	
5-1873	Halcyon		from Cork		Tuskar	
1874	Mary				Rosslare strand	
4-1-1874	River Krishna		Liverpool to India		Tuskar	
20-2-1874	Glide			coal	Kilmore	
18-10-1874	unknown				The Barrels	
28-10-1874	Henry				Coningbeg	
5-12-1874	Annie		Newport to Waterford	coal	Tacumshane	
1-1875	City Of London		San Francisco to London	wheat & salmon	Ballyhealy	
8-1-1875	Zorilla		Liverpool to Palermo		Tuskar	
18-6-1875	Sheil			coal	Ballyteigue	
19-1-1875	Vittorioso G		Cardiff to Constantinople	coal	St Patrick's Bridge	
7-1875	Lizzie Scallan		from New York		South bay Rosslare	
7-1875	Guiding Star				Hilltown bay	
7-1875	New Zealand		to Wexford	coal	Carrig rocks	
25-9-1875	Paquite de Terranova		to Falmouth	sugar	Rusk bank	
11-1875	Mino				Ballyhealy	
30-12-1875	Dante		Liverpool to Bombay		off Tuskar	
4-1-1876	Cape Comorin		Liverpool to Bombay	general	Ballyteigue	
24-5-1876	Pontiac		from New Orleans	corn & cotton	St Patrick's Bridge	
11-11-1876	Orinoco		St Johns to Liverpool	timber	South Bay Rosslare	
11-1876	Alba C				Hilltown bay	
10-12-1876	Sper		Portcawl to Wexford	coal	Carrig rocks	
18-1-1877	Nanta		Glasgow to Trieste		Rusk bank	
22-1-1877	Morning Star				Dogger bank	
22-1-1877	Unknown				Dogger bank	
2-1877	Ullock				Tacumshane	
16-4-1877	Mutlah		London to Halifax	general	Ardamine	
5-5-1877	Sibil			sulphur & phosphate	Rostoonstown	
28-5-1877	Island Queen			flour	Off Carnsore	
25-8-1877	Linda				Near Carne	
19-11-1877	Rainton				Glasgorman bank	
1878	Muircha				Off Tuskar	

CHRONOLOGICAL WEXFORD LIST

Date	Ship Name	Home port or Captain	Voyage	Cargo	Wreck Location	Comment
26-2-1878	Sydne Dubrooachi Montagu		Newry to New York		Dogger bank	
6-1878	Idaho		New York to Liverpool	Horses & Cattle	Coningbeg	
31-10-1878	Helvetia				Tuskar	
8-11-1878	Dawn				Tuskar	
19-12-1878	Fairy		Wexford to Tuskar		Tuskar	
1-1879	Debonnair				Ballyhealy	
1-1879	Helen		Ex Liverpool		Rosslare	
1-1879	King Arthur		Ex Charleston		Bannow bay	
30-1-1879	Brother Jonanthan			steam tug	Small Saltee	
28-9-1879	Langdale		San Francisco to Liverpool	wheat	Carnsore	
2-12-1879	Tempo		Italy	Maize	Hook	
21-12-1879	Chevreuil		West Africa to Glasgow	Dyewood	Carne	
1880	Gem				Carnsore	
12-5-1880	Jonah			wheat	Dogger bank	
22-11-1880	Balla		Labrador to Liverpool	Salt fish	Bar o Lough	
26-11-1880	John A Harvie		from New York	Maize	Tacumshane	
1-1-1881	unknown		Labrador to Liverpool	Dried fish	Bar o Lough	
1881	Morning Light		South Shields to Dunlaoghaire		Tacumshane	
3-1881	Philomine			Barley	Tacumshane	
3-1881	Pinson		Port Talbot to Malbay	coal	Bastardstown	
3-1881	Ethol of Truan			Iron Ore	Tacumshane	
4-7-1881	Brittanic			Passengers	Kilmore	
16-7-1881	Zigana				Dogger bank	
4-11-1881	Liffey		St John's to Liverpool	deal	St Patrick's bridge	
1-1-1882	Laparay		To Liverpool	grain	Carne	
11-1-1882	Regalia		Ex Jersey	flour	Ballyhealy	
18-11-1882	America		Quebec to Wexford	barley	Dogger bank	
20-11-1882	Dazzler			deal	Wexford bar	
23-11-1882	Grandholm		St Malo to Campbletown	barley	Ballyteigue	
29-11-1882	Argentine republic			timber	Dogger bank	
15-12-1882	Landgrig Hall		Liverpool to California	salt	Tuskar	
15-12-1882	Fame				Curracloe	
12-1882	Unknown				Wexford harbour	
12-1882	Hinde				Morriscastle	
12-1882	Oxford				Morriscastle	
17-12-1882	Szepary		Flume to Dublin	flour	Bannow	
22-2-1883	Clementina		Demerera to Greenock	rum & sugar	Ballyteigue	
22-3-1883	Hertford		Troon to Youghal	coal	Carrig rocks	
1-9-1883	Ellen Kerr				Rosslare	
9-1883	Chita				Saltees	
1-9-1883	Slaney				Hook	
24-12-1883	White star		Calcutta to Liverpool	Jute & Jade	Tuskar	
7-2-1884	Egmont			corn	Holden's bed	
2-1884	Stratendrick			coal & iron	Rosslare	
12-2-1884	Sem			coal	Carnsore	

Date	Ship Name	Home port or Captain	Voyage	Cargo	Wreck Location	Comment
8-3-1884	Georgia		from Palermo		Carne	
11-5-1884	Cormorant		from Cork	cattle & general	Tuskar	
11-5-1884	George Bewley		Liverpool to Peru	general	Tuskar	
13-6-1884	Larne		Milford to Dunmore	salt & fish boxes	Great Saltee	
4-8-1885	Roscius		Belfast to Newcastle		4m SW Hook	
12-8-1884	Union		Newport to Cork	coal	20m SE Blackwater LS	
21-10-1885	Highland Mary		Cardiff to Wexford	coal	Rosslare	
1885	Equoit				Wexford harbour	
14-1-1885	Slaney		Wexford to Liverpool	bacon	Dogger Bank	
21-1-1885	Admiral Moorson		Dublin to Liverpool	Blackwater		
18-7-1885	Sea Foam			Herring	Hook	two lost
1885	Roscius				off Hook	crew saved
7-1885	Edith		Ayr to Bannow	coal	Bannow bar	
8-1885	Corsair				Courtown	
8-1885	Vivandiere				Blackwater bank	
20-9-1885	Nora		Newport to Wexford	coal	Wexford harbour	
21-10-1885	Highland Mary			coal	South bay	
1886	Sirius		Liverpool to Waterford		Carnsore	
8-2-1886	Albinus					
24-5-1886	Pontiac		From New Orleans	Maize & Cotton	St Patrick's bridge	
10-1886	Mellery		From North Wales		Tuskar	
9-10-1886	Reliance					
10-1886	Thomas & Sarah				Ballyteigue	
5-12-1886	Six Sisters			timber	Tacumsahne	
14-12-1886	Samanco		Liverpool to Callao	coal	Carnsore	
10-1-1887	Forth		Ayr to Wexford	coal	Blackwater bank	
18-4-1887	Fame				Blackwater bank	
3-5-1887	Mountain Maid		Llanelly to Lough Foyle	coal	Greenore	
9-7-1887	Naiad					
11-1887					Wexford harbour	
3-1-1888	Alfred D Snow		San Francisco to Liverpool	wheat	off Broomhill	
20-3-1888	Lucinda Jane		to Dublin	malt	Hill of sea	all
7-3-1888	Pilot					
16-3-1888	Saltee		Brunswick to Wexford		Dogger bank	13
12-1888	Etta		From St Johns		Waterford	18
1889	Garrydock		to Waterford		Tuskar	all saved
1889	Jewess		Wexford to Dublin		Cahore	all saved
20-2-1889	Elieser		British Honduras to Fleetwood		Ballyteigue	10 saved
4-8-1889	Lillydale		Newport	coal	Kilrane	
16-12-1889	Delphine Melanie		Le Harvre to Glasgow	ballast	Tacumshane	
17-1-1890	John C Wade				Wexford slob	
1-1890	Jenny Lind				Wexford slob	
19-2-1890	Rose				Carnsore	
10-12-1890	Clara & Jessie		Milford to Wicklow	ballast	S of Rosslare	all saved
15-12-1890	Ellen				Tuskar	

CHRONOLOGICAL WEXFORD LIST

Date	Ship Name	Home port or Captain	Voyage	Cargo	Wreck Location	Comment
15-12-1890	Pausilippo				Tuskar	
c1890	Margaret	Liverpool		coal	Blackwater bank	
C1890	Enterprise			slates	Ballyteigue	
C1890	Fairy Queen		to Africa	muskets	Little Saltee	
C1890	Atle				Ballyteigue	
1891	Angharad				Rosslare Fort	
1891?	Telegraph			coal	Wexford Bar	
1891	Commerce				Wexford bar	
7-1891	Emily Winnie		Ayr to Kilmore Quay	coal		
16-1-1892	Marys		Runcorn to Port Talbot		Rosslare fort	
20-1-1892	M. Dabigon Chantenay		Port Talbot to Malbay	coal	Bastardstown	
21-1-1892	Varr	Brevig Liverpool		Ice blocks	Ballyhealy	All saved
16-2-1892	Prima Donna				Wexford Bar	
30-7-1892	Grenadier				Tuskar	
28-11-1892	Daring	Liverpool Waterford			Slade	
12-1892	Monte Videan				Tuskar	
5-1-1893	J.N.Ternan					
2-1893	Violante	Rotterdam Liverpool		Ballast	Morriscastle	
2-1893	Esther			Coal	Tacumshane	
8-12-1893	Vivid	Whitby		Coal	Ballyhack	
12-1893	Sybil					
1894	Hondeklip					
1-1894	Peter Rikmars				Waterford harbour	
1-1894	Christina				Waterford harbour	
8-1-1894	Ellen Kerr		Milfordhaven to Wexford		Rosslare	
5-6-1894	Samuel Dixon				Carne	
6-11-1895	Kate & Mary			coal		collided with Pembroke off Hook only one saved
27-3-1895		From St Nazaire			Blackwater Bank	
20-4-1895	Olga	to Waterford			Broomhill	
20-5-1895	Rapid					
22-6-1895	Marguerite				Off Saltee	
24-6-1895	Mermiss	Glasgow Constantinople			Tuskar	
24-12-1895	Monmouth	from Bristol			Great Saltee	
24-12-1895	Eliza				Cahore	
24-12-1895	Citizen of Youghal		Newport to Youghal		Little Saltee	
26-12-1895					Carnsore	
8-10-1896	Jessie	to New Ross			Hook	
8-10-1896	fishing boats				off Kilmore Quay	all saved
24-3-1897	Jessie			cement	Fundale Rock	
28-3-1897del						

CHRONOLOGICAL WEXFORD LIST

Date	Ship Name	Home port or Captain	Voyage	Cargo	Wreck Location	Comment
31-3-1897	Express		Liverpool -Wexford	Iron ore	Tercheen Rock Carne	19 saved
3-1-1898	Hilda		Swansea-new Ross	coal	Duncannon Pier	
17-4-1898	Hawswater		Liverpool -Natal	ballast	Forlorn Point	all saved
11-1898	Folader			coal	long Bank	all saved
2-1899	Pembroke				Little Saltee	31 saved ship refloated
-	Union				Wexford Bar	
25-9-1822 ?	Selina				Wexford Bar	
26-9-1869	Electric Spark		to San Francisco	salt	Blackwater Head	
unclear	Blue Bone				South bay	
unclear	Muckaloo				Rosslare fort	
unclear	Curlew				Point of park	
unclear	Garreyowen				Ballinoulart	
22-10-1881	Orphan girl		London to Liverpool	cement	Ballymoney	
c1900	Frenchman				South Bay	
c1900	Mermaid				South Bay	
c1900	Orangeman				South Bay	
c1900	Slaney				Wexford Harbour	
26-5-1900	Louisa		from Darthmouth	coal	Saltees	
14-9-1900	Dolphin longboat				Ardcavan	
13-10-1901	L Furlong		Swansea to New Ross	coal	Collough Rock Carne	
26-1-1901	Hannah				off Tuskar	
7-8-1901	Kincora		Limerick to Liverpool	general	Off Tuskar	7 lost run down by Oceanic
1903	Supply				Off Courtown	
10-1-1903	Doris	Milford			Off Saltees	
26-4-1903	Manchester Market		Manchester to Philadelphia	metal	Tuskar	
7-3-1904	Yara Yara		Newport to Wexford	coal	Rosslare	
2-4-1904	Belle				Wexford bar	
1905	Melamphus				Long Bank	
26-2-1905	Clarence		Wexford to England		Near Tuskar	
17-7-1905	Greenock			salvage ship	Off Tuskar	
8-1905	Bonafide		Fiji to Liverpool	copper	Rosslare	
23-1-1906	Gannet				Rosslare	
27-1-1906	ketch				Rosslare	
27-1-1906	ketch				Rosslare	
27-1-1906	schooner				Rosslare	
11-2-1906	Victoria				Ballygeary	
16-2-1906	Fulmar				Wexford	
8-3-1906	Puffin				Rosslare	
7-5-1906	Antelope			pipeclay	Bastardstown	
20-6-1906	Majestic					all saved
8-11-1906	The Wave					4
c1906	JCR		Portmadoc to Waterford	Slates	Splaugh rock	

CHRONOLOGICAL WEXFORD LIST

Date	Ship Name	Home port or Captain	Voyage	Cargo	Wreck Location	Comment
8-11-1906	Young Hudson					-
7-1-1907	Marcello Dias					all saved
	Accra		Tenerife to Liverpool		Tacumshane	all saved
3-8-1907	Topaz				off Tuskar	
22-8-1907	Margaret & Mary				near Tuskar	all saved
24-12-1907	-				Greenore point	all saved
6-3-1908	Ocean Maid				Ballygeary	all saved
6-3-1908	Denbeighshire Lass				ballygeary	
20-8-1908	Helen McGregor				Near cahore	
8-11-1908	trawler	Brixham			Long bank	
28-11-1908	Goacuetta				St Patrick's Bridge	
4-10-1909	Zion Hill				Hill o Sea	
4-10-1909	Harvest Home				Hill o Sea	
4-10-1909	Helen & Ernest				Hill o Sea	
2-12-1909	-				Hill o Sea	
2-12-1909	Gannet				Wexford Bay	
3-1910	Emily				N of Tuskar	
19-12-1910	Annesley				Tuskar	
1911	Iverna				Blackwater Bank	
17-3-1911	Margaret		Newport to Waterford	coal	Hook	
27-10-1911	Alice Latham				Kilmore	
15-2-1912	Clara				Kilmore	
25-9-1912	Eva				Cahore	
18-6-1913	Topic				Tuskar	
1914	Pioneer				Cahore	
2-12-1914	Val de Saire	France	Glasgow to Le Havre		near Tuskar	
1-11-1915	Margaret & Mary		Cardiff to Wexford	coal	Raven Spit	
1-11-1915	Sea View				South bay	
20-2-1915	Mexico				Keeragh Islands	
war	Mary Grace				Off Coningbeg	
1915	Roebuck				Off Tuskar	
1915	U27					
1915	Irsun				off Tuskar	
28-3-1915	Falaha				East of Tuskar	
24-4-1915	The Harmony				Blackwater Bank	
5-1915	Centurion				SW of Barrels	
6-5-1915	Candidate				S of Coningbeg	
16-6-1915	Trafford				S of Hook	
27-6-1915	Indrani				S of Saltees	
17-8-1915	Maggie					
9-1915	Mesaba				Tuskar	
11-1915	John Bull				Rosslare	
11-1915	Friendship				Rosslare Harbour	
11-1915	Harvest King				Rosslare Harbour	
11-1915	Unity				Rosslare Harbour	
11-1915	Advance				Rosslare Harbour	
11-1915	Edward				Rosslare Harbour	

CHRONOLOGICAL WEXFORD LIST

Date	Ship Name	Home port or Captain	Voyage	Cargo	Wreck Location	Comment
11-1915	Seaview				Kilrane	
19-11-1915	Margaret & Mary				Raven spit	
11-1915	Harty				Carne	ships boat ashore
27-3-1916	Manchester Engineer		to Manchester		S of Coningbeg	
28-10-1916	Raylton Dixon		from Christiania	coal	off Tuskar	
28-10-1916	Speedwell 7				Splaugh Rock	
29-12-1916	Lennox		Cardiff to Port Said	coal	Saltees	
c1916	Fingal				SE of Hook	
1917	Coordy				S of Hook	
22-2-1917	Invercauld				Coningbeg	abandoned
10-3-1917	Mediterranean				S of Hook	
10-3-1917	T Crowley				S of Hook	
13-3-1917	Brika				off Coningbeg	
17-3-1917	Guard			fishing	8m SW Coningbeg	bombed by submarine
17-3-1917	Antony				near Hook	torpedoed
22-3-1917	Providence				near Barrels	torpedoed
29-3-1917	Lincolnshire				S of Hook	torpedoed
29-3-1917	Crispin				14 miles S of |Hook	torpedoed
4-5-1917	Pilar de Larenga				S of Tuskar	torpedoed
30-6-1917	Lady of the Lake				S of Hook	torpedoed
1-8-1917	Karina				S of Hook	torpedoed
25-8-1917	Cymrian				S of Tuskar	torpedoed
17-9-1917	Our Bairns				S of Hook	torpedoed
19-9-1917	Ronald				S of Hook	torpedoed
19-9-1917	Ethal Manor			coal	off Hook	torpedoed
26-9-1917	U 33				s of Tuskar	torpedoed
11-10-1917	Keithales			Admiralty yacht	Blackwater LS	Collision
11-10-1917	Rhodesia				S of Coningbeg	torpedoed
13-11-1917	Ardmore		from Cork		Off Coningbeg	torpedoed
13-11-1917	Carlo		Carthagena to Liverpool	lead, fruit	S of Keeraghs	torpedoed
17-9-1917	Ronald			fishing	25m SW Coningbeg	gunfire
17-9-1917	Our Bairns			fishing	25m SW Coningbeg	gunfire
17-12-1917	Coningbeg		Liverpool to Waterford	General	25 miles ESE of S Arklow LV	44 lost torpedoed
2-12-1917	Copeland				off Tuskar	torpedoed
1918	Baron Ailsa			coal	S of Tuskar	torpedoed
7-1-1918	Egda			ballast	E of Tuskar	torpedoed
19-2-1918	Wheat Flower				N of Tuskar	torpedoed
2-3-1918	Havna				off Tuskar	torpedoed
9-3-1918	Nancy Wignall		from Wexford		S of Tuskar	torpedoed
14-3-1918	Tweed			stores	E of Tuskar	torpedoed
23-3-1918	Jane Grey				S of Tuskar	
25-4-1918	U 104			warship	S of Tacumshane	
26-4-1918	Ethel				E of Tuskar	
29-4-1918	Johnny Toole				Near Tuskar	
29-4-1918	Christina Davis			coal	S of Tuskar	torpedoed

CHRONOLOGICAL WEXFORD LIST

Date	Ship Name	Home port or Captain	Voyage	Cargo	Wreck Location	Comment
8-5-1918	Thoralf				S of Coningbeg	torpedoed
29-8-1918	Atxeri Mendi		from Spain	coal	off Tuskar	torpedoed
31-8-1918	Unknown				Off Tuskar	
3-9-1918	Highcliffe			coal	E of Tuskar	torpedoed
7-12-1919	St Margaret		Troon to Waterford	coal	off Hook	
c1920	Union			sand	St Patrick's Bridge	
9-1920	Meridean				carne	
7-1921	Hilda		Swansea to Wexford	coal	Wexford bar	
15-11-1921	Useful	Arklow	from Preston	pipe clay	Carrig rocks	
22-11-1921	Faithful		to Preston	China clay	Carrig rocks	all saved
27-11-1921	Industrial				Churchtown	
late 1921	Meridian		Par to Runcorn		Courtown	
c1922	Miss Williams			coal	South bay	
c1922	Harvest Home				South bay	
c1922	Shelton Abbey			Timber	South bay	
1-1922	Active			Wheat	Off Wexford	
1923	Avance				Off Tuskar	
1-1924	Cymric			bricks	Rosslare	
10-7-1924	Lismore				Carne	one survivor
28-4-1925	Marion				Bayllytrent	
8-1925	Piraeus				Collough rock	
12-1-1926	Valdura			Wheat	Forlorn	
1927	Bracknell			coal	blue rocks	
c1927	Watfarer			ballast	Kilmore	
3-2-1927	Shearness			Whiskey	Tuskar	
27-4-1927	Cluny				St Patrick's bridge	
27-10-1927	Loop Head		Waterford to Limerick	Coal	Tuskar	
10-1927	Pearl				Kilmore Quay	
10-1927	Clara				Kilmore Quay	
2-1928	Mizpah		to London	potatoes	Baginbun	3 saved
15-3-1928	Gartlock		Bristol to Liverpool	flour	Cahore	
28-9-1928	Brackley			coal	St Patrick's Bridge	
3-11-1928	Electric			fish	Kilmore Quay	
5-12-1928	Onward			coal	Kilmore Quay	
10-1929	Spray					
10-1929	Benita				Baginbun	
10-1929	Geisha				Cahore	
20-10-1929	Mountblairy				St Patrick's Bridge	
1930	Earl				Rosslare	
9-1931	Royal Firth			coal	Tuskar	
7-9-1932	Aranci	Coppacks	Newry to Portsmouth		22m SW Tuskar	
1932	Forest Deer			coal	Tuskar	
1933	Swanen			timber	Raven Point	
1933	Clara				Blackwater Head	
19-1-1934	Brerton		Lossiemouth to Barry	oats	Carraig rocks	9 saved
5-2-1936	Elsie Annie		Ayr to Wexford	coal	Dogger bank	
29-2-1936	Wexfordian		to Wexford	coal	Dogger Bank	

Date	Ship Name	Home port or Captain	Voyage	Cargo	Wreck Location	Comment
20-12-1938	ME Johnson				off Splaugh rock	
c1940	Margaret Edna				off Carrigs	
11-1940	Osage		Belfast to Bristol	tanker	Blackwater light	
12-11-1940	Ardmore		Cork to Fishguard	500 pigs	S of Wexford	one saved
19-12-1940	Isolde			light tender	near Barrels	
1-4-1941	San Conrado				Near Tuskar	
1-4-1941	Hildefjord			tanker	SE of Tuskar	
13-6-1941	St Patrick		Rosslare to Fishguard	mailboat	E of Tuskar	
19-10-1941	Rask				Off Greenore	
20-10-1941					off Kilmore	
24-11-1941	Rockabill				-	
9-12-1941	Gertie				Near Tuskar	
21-6-1942	Lanabrone			coal	Great Saltee	
10-1945	Happy Harry			coal	Rosslare	
23-11-1946	Albany				E of Tuskar	
8-2-1947	Ary				S of Hook	
8-5-1947	Muirchu				Near Tuskar	
31-12-1947	Isallt			Fertiliser	Ballymoney	
1948	Mint			fish	Rosslare fort	
26-1-1948	Edenvale				near Tuskar	
1949	Cydonia				Rosslare	
4-1953	Susan Vittery				off Greenore	
1-1955	Minorca		Rouen to Liverpool	General	Cahore	
19-12-1957	Auguste Maurice				Ballyteigue	
26-2-1957	Naomh Seosamh			fish	Hook	
19-12-1957	Les Buissonnets	Lorient		fish	Rostoonstown	
12-1959	Santa Lucia			fish	Hook	
c1960	Andre Peierette				Wexford Harbour	
c1961	Primrose				Wexford bridge	
c1960	Kestrel			fish	Hook	
9-10-1962	Sparkling Wave			Trawler	half a mile North of	Hook Head
2-2-1961	Almajo					
22-10-1961	Halronnell				Black Rock	
17-2-1966	Dredger no 2	Belfast		harbour dredger	Ballymoney	
7-11-1967	Shapinsay				Doornogue point Hook	
27-11-1970	Glenmalure			Trawler		
21-2-1968	Halzeal 3				off Slade	
15-8-1969	El Alamein	Kilmore		Trawler	off Cahore	
c1970	Akme pal				Raven pt	
c1970	Shelburne			wooden barge	Wexford harbour	
1970	Anchorite					
8-12-1971	Lode Star			Trawler	off Hook	Collided
8-12-1971	Castle Bay			Trawler	off Hook	Collided
1972	Tourmalet		Leaving Waterford	Trawler	Hook	sank while being refloated
12-3-1973	Croghan			Trawler		

CHRONOLOGICAL WEXFORD LIST

Date	Ship Name	Home port or Captain	Voyage	Cargo	Wreck Location	Comment
20-10-1973	Margaret Kerry					
16-1-1974	Jadestar Glory					
30-1-1974	Rachel					
14-1-1975	Timber Skipper		Finland to Cork	timber	Cahore	refloated
7-1976	Ruffian					
7-12-1978	ND de Sacre Coeur				SE of Tuskar	
c1980	Success				Rosslare Pier	collided with ferry
1981	Wheal Jeevor			Fish	S of Keeraghs	
14-12-1981	Grainville				Tuskar	
12-1-1983	-			Coal	Tuskar	
	West Rock				Carne	
?	Lately				SE of Carne	

ALPHABETICAL INDEX

ALPHABETICAL INDEX

ALPHABETICAL INDEX